Kwajalein Atoll,
the Marshall Islands
and American Policy
in the Pacific

Kwajalein Atoll, the Marshall Islands and American Policy in the Pacific

RUTH DOUGLAS CURRIE

McFarland & Company, Inc., Publishers
Jefferson, North Carolina

LIBRARY OF CONGRESS CATALOGUING-IN-PUBLICATION DATA

Names: Currie, Ruth Douglas, author.
Title: Kwajalein Atoll, the Marshall Islands and American policy in the Pacific / Ruth Douglas Currie.
Description: Jefferson, North Carolina : McFarland & Company, Inc., Publishers, 2016. | Includes bibliographical references and index.
Identifiers: LCCN 2016041840 | ISBN 9781476663111 (softcover : acid free paper) ∞
Subjects: LCSH: Marshall Islands—Foreign relations—United States. | United States—Foreign relations—Marshall Islands. | Kwajalein Atoll (Marshall Islands)
Classification: LCC DU710 .C87 2016 | DDC 996.8/3—dc23
LC record available at https://lccn.loc.gov/2016041840

BRITISH LIBRARY CATALOGUING DATA ARE AVAILABLE

ISBN (print) 978-1-4766-6311-1
ISBN (ebook) 978-1-4766-2632-1

© 2016 Ruth Douglas Currie. All rights reserved

No part of this book may be reproduced or transmitted in any form or by any means, electronic or mechanical, including photocopying or recording, or by any information storage and retrieval system, without permission in writing from the publisher.

Front cover photograph of Kwajalein Island, Command Flags (U.S. Army Photo)

Printed in the United States of America

McFarland & Company, Inc., Publishers
 Box 611, Jefferson, North Carolina 28640
  www.mcfarlandpub.com

For Ken

Table of Contents

Acknowledgments	viii
Preface	1
Introduction	2
One—America Claims the Pacific	7
Two—National Competition in the Nineteenth Century	20
Three—Versailles and the Japanese Mandate	34
Four—World War II	51
Five—Truman, the United Nations and U.S. Control	72
Six—The Trust Territory of the Pacific Islands	87
Seven—The Congress of Micronesia	102
Eight—Micronesian Status Politics	118
Nine—Free Association	137
Ten—To the Twenty-First Century	154
Epilogue	176
Chapter Notes	179
Bibliography	198
Index	217

Acknowledgments

In a project encompassing so many years, there are scores of people to thank for their assistance. First is Colonel Michael Volpe, who served as Chief of Staff for Lieutenant General John F. Wall, Commander, U.S. Army Strategic Defense Command (USASDC). With a keen appreciation for history, Colonel Volpe required that the Command Historian be part of the General's staff. In that capacity, I attended briefings and had access to many classified reports concerning the Research & Development phase of the Army's efforts in missile defense and advanced research projects. Colonel Volpe asked me to write a brief history of the Army's role in President Reagan's Strategic Defense Initiative (SDI), which I did, aided by my Assistant, Claus Martel, and Administrative Assistant, Ruthie Poe, using the documents available to us in the Historical Office.

Colonel Volpe's next assignment was to write a broader history of the Army's ballistic-missile defense operation and base in Kwajalein Atoll, Marshall Islands. He allowed Claus Martel to travel with me to Kwajalein for a week-long research trip. I thank Claus for his support and assistance in many capacities on that trip. He took many of the photographs that appear in this publication. Later, Colonel Volpe authorized a research trip for me to Hawaii and arranged an interview with Ambassador Fred Zeder, who graciously provided a valuable window into the background of the Trust Territory Government and the contribution of High Commissioner Janet McCoy. While in Hawaii, I did extensive work with the TTPI Archives and Pacific Collection Archives at the University of Hawaii Library. Thanks to Karen Peacock who guided me to many archival sources in the Pacific Collection, especially to the extraordinary collection of German documents from the period of German control of the Marshalls. Karen also arranged an interesting conversation with Stewart Firth, who had translated the German documents and whose own research and writing on the Pacific have been valuable. A week's trip to Newport, RI, and the Naval War College Library provided more depth for my research.

Back in DC, the Army's Center for Military History files were open to me and provided eyewitness evidence for conditions on the ground after the Battle of Kwajalein. Through more years, my thanks for the Army's continued support from friends such as USASDC Public Affairs Coordinator Ed Vaughn and for access to records in the Historical Office after my tenure, including permission to use the research from my trips to Kwajalein and Hawaii. The Army's primary sources of the command's Annual History Reports and Reports of the Trust Territory Government, Congress of Micronesia, and Future Political Status Commission were invaluable in seeing the Marshallese perspective in negotiations.

My thanks to Sharon Watkins Lang in the USASMDC/ARSTRAT Historical Office for help with multiple inquiries and information. Especially helpful was the contact with John Fairlamb, Ph.D., who served as the Army's Representative in the Office of Compact Negotiations in the U.S. Department of State and participated in Compact negotiations for four years. After returning to USASMDC Headquarters, he led critical discussions and advised the Army on implementation of the Kwajalein Land Use Agreement and the amended Military Use and Operating Rights Agreement. My thanks to Dr. Fairlamb for his generous conversation, expert advice and assistance in providing documents for my use.

While I had only begun the work for this broader history in my four years with the Army, I credit Colonel Volpe with enabling the original research that allowed me to go further. Though I returned to college and university teaching, with other priorities and publishing interests, I was now totally intrigued with the history of the Marshall Islands and Kwajalein Atoll. I made U.S. Policy in the Pacific a prime subject for my classes in American Foreign Relations.

I give thanks to my intellectual mentor in the field, Walter LaFeber, whose scholarship and books were important in my own teaching. For this publication, I relied on his masterpiece, *The Clash*, to understand the complex competition between the U.S. and Japan. For the origins of the Strategic Defense Initiative, I looked to the definitive work of Donald R. Baucum, U.S. Air Force historian, and thank him for his service. In the first chapter, I used Nathaniel Philbrick's fascinating story of the Wilkes Exploring Expedition to introduce early interest in the Pacific. Thanks to his map cartographer, Jeffrey Ward, for the use of his map charting the voyages that provided a first viewing of the Marshalls by an American. Francis Hezel's copious work in gathering documents from the American religious influence in the islands was essential for that part of the story. Hezel must be thanked for his many publications on the history and cultures of Micronesia. For tracking negotiations through the long years of the Congress of Micronesia and Future Political Status Commission, I relied on the huge contributions of Howard Willens and Deanne Siemer, Norman Meller, and Masahiro Igarashi.

For his excellent research and several publications over the years, I thank Giff Johnson, Editor of *The Marshall Islands Journal* since 1985. The *Journal* was founded by ex-Peace Corps volunteers in 1970, and has provided an independent voice and report of life and politics on the islands, which I have used to chronicle and understand the history, culture, and prime issues for the Marshallese.

Through a long academic career, my students have joined with me in research and analysis of American policy in the Pacific and I thank them for making it fun. One graduate student at Appalachian State University uncovered an original of Daniel Graham's *High Frontier*, on sale for one dollar in a used-book store. Members of the research class on the history of the Marshall Islands at Warren Wilson College did a superior job. That group included Nicole Connor, Georgia Anton, Sarah Bradham, and Caitlin McQueen. Sarah stayed on for one semester as my research assistant and provided the English translation for the text of an important treaty. Caitlin's extraordinary research on Truman and the founding of the UN proved quite valuable for that topic. Another Warren Wilson student of Foreign Relations, Chandler Jones, stayed on as my research assistant for two years after his graduation. My thanks to Chandler for his excellent work in identifying significant publications and accessing needed primary source documents.

On the Warren Wilson Library staff, I thank Reference Librarians David Bradshaw and Heather Stewart Harvey for their kind assistance over the years. Heather guided the research class through their extensive efforts and has continued to provide for my work numerous Inter-Library Loans and other support services.

I am grateful to all those individuals who shared with me their personal stories related to the history. Art Lindsay served in the Naval Air Corps as an Aviation Radioman, Seaman1st Class. Art was stationed on Kwajalein Island for six months in 1945–1946. Dr. Jim Bryan worked to get Sabin oral vaccine to the Marshallese in 1963. Stanly Godbold is writing volume two of his impressive biography of President Jimmy Carter. Natalie Nimmer, who had taught in the Marshalls as part of the Harvard University World Teach Program, served for a time on the Warren Wilson College staff. In addition to her time with me, she graciously hosted the students in the research class and shared an eyewitness account and photos of her previous work. After leaving the college, she returned to live and work in the Marshalls. I thank these friends and all those listed in the Personal Interviews section of the Bibliography.

Thanks to colleagues and friends who have read sections or chapters in the manuscript pertinent to their special expertise and have made helpful suggestions. These include: Dave Barstow, Philip Otterness, John Fairlamb, Stanly Godbold, and Captain James Y. Wallace III (USN Retired). I wish to thank the anonymous peer reviewers who also made helpful suggestions. I credit them with enabling me to gain new perspective in my analysis of the relationship between the Marshallese and Americans. In the final version of the book, I hope they will recognize positive responses to their insight.

Words are inadequate to express my appreciation for the support and effort of my closing editorial assistants. John Steele proved to be an experienced and professional proofreader. John Morris, Nexus PhotoGraphics, Asheville, NC, has provided awesome restoration for old photos and maps and has done much of the legwork in acquiring permissions. Kristina Trivette has been tireless in sorting the jumble of extensive bibliography and notes. With good humor through countless hours, Kristy has helped me complete the thankless task of creating an index.

Finally, of course, profound thanks for my own friends and family, who have encouraged me through what I am sure they thought was neverending absorption with "the book." Especially I note debt to my dear sister Lynn, who has read it all, heard it all, and is wise in discernment of all—my rock through years of travail. And most of all to Ken, my husband and "dearest friend," without whose support and the joy of our love I could not have persevered.

Preface

In the early years of my career as an historian of American Foreign Relations, I served four years as Command Historian of the U.S. Army Strategic Defense Command (USASDC). One assignment in that office was to write a history of the Army's role in President Reagan's Strategic Defense Initiative (SDI) and the significance of Kwajalein Atoll in the Marshall Islands.

That assignment led to the continuing research into the complex way in which the American Government creates policy, paring various agendas of the State and Interior Departments with competing Military goals for national defense. It also led to an examination of the history of the Marshall Islands and the part they have played in international politics since the nineteenth century. In seeking to understand the perspective of the indigenous islanders, this study takes a broad look at how the Marshallese nation and the U.S. came together to secure America's place in the Pacific.

My research began in the USASDC Historical Office, a research trip to Kwajalein, the Archives of the Trust Territory of the Pacific Islands, and the Pacific Collection Archives of the University of Hawaii. Army records include the Congress of Micronesia and Future Political Status Negotiations. The work of many eminent historians of Pacific history became significant in the quest, as did numerous primary sources and documents, and the record of each American presidential administration. Over the years, my college and university undergraduate and graduate students have joined with me in researching and analyzing this intriguing subject.

Introduction

> "We stand not for empire, but for self-determination."
> —President Barack Obama, 2011

In January 2012, President Barack Obama firmly declared that in the twenty-first century America would remain a strong Pacific power, a familiar claim. Even in the nineteenth century, seeking security for their own nationalism, Americans had joined the exploration of the Pacific Ocean in a quest for new opportunity beyond their shores. In the twentieth century, the major focus of this study, world war and international competition increased America's appetite for hegemony. Policy makers viewed the Pacific with covetous eyes, seeing there the potential for increasing wealth and power, seeking there additional land—America's place and base of operation.

One obstacle in achieving that goal lay in America's own national creed. After the Constitutional Convention in 1788, Benjamin Franklin's response to the question of what form the new government would take is classic: "A republic, madam, if you can keep it." His answer highlights the continuing challenge of American policy to find the balance between idealism on the one hand, and realism on the other. Some scholars have used the parallel terms principle and power to describe the dilemma.[1]

This narrative will offer a case study to highlight the challenge of creating American policy while honoring the balance—seeking dominance in Oceania while denying imperialism, naming it "just cause" even when controlling the property of others. Kwajalein Atoll in the Marshall Islands is the perfect choice to symbolize that contradiction. In the central Pacific, location makes it always essential for strategic planning. And there, the U.S. Army claims a base of legitimate occupation. For this investigation, the issue of land usage must be central, for the American effort to claim territory has been met with never-ending resistance from the owners. In Marshallese history, with its matrilineal culture, the mystic of land is inalienable to the individual, "never regarded as a mere commodity."²

While Kwajalein Atoll will be the focus of this study, the narrative will be broad. Showing the impact of American policy on the indigenous people of the Pacific will spotlight the path by which the Marshall Islands were drawn into the orb of the United States. The beginning chapters cover national competition in the Pacific, Marshallese culture, and America's introduction to the Marshalls. The missionary movement exemplified good intentions gone awry, where religious and economic motives went hand-in-hand to transform islanders into America's image. In the nineteenth century, following the example of the British Empire, Germany would be the prime challenge for the United States. Germany occupied and controlled the Marshall Islands for more than twenty years.

In the twentieth century, America's role in wars and postwar politics illustrated the difficulty of creating unified policy with competing priorities from various branches of civil and military governmental agencies. The story line must begin with the McKinley Administration at the turn of the century, whose intent was laid bare by accession of Hawaii and the Philippines, even while a paternalistic face masked the goal of economic power. Ironically, in the desire to block German access to the Philippines, peace negotiators after the Spanish-American War missed an early chance for additional U.S. presence in the Marshall Islands.

Seeing their strategic location, President Woodrow Wilson sought to avoid that mistake by claiming U.S. access to the islands after World War I. Despite his best efforts at idealistic statecraft, however, Japan, the new competitor in the Pacific, would make that difficult. Stymied at Versailles, Wilson reluctantly watched the Marshalls disappear under Japanese mandate.

For the Marshallese, the era of Japanese occupation would continue for more than twenty years and frame the agony of the Second World War. In 1944, with the Battle of Kwajalein, America finally made a decisive turn toward the winning strategy in the Pacific theatre. After the battle, islanders welcomed the American military as liberators, while the U.S. claimed the necessity of "belligerent occupation" in the Marshalls.

In the post–World War II period, the saga of America's control in the Pacific took hold, justifying its military presence while claiming to support change. President Truman attempted to honor both Franklin D. Roosevelt and Wilson's legacies through the creation of the United Nations (UN), the very embodiment of democratic idealism. When the UN approved the

Kwajalein Island, shore line, 1987 (U.S. Army photo).

Trust Territory of the Pacific Islands (TTPI), however, it gave the Trust Territory to U.S. control, sanctioning its only "strategic trust."

Thus, the modern stage—with the Marshalls one centerpiece of the drama. In the Cold War of the 1950s, the isolation of the outer islands provided the needed site for nuclear testing. In the 1960s, as the U.S. Army nurtured the nation's nascent ballistic missile defense program, Kwajalein Atoll became the heart of military planning because of its deep lagoon and spot-on placement as a target for test missiles fired from California. Inevitably, the military resolve to control Kwajalein, that central "strategic" spot in the vast Pacific, would clash with the expectation of the UN to bring independence to any "trust" under U.S. jurisdiction.

This study will track the political struggle of each administration in the decades needed to secure control of Kwajalein Atoll, each finding resistance with every step. The compelling story of how Marshallese leaders negotiated and bargained for their rights over these years is the heart of the narrative. Finally, they relinquished their atoll for American lease by securing a Compact of Free Association between sovereign nations, as the Republic of the Marshall Islands (RMI). Originally signed in 1986, the Compact did not resolve the legal controversies of land usage in the face of ongoing resistance of Marshallese landowners. The tension of accommodating this basic contradiction would remain until 2011, when the RMI Government and the landowners reached a final Kwajalein Land Use Agreement. With the Mililary Use and Operating Rights Agreement (MUORA) in place, the Obama Administration agreed with RMI to release to the landowners funds then held in Escrow. One result: No Marshallese now may live on Kwajalein Island.

Thus, in the face of profound challenges of the twenty-first century, as America's president proclaimed the U.S. "century of the Pacific," the role that Kwajalein will play in that declaration is yet to be decided. Independence as a "freely associated state" guarantees U.S. protection for the Marshalls, but what is "strategic denial" and what will be the definition of strategic interests? With an assertive Republic of China winning ever-increasing patronage, presence and power, the future of Pacific competition is unknown.

The economy of the RMI is likewise dependent on the grant provisions of the Compact of Free Association. The unintended consequences of dependency and free association may be seen in: Marshallese migration to Hawaii, Guam, and the U.S. mainland; health and wellness issues of the people; residual culpability for nuclear testing; and the impact of climate change on the islands, where rising seas are already alarming.

American language and influence are dominant in the Marshalls, while the people endeavor to recapture the rich texture of their own culture and history. Both the United States and the Republic of the Marshall Islands recognize the bane as well as the benefit of their alliance. Perhaps the true costs in the claim of democratic idealism, measured by the reality of American power, are yet to be fully realized.

One

America Claims the Pacific

With almost two centuries of interaction between Marshallese and Americans, the United States and the Republic of the Marshall Islands have forged a bond they euphemistically describe as a "special relationship." To understand that free association, it will be necessary to follow the events that drew the Marshalls onto the world stage, even as the U.S. became a competitor and sought hegemony in the arena of the Pacific Ocean. Based on America's ultimate success in the Second World War, the U.S. Army now claims Kwajalein Atoll as a base of operation.

After that long and terrible conflict, many of the victors sought the face of "benign colonialism," in the attempt to distinguish themselves from previous occupiers. Still, some academics charge that the United States only masks "empire" in claiming a place in the Pacific and forcing unwanted "economic development" for indigenous island peoples.[1] This chronicle will attempt a realistic examination of the balance between U.S resolve to protect and control, and the Marshallese effort to maintain self-determination in the face of American power.

The Marshall Islands belong to the portion of the western and central Pacific known as Micronesia. Literally meaning "small islands," Micronesia is comprised of four major archipelagos mostly north of the equator: the Marianas, which include Guam; the Carolines; the Gilbert Islands; and the Marshalls. Although its composite name implies homogeneity, this is far from accurate, since within Micronesia there are at least twelve vernacular languages. Anthropologists do not agree totally on the origins of Micronesian peoples, but modern archeological studies conclude they entered the Pacific from Southeast Asia. Language differences include those for some eastern Micronesian cultures as the "generic Austronesian family," formerly called Malayo-Polynesian. Scholars view the language of some western Micronesian people, such as the Marshalls, as "closer to Polynesian languages in origin."[2]

The mapping of the Pacific with categories such as Melanesia, Polynesia, and Micronesia, were the "artificial creations by Europeans," from the nineteenth century. The designations of French explorer/geographer Captain Dumont d'Urville included "linguistic and cultural affinities" and reflected "prevailing European stereotypes about non–Western peoples." Scholars now view these as condescending and racist, "more misleading than illuminating." While recognizing inadequacy, however, the designations continue to be used as "geographic shorthand."[3] As they are located in central Oceania, on the eastern edge of so-called "Micronesia," inclusion of the Marshall Islands in this appellation only underscores its limitations.

Thus, while this narrative will note various parallel and related happenings in other parts of Micronesia, the text will look primarily at the Marshalls, spotlighting the path by which they were drawn into the sphere of the United States, a unique part of the story. To understand national policy of the United States through these centuries, Kwajalein Atoll, with its exquisite strategic location, becomes the perfect vehicle and symbol of the American quest for a controlling role in the Pacific.[4]

Marshall Islands

The land of the Marshallese falls 2400 miles south and west of Hawaii, 700 miles north of the equator. These islands, made up of twenty-nine atolls of "low" coral, with more than twelve hundred small islands, some uninhabited, comprise a land mass of only seventy square miles. The central grouping of islands falls in two chains running North/South. The people know the chains as Ratak (toward the sunrise), the northeastern; and Ralik (toward the sunset), the southwestern. Within each grouping, there has been an amazing linkage between peoples separated by miles of ocean. Thus, while differing dialects of the common tongue may have existed, the history and culture of the Marshallese have bound them together as one people, one nation.[5] Located in the Ralik chain, Kwajalein is the world's largest atoll. In its southern tip, Kwajalein Island, the largest island in the atoll, is crescent shaped, approximately two miles in length, and boasts a deep lagoon.

Marshallese Culture

While never "unified under a single leader" in their early history, one *iroij* (chief) might have several atolls under his command. While the *iroij* held absolute power, his control rested on "loyalty and tribute payment." Examples of establishing leadership and atoll holdings will be noted below. A generous people, travel and hospitality for the extended family have remained characteristic. Travel between islands was commonplace, made possible by superior navigational skills in outrigger canoes, the "most impressive achievement in Micronesian technology" because of their "carefully proportioned and finely hewn multi-piece hulls" often more than forty feet long, the pieces lashed with coconut coir.[6]

One artifact extant from the pre-colonial era, the Marshallese stick chart, was a mnemonic device of sticks and cowrie shells that represented wave patterns and location of islands. The Marshallese employed the chart for instructional purposes, but after an apprenticeship learning the "roll of the boat" and "appearance of the waves" and committing its secrets to memory, no boatman ever took it on a sea journey. Impressed and fascinated by their ability to steer a course by the feel of the waves, German sea captains sought to document the achievement and left the best record of the early navigational knowledge of the Marshallese.[7]

In the 1990s, the Youth to Youth in Health movement in the islands sought to empower young people to recover their traditional culture in song, dance, and also outrigger canoe skills as one example. Marshallese leaders have sought to recapture pride in this former skill by teaching shipbuilding and holding exhibition races with outrigger canoes, attempting to relearn the earlier ability. In the twenty-first century, with admiration for learning "wave navigation," scholars in the fields of physics and oceanography have established research seminars to borrow and learn. Grants from the U.S. Ambassador's Fund for Cultural Preservation and the National Geographic Genographic Legacy Fund continue to support ongoing revival efforts of this unique Marshallese canoe and navigation mastery.[8]

The culture of the Marshalls has been determined by two primary, interlocking characteristics, both initially unknown to Western patriarchal societies. First, the Marshallese are matrilineal, with deep reverence for the female as life-giver. Their religious mythology attributed the people's origin to Tobolar, the Mother of Mothers, linked to the life-sustaining milk of the coconut. Ancestral sisters became associated with the two island chains and represented the two oldest *jowi* (clans) or lineage. In the approximately fifty *jowi* in the twenty-first century, offspring are "born to his or her mother's *jowi*, a feature of this matrilineal society." However understood, the Tobolar Copra Company in the Marshalls conducts a significant business in international trade. A typical Tobolar advertisement may read: "Copra Products from the Marshall Islands."[9]

Traditionally, nevertheless, the Marshallese considered the public role appropriate for the male, each *bwij* (lineage) headed by its *alab* (clan head), a role most often filled by the eldest male of the matrilineage, who acted at the request of his sister, the eldest female. The male, therefore, frequently represented the "kin group" in community affairs.[10] Remnants of this heritage of the female's powerful position in counsel may be seen in the effort following the 2012 elections to guarantee that a certain percentage of office holders in the Marshallese Nitijela (parliament) would be female, guaranteed by constitutional amendment. That the effort has thus far been futile reveals a modern weakening of the traditional role. On the other hand, the organization Women United Together in the Marshall Islands, shows a determination to fight for women's rights, seeking to maintain the matrilineal heritage of respect and combat the impact of Western patriarchal culture.[11]

The second salient cultural characteristic, land tenure, was fundamental to Marshallese identity and security. Again, this may be understood only through the matrilineal lens, as all children, both male and female, with *jowi* (clan), belong to the *bwij* of their mother, with land rights gained only through the female line. Land ownership could have as many as "four strata of titleholders," sometimes sharing a single *wato,* a "slice of land one to five acres in size that usually runs from the lagoon side of the island to the ocean side." In the twenty-first century, land tenure and land control issues remain paramount. Even as pure *iroij/leroij* (male/female) lineage has become practically extinct, in Marshallese courts, complex land claims based in matrilineal lineage show the continuing deep-seated traditional heritage. In each atoll, including Kwajalein, "virtually every location on the atoll" is of "critical importance to someone."[12]

The issue of land ownership will be central to this study. The American attempt to claim land in Kwajalein Atoll for its own defense needs would run headlong into the cultural mores of the Marshallese people. The complex issue of landowner rights vastly complicated settlement of the elusive Kwajalein Land Use Agreement over decades of negotiation to final resolution. To add to later travails, Americans would inherit the land tenure structure already bearing marks of interference by the effort of previous colonialists.

United States

Born a rebellious colony in the far-reaching British Empire, America itself was a victim of European cultural racism. In 1776, the founding documents demanded recognition that Americans were "created equal," with the right to find their own happiness outside the empire. In forming a nation, they would seek "a more perfect union," and later expand the claim that the United States was indeed "exceptional" in all undertakings. Unfortunately, such a claim appeared hollow justification for the way in which American colonists savaged the forests of the new continent and decimated the indigenous Native Americans, seizing their tribal land under the banner of white "civilization." The additional shame and evidence of its own bias was African slavery in the colonies from the beginning and continuing until outlawed by the thirteenth amendment of the Constitution at the close of the Civil War. Rarely entirely eliminated, the record of prejudice and racism between peoples and cultures becomes a notable theme in U.S. history.

In forging a national identity, the American Revolution, if anything, was a fight for economic gain in domestic and international trade. Just as the motivation of European nations had been expansion of their wealth in the New World, the colonial traders sought that same benefit for themselves. As the Atlantic Ocean had been the avenue for discovery, the Atlantic became the initial avenue for trade. American seamen and traders took their place, finding that "the sea leads everywhere." Its commerce had "accumulated capital," while "mastery of the sea, when the sea was highway to the world, meant mastery of sources of raw materials."[13]

The thirteen colonies claiming independence hugged the Atlantic coast of a huge continent where European monarchies had struggled for more than a century for a foothold; they would not relinquish their claims easily. The new nation quickly realized that the expanse of land required pushing westward, for "the continent too was an ocean." In 1787, even before the Constitution was ratified, with leadership from Thomas Jefferson, lawmakers passed the Northwest Ordinance, seeking revenue as well as process in the settlement. The Congress pressured states to cede to the nation their claims to land not yet explored by Americans. The Ordinance "forced Congress to go into business even before it knew what it had to sell," the land itself "more varied…" than members "dared imagine."[14]

In 1803, a then President Jefferson, having contracted Meriwether Lewis and William Clark to explore westward, secured the Louisiana Purchase from France, doubling the size of the nation. The exact boundary of the purchase was dubious to all. In negotiations with Spain, France had long claimed its possession reached the west coast; Jefferson himself, "as he indicated in his instruction" for the Expedition, "seems to have thought" the purchase "probably extended to the Pacific." Whatever his thoughts, in his message to Congress, the president admitted the "very boundaries to be obscure."[15] By 1805, Lewis and Clark did reach the Pacific Ocean, "highway to the world," but it would take more settlement and struggle with Great Britain, as well as Spain, before the U.S. could make the crucial claim to that highway. After securing freedom of the seas for trade in the Atlantic by the War of 1812, in the Adams-Onis Treaty of 1819, the U.S. pushed Spain from the California sea boundary. Mexican claims continued until 1848, when settlement of the Mexican War gave control of the entire California coast. The complex domestic politics of the 1840s dealt with multiple issues, including "Manifest Destiny" and conflict over slavery in the Southwest, and were a part of America's expansionist mentality.

For this focus, the issue is the Marshall Islands and how far the expansionist mentality would reach. "America's first frontier was not the West; it was the sea." European countries continued their international commerce and exploration, while American administrations fretted that the U.S. should have a role as well. As early as 1785, future president John Adams had encouraged American merchants to push "their commerce to the East Indies as fast and as far as it will go."[16] Seamen had already followed that advice, as the first American ship to reach China was in 1784.

John Quincy Adams went further. In 1825, in his inaugural address, this President Adams proposed a pioneering program of exploration in the Pacific, expeditions to "further the cause of education and science," in order to compete with European nations and support American commerce. Adams' efforts laid the groundwork, but in his term of office, other concerns delayed results. It was the unlikely supporter of a strong navy in the person of President Andrew Jackson, who "began to see the importance of science and exploration" for the nation, for science and for new markets.[17]

Still, it would be President Martin Van Buren who finally commissioned Lieutenant Charles Wilkes to lead the great United States Exploring Expedition of 1838–1842, the voyage that gave America its first credibility as a Pacific nation. The decade of delay since the effort of Adams in 1828 involved intrigue, personal frictions, and competition. In retrospect, however, it seemed historic destiny that Wilkes was chosen for the leadership. As a youth, explorer James Cook had been his hero, and Wilkes yearned to follow in Cook's footsteps of exploratory voyages. As a Lieutenant he had cultivated friendship with Navy personnel, learned scores of detail about ship instruments, always seeking "full knowledge" of everything that had already been done in exploration. To seal the resume, Wilkes was a strong Andrew Jackson supporter. In 1837, former President John Quincy Adams, now a representative in the U.S. House of Representatives, had not

One—America Claims the Pacific 13

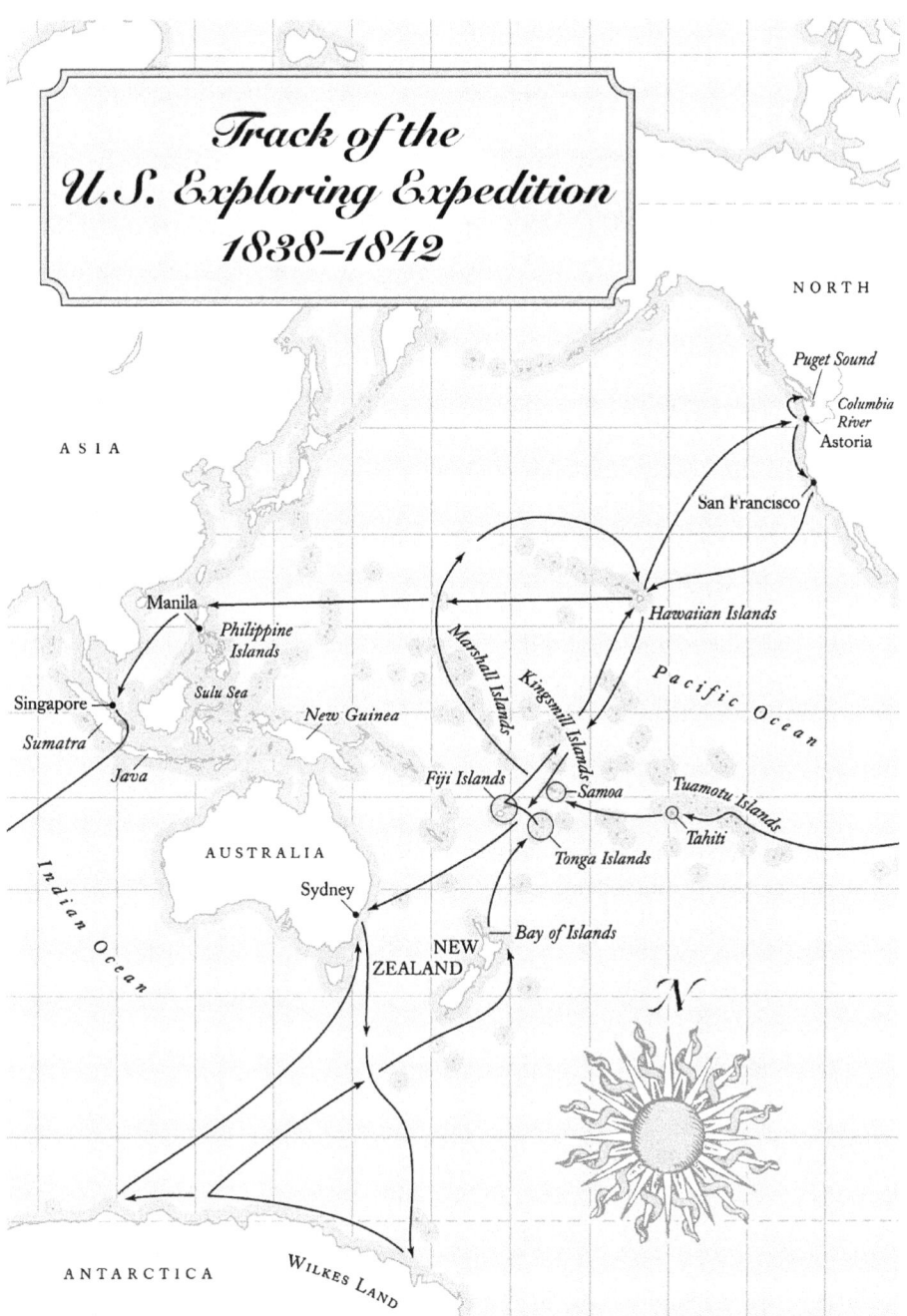

U.S. Exploring Expedition, 1838–1842 (© 2003 Jeffrey L. Ward).

forgotten. In his diary Adams wrote: "…all I wanted to hear about the exploring expedition was that it had sailed."[18]

Sail it did, and it was an extraordinary voyage, including Antarctica, the Atlantic, and Pacific Ocean, where the Marshalls awaited American eyes. The venture included six ships and 346 men, lasted four years, and returned amazing information and artifacts for the U.S. president. The officer who may be credited with saving the expedition from the excesses Wilkes came to exhibit was Officer William Reynolds. From the Reynolds personal diary, historians have learned most about the Wilkes saga from the inside.

More importantly for this telling, when the entourage separated into two groups, it was Reynolds, commanding the *Flying Fish*, along with the *Peacock*, who took a separate route from Wilkes, and actually sailed and mapped the Marshall Islands. This first viewing of the Marshalls by an American produced a sketch of an unnamed "Pacific Island." The drawing looks amazingly similar to the outline of Kwajalein.[19] But while the Wilkes success was impressive, at that point, American commitment was tenuous and unsustainable.

Still, the lure of the Pacific was ever before them. It would take more years of politics and another president's zeal to compete for control of the continent's northwest coast and gateway to the sea. In the 1840s, conflict with England again seemed probable or at least possible over dual claims for Oregon. Neither country was eager for another war, but national politics would play a role in the debate. Newly elected President James K. Polk's political opponents had sought to tarnish his reputation by charging a scheme of expansionism, goading Great Britain with the slogan: "fifty-four forty or fight." Polk did not shy away from the confrontation, while the British agreed to settlement, just at the fifty-four forty parallel. Joint occupation ended and Polk took the credit. In 1848, the Congress clearly defined for America the Oregon Territory. President Polk now saw the northwest coast as an open door for ocean frontiers.[20]

Clash of the West with the Marshalls

Spain had led the way in exploration of the Pacific, including in the Marshall Islands. Although initially claimed by the Spanish as part of its Pacific empire, in truth, the Spanish influence barely touched the Marshalls, in the eastern reaches of Micronesia. Despite first efforts at exploration, Spanish charts generally guided sailors north of the islands until the end of the sixteenth century, when early contact with Spanish sailors gave the Marshallese a reputation for violence and hostile behavior.[21]

As was frequently the case in such chronicles of Western contact with indigenous peoples, the justifiable reasons for inhospitable behavior were rarely publicized. One account showed that locals burned two Spanish ships after the Spanish made attempts to abduct "island women for sale to plantation owners in other parts of the Pacific," clearly violating Marshallese culture and matrilineal values. Reports concerning the character of the Marshallese, a sanguine and genial people, would change by additional interaction with the West. Further, reclaiming its past, in 2013, the Marshalls would hold a "500-Year Celebration," recognizing Spanish "exploration and legacy."[22]

By the eighteenth century, Great Britain had surpassed the forerunners Spain, Portugal, and the Netherlands in Pacific exploration. The British Empire stretched from India to Asia to North America. Even so, it was not until late in the eighteenth century that the British "discovered" the jewel Hawaiian chain. In 1778–1779, Captain James Cook surveyed the islands, claiming them for the empire and first bestowing the name "Sandwich Islands," to honor the British Lord of the Admiralty. Seeking ocean passage between the Pacific and Atlantic, Cook sought the ease of conveyance for his cargos of "criminals and social undesirables" en route to Australia. Cook and other British captains explored the equatorial islands as well, even assuming naming rights as in the case of Captain John Marshall. British contact with the Marshallese reportedly was "relaxed and cordial," dispelling former reports of savagery. The previous reputation reported by Spanish sailors, nevertheless, had afforded the Marshallese two centuries of protection from colonial zeal. Now, on the map a "location marked," thanks to the sea captains, they became an alternate route for the China trade. Again in recognizing their history, in the twenty-first century, some wish to reclaim their Marshallese name, Aelon Kein, "Our Islands."[23]

Religion

In the early part of the nineteenth century, a means other than trade for drawing the future of the Marshall Islands proved deeper and more lasting: that of religion. The impact of Christian missions on the exploration of the Pacific and on American policy was substantial in both subtle and direct ways. Often missionaries were among the first to the islands, as in Hawaii starting in 1820, joining merchants, traders, and whalers who made official Washington aware of the significance of the ports and natural resources. In the Marshalls, the Spanish lack of interest in administering governance control opened the way for an early American influence through its missionary effort. Regrettably for Spain, its lack of oversight by mid-century accounted for a Protestant majority among the indigenous population. The first Roman Catholic mission, at Jaluit, would not enter the Marshalls until 1899.[24]

In 1857, preceding the German presence by only a few years, and the Roman Catholic Church by more than twenty years, the American Board of Commissioners for Foreign Missions out of Boston, Massachusetts, visited Ebon Atoll, Marshall Islands, in the persons of Dr. and Mrs. George Pierson and Mr. and Mrs. Edward Doane. Notably, this group represented the same band of Congregationalists that indelibly stamped the Hawaiian Islands with a stern puritanism. There, at first resistant to the message of the Americans, so foreign to their beliefs, the turn came with the conversion of the strong female leader Kaahumanu, queen regent and prime minister at the time of a severe illness. After healing attributed to a female missionary's medical assistance, Kaahumanu converted to Protestantism, changing forever Hawaiian history. By the end of the nineteenth century, the influence of missionaries and their descendants would lead to complete control of the government and betrayal of the Hawaiian culture.[25] The conclusion of the Hawaiian accession to America will be seen in context in the next chapter.

The carry-over missionary influence in the Marshalls is the subject here. In 1855, Pierson had scouted the prospects for a Protestant mission with the help of Captain Ichabod Handy, a pious whaler knowledgeable of the Marshalls and claiming "about seventeen years" of "occasional trading calls" and living in the islands.[26] Through enormous good luck, or providence as they would have seen it, Handy landed Dr. and Mrs. Pierson on Ailinglapalap, the traditional "main residence" of the paramount *iroij* of the Ralik chain, which included Kwajalein Atoll. There he met Kaibuke himself, according to Pierson, "a crafty old chief," who apparently sensed some benefit for himself and his people. Surprisingly, Kaibuke denounced his previous war on whites and "promised Pierson his personal protection if only he and other missionaries would make their home" in the islands of the Ralik.[27] For their part, the missionaries saw the islanders as "not absolutely savage, but hardy and fighting...." Ironically, considering later Japanese assessments of their being "less-civilized," the early missionaries saw the Marshallese as:

unmistakably of Japanese extraction.... Their features and physical organization are most strikingly similar.... Like the Japanese and Chinese, they are remarkably industrious. They are constantly at work, whether upon the land or sea.... This trait is most strikingly in contrast with all the Polynesian tribes, so proverbially indolent.[28]

No doubt, this trait would be impressive for those who carried with them the Calvinist work ethic.

Hiram Bingham, who had begun the Boston Congregationalist mission in Hawaii, and his Hawaiian protégé Kanoa, both bound for the Gilberts, accompanied Pierson when he returned to Ebon in 1857, with Edward Doane. Ebon, south of Ailinglapalap, proved the ideal starting point, since Kaibuke made his home there, ensuring the missionaries' safety. Kaibuke's influence "had not peer" and his assistance was essential for their success. "It must be said to his credit," the 1858 reporter insisted, "that he has always kept his word, originally made to Dr. Pierson, that he would protect the mission. He took Dr. Pierson for 'his son' and Mr. Doan for 'his friend.'"[29]

Another indication of the real bond between the religious and the islanders, in light of the power of sisterhood in the Marshallese matrilineal culture, was comparable to the incident in Hawaii related above. It was striking that Nemaira, the sister of Kaibuke, formed an equally touching friendship with Mrs. Pierson. One reporter honored Mrs. Pierson as the "first white female who ventured to risk her life amongst the [people] of the Marshall Islands. Her mission was a noble one...." Her "influence with Nemaira, the sister of Kaibuke, was very great...." Pierson's account from the 1860s explained the honored role: "Among the chiefs, everything, in regard to rank, depends upon who was a chief's mother. The female gives rank."[30]

While Kaibuke's protection was the salient factor allowing for survival for the foreigners early on, the chief's "conversion" may have been primarily pragmatic for peace in the *bwij* (lineage). Traditional warfare continued for a time despite teachings of humility and peace; attendance in religious services could be affected by other, secular concerns on a Sunday. "Every so often Kaibuke would sail off to one of the northern islands of the chains with virtually all the lesser chiefs and a party of three or four hundred retainers to reassert his claims and collect tribute." Despite the resulting poor attendance at worship, in the long run, this chance for interaction did more to spread the word of the new religion than any American effort could have.[31]

Meanwhile, Kaibuke kept his promise of protection for the missionaries, which would result in a continuing link with one brand of Protestant

America. The "puritans" left a profound mark on the culture of the Marshalls, roundly denouncing the habits of infanticide, tattooing, and insisted on abstinence from alcohol, tobacco, and firearms. Even if not totally successful in implementation, the imprint was unmistakable. After the Roman Catholic mission was established in Jaluit, competition between the churches would continue. Counter to the nineteenth century reduction in population after contact with Western diseases, the impact of the Roman Catholic aversion to birth control would disrupt the traditional, common-sense methods and create problematic over-population by the late twentieth century. In the twenty-first century, casual sex and teenage pregnancy were issues for concern.[32]

Ultimately, however, it was not the Americans themselves who guaranteed success for the conversion effort, since by 1877 they had left the central Pacific. Rather, the first critical factor was that the American pioneers were supplemented by their protégé Hawaiians. Without the work of these "energetic and resourceful" islanders in the "critical first fifteen years," the mission would have failed. In fact, Pierson and his wife left the Marshall Islands with serious health problems in fewer than five years; Doane journeyed on to the Caroline Islands, to do battle in competition with Roman Catholic missionaries, under imperious Spanish authority. In 1861, he sent his family to Hawaii and followed there himself in 1863, where he died without returning to the Marshalls.[33]

In addition to the cultural impact, the second factor of influence of the Protestants in the Marshalls was the success of the mission school in teaching some locals to tutor others. In later years, superior Roman Catholic schools would compete and surpass these initial efforts, but it was the Protestant mission that made the first impact and opened the doors of education for islanders. Marshallese youth, thrilled with reading "their letters," quickly learned to read and write, becoming instruments for education and religion in the second and following generations of converts. After 1863, and Kaibuke's death from typhoid fever (the result of other traders "discovering" the Marshalls), the chiefs became less enamored with the American religious message and presence. Pierson reflected that it would be "no surprising thing if the mission should be violently opposed" by the powerful *iroij*, "who look with a jealous eye upon the fact that their subjects are learning to read and acquire knowledge." In the 1860s, even with the developing lukewarm attitude of the *iroij*, the church grew rapidly. By the end of the decade, there were "more than a hundred communicants." By the mid–1870s, there were over two hundred members and missions on most inhabited islands in both chains.[34] The Marshallese people would continue to value education, which would be a major contribution of United States policy in the twentieth and twenty-first centuries.

The missionary influence on the culture had been enormous, and more importantly for the future, the American presence remained. English was almost a universal language in the Marshalls, while "all things American" were dominant. The United States had achieved the positive reputation of "patron" without a single warship or embassy official.[35]

Two

National Competition in the Nineteenth Century

As often the case, the sparring of religious factions in the Pacific was but a reflection of the international politics that would have a major impact on indigenous peoples. Equally ubiquitous were the commercial sea captains, who planted their country's flag, competed for islanders' allegiance and markets, and then called for and expected governmental protection for their ventures. Such adventurers led the way for national claims. In following this process in the nineteenth century, focus here will be on the competition that would have the greatest impact on the Marshall Islands, and on the rising aspirations of the United States to seek its share of Pacific wealth and control.

While Spain had been a forerunner in overseas empire, the harbinger of its eclipse in both oceans was at hand. First, America was now coming of age. In the Monroe Doctrine of 1823, the United States declared its hegemony in the Western Hemisphere, portending conflict with Spain by the end of the century. Second, Germany's power triangulation, excluding Spain, would shape the future of the Pacific. Newcomers to imperialistic nationalism such as the United States and Germany carefully observed the extent of the British Empire, not failing to note that colonies and trade were integral to its control and national wealth.

Germany's primary interest in the Pacific would be in commercial venture that would grow rapidly. Though it never reached the expected success for the Imperial treasury, it did serve to introduce a national "presence in the world," and several key investors "benefited enormously." The colonial economic investment became three-fold: commercial, as traders with Pacific islanders and general port merchants; agricultural, as planters, mainly of copra; and extractive, as mine owners.[1]

In 1859, the first strike in the Marshalls had been made by trader Adolph Capelle of Hanover, who settled on Ebon and worked for the firm of Hoffschlaeger & Stapenhorst. When that firm failed, Capelle joined with another newcomer, Jose deBrum, and together they created their own business, quickly expanding their trading stations in other islands. Various German companies discovered the potential in the Marshalls, sometimes trying and failing. The two largest, Deutsche Handels- und Plantagen Gesellschaft (DHPG), and, on Jaluit, Robertson & Hernsheim, claimed a large share of the copra and retail trade in the Marshalls. By the 1880s, with pressure from the Imperial government, the two formed a joint-stock company called the Jaluit Company. Eventually, the chancellor would allow the Jaluit Company to actually administer the Marshalls, running the operation "like a company store."[2]

The competition and conflict between nations for the Pacific trade would bring major change for the Marshallese generally, and uniquely for the religious. German plans for a lucrative business ran headlong into the faith-based dictum against alcohol and tobacco, the primary trade for copra. Clearly, the captains did not appreciate the interference of the Protestant church in the financial scheme, subjecting missionaries to "annoying inconvenience and extra expense" to register, even attempting to confiscate part of Congregational Church offering. Some thought it clear the Germans were "trying to drive ... American missionaries from the Marshall Islands. They do not want anybody or thing there which will in any way hinder their money making."[3]

German colonial policy had awaited the consolidation of the nation in 1871 and leadership of Chancellor Otto von Bismarck, the architect of unification. Bismarck trod lightly around the German Reichstag's aversion to the "expense and friction" of overseas adventurism, while grandly engaged in a "duplicity of style." Publicly and shrewdly he eschewed such actions, even as diplomatically and secretly the chancellor jockeyed for control in the arena of Pacific trade.[4]

In the 1870s, and "anxious not to be left out," the first phase of Bismarck's competitive strategy was deference to England's mastery of the seas, even while gaining Britain's essential cooperation.[5] After secret negotiations the previous year, in April 1876, England and Germany baldly divided the Pacific between them. Ignoring Spain, as well as any overlapping ambitions of France, its European rival, Germany accepted British claims to the west, and in the South Pacific recognized the Empire's colonies in Australia, New Zealand, and New Guinea. Germany's "half" would be the eastern portion, with the Carolines and Marshall Islands to be considered in Germany's "sphere of influence." Ultimately, the unintended consequence of this division, not visible at the time, would remove British competition and enable Japan to claim control over the southern Pacific routes, followed in the next chapter.[6]

Despite Spain's attempt to regulate German Pacific commerce and protests as early as 1873, the tide had turned. German captains already knew well the routes through the Carolines and Marshalls and dominated the trade routes of the equatorial islands. Then, in 1876, Chancellor Bismarck obtained his Reichstag's approval for "government protection to all commercial enterprise overseas." It would be their "duty" not to leave "German enterprises in the Pacific entirely to their fate…" but to make sure "one or more German war-vessels continually operated in that region." This modus operandi already was apparent with German traders in the Marshalls.[7]

Following, the Madrid Protocol of March 1877 addressed the continuing question of Spanish sovereignty, with signatories Germany, Spain, and (notably) England. Spain settled for the protocol's language that guaranteed "freedom of traffic" in "all areas not actually under the occupation of any country," the commercial intent of the three signers in any case.[8] Not fully put to rest, however, the questions of Spanish rights would return in the next decade. Bismarck's treaties and protocols were merely delivering the imperial protection expected by citizens abroad and basic to colonial control, cementing the "golden age of German commerce in the Pacific." By the 1880s, Bismarck had developed "diplomatic mastery," and perhaps less need for deference to Great Britain.[9]

Following the 1877 Protocol, Bismarck's warships made the difference in gaining the attention of indigenes and some response in allegiance to the new power. The Germans had great ambitions for more, more efficient, and thereby more lucrative copra plantations. They were aware, as well, that "free," that is, unimpeded trade, depended on "continuous peace with the natives."[10] Their "political intervention" came in the form much like that the missionaries had sought for religious inroads: the authority of traditional *iroij* (chiefs). Bismarck would attempt so-called "treaty" and then simply make the Jaluit Company the governing agent.[11]

In 1885, German Commander Rotger of the SMS *Nautilus* signed an official "treaty of friendship" with *Iroij* Kabua of the Ralik, the chain that included Kwajalein as well as Jaluit. The treaty guaranteed the "protection of the German emperor" for Kabua's Marshallese subjects; the purpose, as well, "to protect the legal trade" and "to provide the German traders with full security.…" To seal the agreement, a ceremony in Jaluit included the concurrence of "other high chiefs" and a twenty-one-gun salute to the *Iroij*, dubbed "King Kabua" by the Germans.[12] This gesture of respect paid off handsomely in gaining Kabua's loyalty, but also led to complications when conflicts arose in the inevitable land claims.

The simplicity of the European idea of feudalism could not comprehend the complexity of Marshallese land traditions or appreciate the ways in which warfare had reflected internal *iroij* strength in settling disputes. Thus, building on the ethical teaching of the missionaries to accommodate their own commercial ends, the Germans effectively ended warring between competitive local *bwij* (lineages) over land. But when the warring ceased, the *iroij* and *leroij* in power at the time remained fixed, locking in perpetual disputes, requiring a new method of settlement. This would be one source for much of the frustration of later American efforts to sort out land claims on the islands, especially for Kwajalein. When he died in 1910, the Germans would remember that Kabua had "kept the loyalty he promised to the Empire"; and "it had never been necessary to intervene with armed force," though dangerously close on occasion.[13]

The introduction of the Jesuit mission in the Marshalls in 1899 further complicated the negotiations for land settlements, as had German legal jurisdiction.[14] In one case, which the German administrators documented extensively, the Roman Catholics took the opposing side of one challenge to Kabua's land claim, that supported by the Protestants. The dispute required a German ruling, which initially went against the aging chief. After more than five years of hearings and charges based on "native law," the Germans reversed the judgment and acknowledged Kabua's claim. Internal documents reveal how the foreigners struggled:

> more importance has to be placed on the fairness of the law than on its strict application.
> A settlement of the entire property situation with the goal of apportioning the land to the commoners will be opposed by the entire population as long as a legitimate *iroij* lives.... Acquiring a command of the language ... is absolutely necessary, [but] takes a fairly long time.... Close contact with natives is necessary....

After this incident, Germans pondered the implications of superimposing the Empire's law on traditional mores. One bureaucratic solution had suggested deporting Kabua to New Guinea if he did not comply with the German ruling. The negative response was predictable: to have removed Kabua, the imperialists discussed darkly, "would be ... a measure whose consequences cannot be predicted." Equally unpopular was the plan to move some *rejerbal* (local workers) to outer islands for copra production.[15]

The legal procedures themselves brought a worsening of German/

Marshallese relations and "great distrust of local natives" resulted. Fear of an uprising in the face of insult to Kabua made the Germans decide "'to display the flag' on several important atolls." Kabua's influence "is so great," wired a worried Commander Ahlert, "that any measure against him on the part of the government could lead to an insurrection," a sobering reminder of the vulnerability of colonial rule.[16]

The other dilemma building for German control was the growing power of the United States that could not be ignored. Already noted was the competition of the Marshallese Protestant missionaries, understood as American influence, with officials noting that: "consciously or unconsciously the islanders will prefer things English or American...."[17]

Hawaii and Samoa

With unmistakable determination, the United States intended to be a competitor for a two-ocean economic advantage. Through multiple presidential administrations through the nineteenth century, America carried on its own manipulative diplomacy concerning the Pacific, as illustrated in the examples of Hawaii and Samoa.

First Hawaii. These islands had intrigued Europeans from their finding in 1778, amazingly late in the age of Western exploration. Americans were no less fascinated by the awesome beauty of the islands, as well as their location in the northern waters of the Pacific, seductively close, only 2000 miles from the Northwest mainland. As noted, America was gaining its sea legs in the early nineteenth century, with reports of traders, missionaries, and whalers. In his voyages, Naval Lieutenant Charles Wilkes, in addition to the Marshalls, made several passes and stopovers in Hawaii. Wilkes' discovery of a plaque there honoring Captain James Cook, his own hero, further endeared the islands to him.[18]

As early as 1840, he had underscored potential for a harbor at the mouth of the Pearl River, as had the British. Wilkes noted that the name derived from the fact that "the pearl oyster is found there." Further, that "after passing" the "coral bar" at the mouth, "which is four hundred feet wide, the depth of water becomes ample for large ships..." and "would afford the best and most capacious harbour [sic] in the Pacific."[19]

With that claim, President John Tyler warned Great Britain and France against annexing the chain, subtlety implying little American interest in annexation itself. Tyler's Secretary of State Daniel Webster, explicit and eloquent as always, noted:

> A great majority of vessels visiting the Sandwich Islands were American. Further, the United States would be "more interested in the fate of the islands, and of their government, than any other nation can be...." Therefore ... no power ought either to take possession of the islands as a conquest, or for any purpose of colonization ... or any exclusive privileges in matters of commerce.[20]

In his message to Congress, Tyler himself reiterated the message: the U.S. would harbor "dissatisfaction" if there were "any attempt by another power, should such attempt be threatened or feared to take possession of the islands, colonize them, and subvert the native Government." The U.S.

> possesses so large a share in the intercourse of those islands, it is deemed not unfit to make the declaration that their Government seeks no peculiar advantages, no exclusive control over the Hawaiian Government, but is content with its independent existence, and anxiously wishes for its security and prosperity.

In what became known as the Tyler Doctrine, the president continued by making the argument that the China trade would justify such protective status. The U.S. would allow no other nation to control the Hawaiian Islands. A young newspaper editor in Maine, James G. Blaine, was among those who by the 1850s were "infected by the Hawaiian annexation fever," while the fulfillment of Tyler's vow would be seen by the end of the century.[21]

The details of the sad story of the sabotage of Hawaiian culture and government by the missionaries and their descendants is beyond the scope of this work, but remains an essential part of this policy narrative. The impact of the foreigners in those islands created "literally a land of death..."—western diseases decimating the indigenous population, making the people even more vulnerable to the aggressive commercialism of the invaders. Hawaiian trust in the missionary "advice" and then "a gradual accommodation of the *haole* [not indigene], first their presence, their religion, their legal system, and finally their economics" led to final control by the white oligarchy.[22]

The expanding search of the U.S. naval fleet for a coaling station in the Pacific merged the two major American interests, military and economic, into a death knell for any Hawaiian independence. The growing power of the sugar industry, stepchild of the missionary zeal, pushed for a U.S. market guarantee through the Reciprocity Treaty of 1875–1876. Reciprocity "meant American duties on Hawaiian sugar in exchange for Hawaiian concessions on imported American goods." Despite their objection to that preferential treatment, essentially making Hawaii an American protectorate, the British chose not to contest growing U.S. control at this point. The continuing story of the U.S. capture of Hawaii through annexation will be told below.[23]

A second example of America's Pacific adventure was in Samoa, where the nation's attention again had begun through individual seaman's discovery of "the lazy delights of South Sea life." Competitive interest by France and England had long preceded Germany's, though German traders had arrived by 1857. American voyager Lt. Wilkes had included Samoa in his expedition and mapping in the 1830s. Wilkes noted economic promise, while missionaries added their input with claims on "native" sensibilities—all familiar red flags for future conflict.[24]

For the United States, the attention regarding Hawaii ran parallel to that for Samoa. While Secretary of State William Seward had been successful in convincing a reluctant Congress to purchase Alaska in 1867, President Ulysses Grant's plea for also valuing potential for the Samoan harbor of Pago Pago had fallen on deaf ears. Other individual efforts to keep the islands in national consciousness found little support. In the meantime, the late 1870s were replete with local intrigue between rival German, English, and American efforts to sway indigenous leaders.[25]

After success with the Hawaiian Reciprocity Treaty in 1875–1876, some hoped for a Samoan port as well. With additional endorsement of the Navy, and despite British support for Germany's claim, the U.S. ignored German desire for the harbor. In January 1878, the U.S. Senate unanimously ratified a treaty of friendship and commerce with Samoa that laid the groundwork for the later effort to secure the desired potential naval station on Samoa's Tituila Island. James G. Blaine, foreign policy disciple of Seward and by that time a U.S. Senator (R–ME), had "finalized his blueprints" for empire. The United States "would control two of the potentially finest naval stations in the Pacific—Pearl Harbor in Hawaii and Pago Pago in Samoa." Commodore Robert W. Shufeldt expressed the Navy's delight: "the Pacific Ocean is to become at no distant day the commercial domain of America."[26]

Spain clearly began to rethink relinquishing its stake in the Pacific. Spain's growing resentment over the actions of German traders, success of the Jaluit Company in the Marshalls, and controversy on Yap in the Carolines, increased tension. With the nation's legitimate claim of first discovery, Spanish sovereignty was again the issue.[27]

One must admire Bismarck, who "acted on his beliefs" at "the exact moment they served a practical need," as well as the chancellor's basic need to balance domestic with foreign policy goals. Facing the hostility of America in Samoa and Spain in the Carolines, Bismarck turned for assistance to the Roman Catholic Pope Leo XIII, whom he had previously sought to suppress, and with whom he had been sparring at home in Germany for years over the "temporal power of the papacy."²⁸ Asking that Pope Leo XIII handle arbitration in the dispute was a coup: an offer the Spanish found hard to refuse and recognition Leo coveted. Thus, by "bowing" to the papal ruling, with the mere acknowledgment of Spanish "sovereignty," Bismarck achieved his goal: "freedom of trade in all areas not actually under the occupation of any country," basically a restatement of the 1877 ruling.

Also, ever mindful of Pacific triangulation, Bismarck gained "prior agreement with Britain and the United States" before agreeing to the settlement: Germany would accept Spain's sovereignty over the Carolines, but gained "freedom of trade" and "the right to establish coaling depots and naval stations." The British gained the Gilbert and Ellice Islands (Tuvalu), in exchange for British approval of German annexation of the Marshalls.²⁹

Still, Bismarck chose not to confront the United States. The Americans, well aware that their Protestant missionaries held superiority in numbers of converts but would have no administrative support, gained the promise of "freedom of conscience and freedom of religious worship."³⁰ Spelled out in the ruling, and signed at the Vatican in December 1885, this would be the German means for continuing control of the Marshalls, still to be made official by treaty between Spain and Germany in 1899 (document below).

The Vatican ruling consoled Spain for a time, but conflict continued on the Samoan Islands. In 1887, at the Washington Conference, an American effort at negotiated settlement failed, as Germany and England did not agree to America's scheme for a "tripartite agreement" based on distinctive zones in Samoa.³¹ Further, while foreign offices exchanged tense diplomatic notes, tensions among rivals on the islands escalated until 1889. Galvanized by the new emphasis on the perceived need for naval expansion, the American press as well as the U.S. Congress railed against Bismarck's "alleged German affronts," insisting that President Grover Cleveland hasten to construct the naval port at Pago Pago. One senator even proposed extending the Monroe Doctrine to include both Hawaii and Samoa.³² The growing competition with Germany would turn venomous again with America's taking of Hawaii. Meanwhile, the new Benjamin Harrison Administration included "architect of empire" James G. Blaine, again Secretary of State. Having served in the role for a brief nine months in the Garfield Administration, Blaine now continued his plan to gain dominance in the Pacific arena. In Samoa, the fortuitous hurricane of 15–16 March 1889 demolished the navies of the three rival nations in the Pago Pago harbor, cooling passions perhaps; but, in truth, Bismarck, as well as Blaine, was playing from a different score. His last speech as Chancellor was 18 May 1889. After the elections of February 1890, when he lost his majority in the Reichstag, Wilhelm II forced his resignation in March 1890. Later, in assessing his career, the German Chancellor admitted: "In politics, you cannot focus on a long-range plan and proceed blindly ... but draw the broad outlines...." These "keep unswervingly in view, even though you may not know the precise route that will get you there...." For him, diplomacy could not "prevent war; it can merely" make "peace more attractive."[33]

Thus, two years after the failed Washington Conference in 1887, with increased pressure from Blaine and the United States, Bismarck suggested another meeting to resolve the issue. In Berlin, "the three powers recognize[d] ... the independence of the Samoan Government and the free right of the natives to ... choose their form of government." Also, the agreement included "prohibition" or power to "regulate" in the "importation and sale of firearms and alcoholic liquors."[34]

Seen another way for the purpose of this study, Bismarck had gained Germany a foothold in Samoa. More importantly, the now recognized, uncontested prize was total control in the Marshalls—discounting any resistance from the islanders, of course. Having vanquished all national contenders through negotiation, the Empire could now focus on what it viewed as the greatest profit from monopoly that "appeared to hold promise," the most lucrative market of the Pacific: "the copra plantations business in the Marshall Islands...." And by the twentieth century, the investment would include phosphate mining in the islands. On the other hand, while the German military intent could be measured by its General Staff's potential war plans against the U.S., the final version of the destructive competition between the U.S. and Germany yet lay in the future.[35]

Instead, still absorbed with finalizing their Samoa venture, the Hawaiian "fruit" was about to ripen, as Americans perceived Hawaii the key to American Pacific interests. In 1888, Thomas F. Bayard, Secretary of State in President Grover Cleveland's first term, quoted John Quincy Adams' analogy: the U.S. only had "to wait quietly and patiently and let the islands fill up with American planters and American industries until they should be wholly identified with the United States. It was simply a matter of waiting until the apple should fall."[36]

Annexation would require U.S. control of domestic politics in the islands. Descendants of missionaries, Lorrin A. Thurston and Sanford B. Dole, had joined with other planters and businessmen in the 1880s to foster discontent by creating the Hawaiian League. By 1892, these same members went further to organize a secret Annexationist Club. Over the century, with increased *haole* power, the fragmentation of the Hawaiian government had resulted in the minority white (read American) intent on revolution against the monarchy in the person of Queen Liliuokalani. The manner of U.S. intervention that guaranteed the loss of power for indigenous rule, however interpreted, resulted in the "hard fact" of American hegemony.[37]

For those eager to close the deal, the re-election of Grover Cleveland as U.S. President in 1892 proved frustrating as it stalled annexation for a time. The death of Blaine in January 1893 punctuated the changeover to Cleveland, reluctant imperialist, who took the incredulous step back to seek input from the Hawaiians themselves regarding the looming American takeover.[38]

Whatever the view regarding the efficacy of the Cleveland effort, the years of his administration provided new grist for the argument pro annexation. The military interest in a Pearl River harbor, not yet a reality, grew with the demand for naval expansion. In addition, the Americans eyed the emerging racial diversity in the islands with anxiety. Blaine himself had feared "continued Oriental migration" and the overwhelming influx of Indian workers to the insatiable sugar plantations. Various European nationalities, as well as the Chinese, supplied laborers, while the McKinley tariff of 1890 had "stripped" Hawaii of its reciprocity advantages, "putting foreign sugar on the duty-free list," just as Hawaii sugar had enjoyed with the previous treaty.[39]

The Turning Point and War

In the United States, the political atmosphere through the decade of the 1890s created the context for a major turning point for American foreign policy: the decision to join full bore the international competition for trade and bases in the Pacific. The confluence of factors proved compelling. First was Alfred Mahan's persuasive history of the British Empire, with the conclusion that dominance rested on "Sea Power." The U.S., Mahan insisted, should take its place as "world power," evidenced by America as the "citadel of Christian civilization," taking on the "great task" for "the westward course of empire" in the Pacific.[40] The growing pains of the U.S. Navy, eager to be the cutting edge of American presence in the Pacific as well as mainland costal defense if needed, had found the leadership of Secretary of the Navy Benjamin Tracy in the Harrison Administration. Tracy responded to Mahan's trumpet by requesting more battleships for the arsenal. Mahan's continuous publications on duty and destiny further increased domestic public support.[41] Second, others such as Congregational minister Josiah Strong stirred toxic racial patriotism with his paean to "Our Country: Its Possible Future and Its Present Crisis" adding to Mahan's chorus. Mahan as well as Strong bolstered the myth of Anglo-Saxon superiority to redeem the Asian world. Couched in the ethical language of mission and principle, even the religious community could buy into the resulting move to empire.[42]

Third, and perhaps most significant, was the planning and strategy of President William McKinley, the reassuring public presence of a genial preacher coupled with cold realism in private consultation. After the electorate of 1896 chose the Republican party's combined platform of military strength and economic opportunity, the die was cast. McKinley's jingoist Navy advisors Teddy Roosevelt and Secretary John D. Long, both stewards of Blaine in their thinking, pushed hard for a Pacific strategy to serve the Monroe Doctrine—meaning a two-ocean U.S. Navy. Additional "war lovers" in Senator Henry Cabot Lodge (R-MA) and William Randolph Hearst, whose newspapers enflamed passion, would provide the justification.[43] McKinley was the perfect placid face for an underlying brutal strategy: it would be America's duty to save Western civilization by acquiring colonies in the Pacific. For American officials, the Marshalls were not yet on their radar screen. Leaving the islands in the grasp of the Germans, the military advantage at Kwajalein was yet to be realized. Hawaii, on the other hand, was a must.

It would be the growing number of Japanese laborers that crystallized the issue for the U.S. Fear of the emerging ambitions of Japan, America's new Pacific competitor, supplied the final rationale for American annexation of Hawaii. In these years, naval planners, sensing the threat, would draw up the first Code Orange plan for defense of Hawaii from Japanese attack.[44] In the twentieth century, Japan would provide the next version of imperial control for the Marshall Islands and would supply the nexus of the United States with the Marshalls. A full discussion of Japan's rise will be covered in the next chapter.

With the growing number of Japanese in Hawaii, Japan demanded that Japanese migrants be more than laborers in the sugar plantations and perhaps even vote. But the Japanese attempt to guarantee equality for these migrants as citizens provided an avenue for an even greater Japanese presence, one that was unacceptable to the United States. As the number of Asian workers surpassed both whites and islanders, fears of losing control through actual civil rights for plantation hands stoked the fires for greater

American control.⁴⁵ The U.S., of course, was not alone in fearing Japan's move west and its rise to imperial status. Britain and Germany, each with covetous eyes on the Hawaiian chain, watched the match being played out.

Timing is everything. The Japanese threat in 1897, coinciding with the growing antagonism with Spain over Cuban policy, brought the perfect opportunity for the McKinley Administration to build on and bring to fruition the work of previous long-term Pacific planners from John Tyler to James Blaine. In 1898, the perceived crisis convinced McKinley to move on the annexation of Hawaii, guaranteeing that the islands remain secure in American control if or when war came, which it did in 1898. America's defeat of Spain would even bring the Philippine Islands into play, as well as a new chance for Germany to realize the colonial strategy carefully laid by Bismarck. The effort to secure a sphere in China made the nearby Philippines as attractive to Germany as to the U.S. and England.⁴⁶

Thus, American strategy to attack Spain first in the Philippines brought Germany and the United States close to war. A "host of foreign spectators" converged in Manila Bay, to be sure, but the "German presence was most keenly felt by Dewey." Frantic cables during the confrontation appeared to little avail, but tension abated with the victory of the Americans and then Germany's reconsideration in quest of some alternative sop. The debate thereby moved to the peace talks. There, Germany "firmly resolved not to be left out of the Spanish 'liquidation.'"⁴⁷

Here the Marshall Islands again entered the equation. After the cease-fire between the U.S and Spain on 12 August 1898, the American Peace Commission convened in Paris, under the direct supervision of President McKinley from Washington.⁴⁸ The high-stake negotiations began behind the scenes between the three big players: Germany's attempt to gain Spanish colonies; Spain's attempt to save face as well as some territory; and the U.S. attempt to gain maximum benefit in Pacific islands from its victory. America expressed interest in the island of Kusaie in the Carolines, with an eye to securing underwater cable, a new possibility of conflict with Germany, whose interest was a coaling station in the Sulu Archipelago of the Philippines. The British, always the guarantor of any Pacific agreement, would attempt to keep careful watch over its colonial interests and German ambitions in Africa. Antecedent to struggles yet to arise, the Brits also were anxious that the U.S. retain the Philippines because of their geographical location near China.⁴⁹

In the Paris negotiations, Germany's relentless attempt to secure its place in the Pacific arena of control, specifically in the Philippines, prompted a new tactic employing the one island group it did control, namely the Marshall Islands. How about an island in the Marshalls in exchange for an island in the Philippines?

Thereby, a toehold in the Marshalls was dangled before American eyes, in the person of John B. Jackson, official from the American Embassy in Germany. Bismarck's successor Foreign Secretary Bernhard von Bulow drew a straight line from the Northwest United States coast to Hawaii and then through the Marshall Islands to the Philippines and China: "Germany was willing, said von Bulow, to negotiate with the United States for one of the Marshall Islands ... in return for Germany's right to a coaling station on one of the Sulus." The island named was Gaspar Rico, Taongi Atoll in the Ralak chain.[50]

Despite visual map evidence of the strategic location the Marshalls enjoyed, the U.S. was reluctant to deal. Some officials saw Wake Island as a better prospect for a proposed cable route; others were reluctant to offer any foothold to Germany in the Philippines, even in the southern Sulu Archipelago.[51] American doubts prevailed. From July to December 1889, negotiators attempted "to harmonize Germany's appetite for territorial acquisition with America's annexationist plans and aims." But Kaiser Wilhelm's instructions were: to "avoid difficulties any misunderstandings with the United States so long as that is compatible with the dignity of the empire."[52]

The moment for diplomatic agreement between the U.S. and Germany dissolved, and the Marshalls moved away from the U.S. sphere, a mistake America did not recognize for years, when advisors to future presidents would again draw von Bulow's straight line in the Pacific through the Marshalls and Kwajalein Atoll.

In December 1898, the U.S. and Spain signed their peace agreement, while McKinley claimed the Philippines by Executive Order, sealing the fate of the Filipinos. In February 1899, after a long debate over the "rightfulness of the administration argument," the U.S. Senate ratified the treaty. America "had forged a new empire."[53] Spain reluctantly relinquished control of the Philippines, Wake Island, Puerto Rico, and Guam, consoled by twenty million dollars and the promise of a more lucrative sale to Germany pending the settlement.

To quell the Kaiser's fury, in secret talks, Spain "promised to cede to Germany all of the Carolines, Palau, and Marianas, with the exception of Guam, for a price...."[54] Mollified if not satisfied, the Spanish Cortes ratified the treaty on 11 April 1899; the German Reichstag on 22 June 1899. The Treaty of 1899 included:

First. The German Empire will recognize in said islands the Spanish religious orders the same rights and the same liberties that recognize the missions of the German religious orders.

Second. The German Empire will give to the commerce and the Spanish agriculture establishments the ... same facilities ... to the commerce of German subjects.

Third. Spain will be able to establish and to conserve ... a deposit of coal of the navy and merchantmen....

Fourth. The German Empire will compensate the transfer of the aforementioned territories ... the sum 25 million pesetas, that will be credited to Spain.[55]

The final unresolved piece regarded Samoa. At the initiation of Germany, the three contestants, Great Britain, Germany, and the U.S., once again convened in Washington on 2 December 1899 and agreed to annul the Berlin General Act which only a few years before had created the tripartite arrangement. Indeed, the three annulled "all previous treaties, conventions and agreements" related to Samoa. The new understanding recognized "the independence of the Samoan Government and the free right of the natives to ... choose their form of government."[56] Then, with England's withdrawal, Germany and the United States divided the islands at the "Longitude 171 west of Greenwich," agreeing to U.S. control of what became American Samoa. As in previous settlements, the three signatories agreed "to continue to enjoy all privileges in the Samoan group 'equal to those enjoyed by the sovereign power in all ports which may be open to the commerce of either of them.'"[57]

After the negotiation, John Hay, now President McKinley's Secretary of State, chortled privately that he was satisfied the Americans had bested the Germans by gaining "Pago Pago, which was of the most vital importance. It is the finest harbor in the Pacific and absolutely indispensable to us." He concluded, "Germany has the least valuable bargain." Whatever that assessment, Hay was perhaps less accurate when he surmised, "they have somewhat lost sight of their material interests in the case...."[58]

Not so much. It was Kaiser Wilhelm II who took credit for vindicating the Pacific balance of powers Bismarck had nurtured. America claimed its Samoa and Hawaii treasures, as well as its pick of Spain's possessions, including Guam and Wake, but the U.S. had now recognized the "legitimacy of Germany's claims in the Pacific." Further, Spain no longer contested Germany's ownership of the Carolines, while the other half of Samoa belonged to Germany. Most pertinent of all, back in 1885, the British had agreed to Germany's unencumbered economic control of the Marshall Islands.[59] German claims were uncontested except by the essential constituency: the Marshallese themselves.

Three

Versailles and the Japanese Mandate

Left for a time under the control of the German Empire, again, international politics would determine the future of the Marshalls. With American President William McKinley's triumph in the Spanish-American War came a new awareness of the blueprint for America's foreign policy in the Pacific. Humanitarian and missionary motives for exploration moved to background status. First and foremost, the "China market" now held America's full attention, despite its rather exaggerated value at the time, as only about one percent of U.S. exports went to China. The plan for expansion was the ticket, with the Hawaiian Islands now under total American jurisdiction for re-coaling benefit. Then, with the ransomed "purchase" of the Philippines and Guam, the last steppingstone was in place. With great celebration, final dredging of the essential Pearl Harbor would shortly follow.[1]

In 1899, McKinley's "Open Door" notes, had demanded an equal place with other European traders in the Asian trade, putting on notice the entire set of world players that the U.S. would not be denied. After a no-answer response to the first round of notes, and in the face of indigenous Chinese resistance to Western trade by the Fists of Righteous Harmony (Boxers) in 1900, with a second round of notes, Secretary of State John Hay added the ominous and impossible clause that the U.S. would: "preserve Chinese territorial and administrative entity ... and safeguard for the world the principle of equal and impartial trade with all parts of the Chinese Empire." Such a guarantee! The stage was then set for "the clash" between Japan and the United Sates in the twentieth century.[2]

This struggle in Asia and the Pacific had been building for decades, "the simultaneous development of Japan and the United States as empires...." America's decade of self-awakening in the 1890s was occurring even while Japan was reviving its own colonial aspirations born as early as the sixteenth century, when "Japanese merchants, warriors, and adventurers" left to the future their dreams of "overseas settlement and colonization."[3] More recent were the trade voyages of the 1880s and exploration of various atolls in the Marshall Islands, including Kwajalein. The Suzuki-Goto Expedition in 1883 produced "copious notes and sketches" of Marshallese villages and harbors.[4] Japanese trader Ukicho Taguchi's insistence on the importance of his nation's control of the "South Pacific" as well as popular literature of the era only further inspired the political strategy building toward Japanese imperialism.[5]

After 1868, the keys to the nationalism of the Meiji Restoration and determination to modernize Japan were threefold: first, avoid being a target of Western imperialism by emulating and surpassing Western encroachment in Asia. Seeing the world divided into the powerful (i.e., the West) versus colonial or semi-colonial, Japan would not be one of the weak.[6]

Second, link territory to trade, noting "overall economic expansion ... after the pattern of the West," the American so-called "peaceful" strategy.[7] The economic effort of Japanese merchants from Marianas to Marshalls through the "South Sea Islands Company" betrayed the Japanese intent through these "commercial pioneers" to compete, even while "wrangling" with the Germans for access. Marshallese *Iroij* Kabua, already noted for his skill in dealing with Germans, was not to be one of the "poor and primitive savages" of Japanese reports. Wary of colonizers, Kabua cleverly warned these new invaders that the Marshalls were "closed to foreigners" except in Jaluit.[8] Jaluit Atoll, of course, was exactly the center of German commercial enterprise through the Jaluit Company. Remarkably, while maneuvering around German claims, the "commercial network" of the Japanese up to 1914 "had gained a near monopoly of trade in central and western Micronesia"—except in Palau and the Marshalls, where the German claim was secure.[9]

In the third key to Meiji modernization lay the destiny of the Marshall Islands, derived from the internal competition between the Japanese Army and Navy. The debate was "landward pull of the neighboring continent" versus the "maritime impulse to move out upon the open seas," exactly the issue of the "northern" land option versus the "southern" ocean strategy.[10] In fact, according to some, most Japanese did not necessarily consider the Asian continent at all when they considered broadening their reach. "The wider Pacific region was more frequently mentioned as an ideal area for undertaking peaceful expansion." Navy Commander Sato Tetsutaro counted Pacific expansion as the link between the three keys: "serious concern of economic advantage, national security, and geopolitics." Japan's future would be "on the ocean"; they would "turn the Pacific into a Japanese lake." This would, of course, require "an increase in Japanese naval strength, trade routes, and opportunity for emigration."[11] Ironically, that same desire for hegemony would color the later U.S. effort to create there "an American Lake."

As that "ocean strategy" expanded to the wider Pacific, a case in point lay in the Hawaii story previously recounted and the Japanese role there. Japanese workers had flocked to the plantations of the white landowners in the islands. At the time of the U.S./Hawaii Reciprocity Treaty (1875–76) that locked the Pearl River lagoon into the American sphere, there were 65,000 Japanese in Hawaii. The growing inevitability of U.S. control infuriated the Japanese government as it protested and then helplessly watched the American takeover. In the end, Tokyo settled for language to protect the "rights" of Japanese workers in Hawaii as well as national Japanese "trading rights." Japan's willingness to "back down" from confronting the U.S. over Hawaii may have been inspired by the internal ascendancy of its "northern strategy," that is, a continental toehold in Manchuria.[12] Clearly, there was no consensus in Japan on the best strategy for accomplishing the goals of modernization.

Crucial to the debate, moreover, was the "emergence ... of Japan as maritime power of first magnitude," while the significance of Japan's two wars at the turn of the century cannot be overemphasized. With the Sino-Japanese War of 1894–95, Japan staked out the strategy of expansion and strength. At the time, the view of China as weak and vulnerable made the mainland an inviting target.[13]

While the war's treaty ceded Taiwan (Formosa) to Japan, the "triple intervention" by Russia, France, and Germany forced the Japanese to return the Liaotung peninsula in southern Manchuria. Three years later, when the Russians leased the same peninsula for its own naval base of Port Arthur, Japan had received its "first major lesson" in what it saw as modern "western imperialism."[14]

Seeing itself confronted by a "colossus of the north," Japan retaliated in the Russo-Japanese War of 1904–05, notoriously initiated by surprise attack at dawn on 8 February 1904. With American support, Japan's success in that conflict added additional weight to the Manchurian path for expansion. Over the opposition of the Chinese, with the American brokers at the Portsmouth Peace Conference in 1905, Japan won controlling rights to the Chinese Eastern Railway, which linked it to the city of Harbin, and renamed it the South Manchuria Railway. The "strategic importance" of that coup was evident.[15]

In 1901, the assassination of William McKinley brought to the U.S. presidency Theodore Roosevelt, brandishing his own "fascination with war." TR himself had guided the American brokers at Portsmouth. Then, in 1907, with his love of bravado and eager to flaunt the potential power of the Navy, he sent an American battleship fleet around the world, in the face of Japanese resentment and seemingly oblivious to the risk of growing anti–Japanese sentiment in California.[16]

American civilian and military leaders, eventually sobered by the obvious and growing Japanese power, stumbled through a decade of cautious accommodation, with gradual realization of the dilemma created by anchoring the U.S. Pacific trade to the Philippines, which clearly were vulnerable to any Japanese expansion southward. Initially, it would be in Korea that the U.S. compromised the unrealistic promise to protect China's territorial integrity.

First in the secret Taft-Katsura Memo of 1905; then, in the official Root-Takahira Agreement of 1908, which bluntly balanced U.S. control of the Philippines with that of Japan's in Korea, the U.S. acknowledged its inability to challenge Tokyo's claim, a "dagger pointed at its heart." Apparently, TR himself had expressed his willingness that Japan have the peninsula. Japan, of course, viewed the taking of Korea as "defensive strategy," protecting Korean "independence," i.e., from Western control, which included Russia. After the strong American missionary efforts through the nineteenth century, with their familiar implied promise, Korea would be disappointed that the U.S. did not attempt to save them from the Japanese.[17]

Having already accepted the sop of reciprocity in the Root-Takahira Agreement, Japan's promise to recognize without revenge America's colony in its own back yard, the U.S. could only watch with increasing apprehension as Japan annexed Korea in 1909; Secretary of State Lansing's recognition of Japan's "twenty-one demands" for China as its "special interest," with the Lansing-Ishii notes, only compounded the problem, as discussed below.

It was in the shadow of imminent world conflict in the next decade that the noose would tighten for the Marshall Islands. The European war provided the opportunity Tokyo had been awaiting to occupy German territory in the Pacific. The trick would be to do so without antagonizing the Allied powers. In the Anglo-Japan Naval Alliance of 1902, Japan had cultivated the needed British support, again with Roosevelt's sanction, an "informal understanding." Despite that treaty, England itself was "suspicious of Japan's intentions and apprehensive of its appetites."[18] Nevertheless, at the outset of the conflict, made apprehensive by the worldwide naval power it confronted in a German opponent, England invited Japanese aid, immediately after which the leadership regretted activating the alliance. Alas, it was too late, for the Japanese acted quickly. "Japan must take the chance of a millennium, to establish its rights and interests in Asia." On 23 August 1914, Tokyo agreed to back the British and their allies at the onset of the Great War.[19] Britain's immediate repentance for the offer was to no avail. By October 1914, Japan had invaded the islands formerly claimed by Germany, including the Marshalls and Yap in the Carolines. This increased the naval presence in the southwestern Pacific to six battleships and destroyers, as it seized and occupied the islands "with no resistance" and assumed jurisdiction of the area. It was "swift, bloodless, and easy."[20] After such tepid resistance to its expansion prior to 1914, the U.S. was in no position to object to the Japanese takeover.

By the end of the war, Japan would have assisted Great Britain but little, "refusing to move its navy to … where it would be of most use." Instead, Tokyo would use the conflict in Europe for the consolation of its own interests. Even by 1912, there had been 122 Europeans and already seventy-three Japanese in Micronesia; seventy-five percent of Micronesian imports were from Japan. As noted, the Japanese had maintained a presence for years through traders, whalers, and military concerns, but with emigration one goal, it was rather surprising then that their "aggressive … commercial drive" had left so small a Japanese population in the islands, and those in the Mariannas and Carolines.[21]

Still, with the green light in 1914, the Japanese quickly built on this limited presence maintained for years. Further, in anticipation of the war's end, the Japanese prepared for any resistance to its keeping the islands, by seeking to guarantee instead support for claims. British efforts to forestall the stranglehold were met by Japan's reply that they "naturally insist on the permanent retention" and would, in fact, "rely on the support of the British government," as an ally. Further into the war, unknown to the Americans, the Japanese obtained the same assurance "in the secret understandings of February and March 1917, with Great Britain, France, Russia, and Italy," claiming that a necessity "because she knew that her European allies had, in 1915, made agreements as to the disposition of the German spoils in Europe." Japan had no intention of being left out again, not "when the Far East was under discussion."[22]

Versailles

In 1919, at the Versailles Peace Conference, U.S. President Woodrow Wilson found himself in a dilemma not of his choosing. While he profoundly feared sanctioning Japan's continued hold in the Pacific, regrettably, at that stage, the president himself did not possess the leverage to avert that result. At every turn, in each nuanced decision before him, he agonized with the reality of untenable or undesirable choices. Which course would best check Japan's coming aggression?[23] Japan's paltry assistance to the British effort during the war had only validated the British ambivalence in the request at the outset. Nevertheless, the British, after all, had allowed the Japanese move in 1914, and the unintended consequence was entrenched Japanese occupation of Germany's Pacific islands, including the Marshalls, now for nearly six years. Practically and diplomatically, it would be difficult to dislodge them. Their control of Yap Island would bring a major dispute over transatlantic cables that had been sanctioned by the Germans. Wilson well recognized the situation but still struggled against granting legitimacy to permanent Japanese control.

In Paris, the President's assistant, David Hunter Miller, kept an exhaustive personal diary with intimate and revealing details of the closed-door conversations and Wilson's deep involvement with the negotiations, including his serious misgivings. "The President said he did not trust the Japanese; that he had trusted them before,—in fact they had broken their agreement about Siberia…." And "that he would not trust them again."[24]

The departments of State and War were equally concerned. State warned of not only the loss of cable communication integrity if Japan controlled the central Pacific, but more ominously, that America might be cut off from its own colony. A confidential memo from Under Secretary Long noted: "in time of war" the islands groups "Marianas, the Carolines, and the Marshalls" form a "screen separating the Philippines from the Hawaiian Group and from the United States." Long reported rumors that Japan may have already fortified the islands.[25]

Wilson's aides, full of conflicting advice, did not solve the problem. The ghosts of previous mistakes in judgment or dubious decisions haunted present choices like a Dickens Christmas tale. Everyone agreed: "the Japanese had to get something," but what would be least damaging?[26] The future of the Marshall Islands hung in the balance.

Wilson's first ghost was the specter of McKinley's Paris team in 1898–1899, letting the Taongi Atoll (Gaspar Rico) in the Marshalls slip away.

One would remember von Bulow's straight line from the Marshalls to the Philippines, noted in negotiations ending the Spanish-American War. The U.S. "might have obtained possession of all the islands ... had it been fully alive to their strategic value." With words essentially quoted from Long's December memo, the president reflected with chagrin that "these islands lie athwart the path from Hawaii to the Philippines ... nearer to Hawaii than the Pacific coast..."; moreover, that "they could be fortified and made naval bases by Japan." In fact, perhaps "they were of little use for anything else..." while "we had no naval base except at Guam."[27]

The second ghost appeared from Portsmouth Treaty negotiations in 1905. Tokyo had not forgotten the seemingly sage advice from U.S. President Theodore Roosevelt that Japan should develop its own regional Monroe Doctrine.[28] This past encouragement clearly compromised Wilson's effort to minimize Japanese control in 1919, while only raising the fear for their renewed claim to hegemony in Asia. Wilson's advisors had even contemplated using the specific language in the Covenant as a way to encourage recognition for existing treaties such as the Monroe Doctrine, "if we could get away with it." But Wilson reminded them of the ambiguity of the Monroe Doctrine—not a treaty at all. To mention it would hardly dissuade the Japanese, who "viewed the doctrine as a convenient rationale for controlling neighboring territory."[29]

Wilson, in fact, remembered his dual problems with his own Senate Foreign Relations Committee and feared a discussion on the subject. Japan might wish to "acquire a harbor for a naval base in Magdalena Bay" in the Philippines, other powers deciding "it would be an insult to Japan to suppose" the reason for the harbor "anything but commercial purposes." Thinking further on the issue, Wilson concluded: "it would be impossible to put in the Covenant a reservation of the Monroe Doctrine without a similar reservation of an Asiatic doctrine of the Japanese...."[30]

The third ghost was the Lansing-Ishii Agreement. In 1900, America's vow to reserve Chinese territorial integrity naturally had elevated Chinese expectations of U.S. protection. Thus, when Secretary of State, Robert Lansing responded to Japan's "twenty-one demands" for recognition of its special regional role regarding China, it raised the stakes even higher. On 15 March 1915 the Americans had accepted "the first four sets of demands (and thus Japan's new hold on Manchuria and even Shantung) by using a fateful phrase. The Japanese 'territorial contiguity creates special relations between Japan and these districts.' The phrase had been suggested by Lansing...." The Japanese would even improve on "special interests" to add their "paramount interests" over China. In 1919, with great hindsight into the impact of his Lansing-Ishii notes, the secretary now advised the president to get tough, "to have it out once and for all with Japan."[31]

Such was looming disaster. The Chinese spoke with Miller "very confidentially of the hostile feelings existing between the Chinese and the Japanese." While the Peking delegates accepted the necessity for their having "the support of the American and British Governments," he was "very anxious that the twenty-one demands of Japan should be annulled," with which Miller privately agreed. In the same confidential tone, this spokesman advised that Japan expansion could be accommodated in northern Korea! Toward that end "he showed me on a map the region north of Korea along the coast which anciently belonged to China, and which he said was sparsely settled and would be suitable for Japanese expansion."[32]

Wilson's fourth ghost was, of course, the matter of California immigration and race, the issue that had complicated all international relations for decades. With the closed door of Hawaii, and then in Caucasian opposition to Asian immigration in California, the Japanese saw the bitter truth: indeed, no, they would not be exempt from the dread "yellow peril" mantra. Nor would America be the only country to exhibit it, as Russian and German competitors held equally racist views. One Japanese novelist noted with dismay, "how the whites despise us."[33] At Versailles, therefore, this underlying issue, so painful to the Japanese, returned in the form of their request made by British Lord Robert Cecil to Australian Prime Minister William Hughes for a "racial equality" clause for the new treaty. Faced with a "determined Japan," Wilson still resisted even an "equality of nations" phrase, claiming it already existed in the Covenant's preamble.[34]

Because of the endemic prejudice in American culture, evidenced north and south in racial violence and segregation, which Wilson did little to dissuade in his domestic policy, some easily dismiss him as "racist" in regard to the Japanese. This facile condemnation of Wilson has failed to adequately note, however, that the expectation of white Western superiority over Asian people had long been part of U.S. foreign policy in general, reflected before this president in Mahan, McKinley, and Teddy Roosevelt.[35]

Somewhat callously, in fact, the nation builders in the McKinley Administration's "pragmatic expansionism" simply assumed the attitude of white superiority, while focusing on commercial goals of ports and markets. The "benefits of empire could be had without the entanglements of race." Humanitarian instincts of various missionaries, as well, held their own patronizing racist assumptions. These could conveniently be put aside by political leaders, even while they welcomed the support of the religious in various mission fields, Hawaii being a case in point.[36]

It is also instructive to note the equally dismissive attitudes of Western delegates such as the comment of Britain's Foreign Minister Arthur Balfour regarding the equality clause. Confronted by Wilson's aide, Colonel House, with the American Declaration of Independence proposition that "all men are created equal," Balfour maintained that this was only "an eighteenth century proposition which he did not believe was true." Perhaps "in a certain sense all men of a particular nation were created equal, but not a man in Central Africa was created equal to a European."[37]

Rather, the fight of the "equal nations" clause should be seen in the context of the entire "Wilsonian Moment" and Wilson's wider sense of responsibility and duty that lay in American imperialism, expressed in a speech before Congress as early as 1913 as "obligations toward our territories," where we are "trustees," with "responsibility" for the "performance of our duty." He continued by listing Puerto Rico, Hawaii, and the Philippines as the U.S. "domain of public conscience."[38]

After the war, the effect of his own vision having "enthralled and inspired an entire generation before the conference with the desire for 'self determination,'" Wilson himself feared that his rhetoric had engendered a hope that would not be realized in the treaty, despite his faith in the League of Nations. He feared the inevitable disillusionment when the "terrible urgency" of past victims of colonialism would seek to "tear their deliverers to pieces if a millennium is not created immediately.... What I seem to see—with all my heart I hope that I am wrong—is a tragedy of disappointment."[39] Wilson's fears were amazingly prescient, as will be seen, while his language of "self determination" and concept of "trustee" later would be reflected in the League's Covenant and then appropriated by the United Nations after World War II. This terminology would define the future of Kwajalein Atoll and the Marshall Islands.

No, the "equal nations" debate at Versailles was much larger than Wilson's private prejudices. Each of the major players—and sideline aspirants—came with their own dedication to a cause. "Framing the Wilsonian moment in the colonial world as an international and transnational event is not merely an analytical device ... the moment was inherently international...."[40]

Still, each of the American ghosts had added to the toll. The complexity of the "equal nation" dilemma was well illustrated by the Mandate system itself, first devised by South African delegate Jan C. Smuts. Another case in point, Smuts offered it to cover not the Pacific islands, but only the German African colonies, which he said were "inhabited by barbarians." By then, also, the jealousies of Australia and New Zealand and their own fear of Japanese power played a role, insisting on their colonies south of the equator. With the British acquiescing, the Japanese "simply asked for equal treatment in the Pacific north of the equator."[41]

Japan had come into the negotiations with an ace, unknown to Wilson: the secret treaty with the allies in 1917 had already determined the fate of the German islands. Learning of the Japanese alliance, the president "was by no means prepared to accept" it. Still, with little room to maneuver, and "a victim of forces beyond his control," he dreamed that under the supervision of the League, the Mandate system would meet the duty of his conscience.[42]

While less than satisfied with this outcome, Tokyo accepted the system for mandate class determined by "population," "size," and "remoteness."[43] Ironically, the Japanese, who had chaffed under the opprobrium of white racism, carried the same prejudice against the people of their mandates. There is little doubt that the Japanese saw the Marshallese described in the Class C category, the designation for those deemed "less equal" and in need of oversight—less able to govern themselves. Confident that they would bring "civilization" to the indigenes, Japan would use the islands as an escape valve for its growing population, and like California, it would segregate from its own citizens the residences, life and schools of the Marshallese.

Confirming the settlement, Tokyo began close-to-total control over Micronesia that would not be broken until the waning years of World War II. The exceptions: the U.S. held Guam in the Marianas; the British held the Gilbert Islands. The controversy over Yap Island and the loss of cable rights could not be settled in Versailles. In his diary, Miller had commented on the dilemma. "That the remaining islands should not become naval bases and that we should have privilege for wireless communication in the Island of Yap were about all that, from the point of view of self interest America could ask."[44] But it could not be accomplished.

Wilson was forced to lamely admit to his Republican opponent Senator Henry Cabot Lodge, Chair of the U.S. Senate Foreign Relations Committee, that the base and "one of the centers of cable and radio communication on the Pacific" would need to be "reserved for the general conference" to be held "in regard to the ownership and operation of the cables." Senator Lodge was not pleased. As though the President needed such, he reminded Wilson of the "importance" of the matter, that "we should have a cable station there," and no secret treaty should "thwart that purpose."[45]

Not until the Washington Naval Conference in 1921–1922 did former

Wilson opponent and then Secretary of State, Charles Evan Hughes, secure the agreement with Japan for U.S. access to cable communication on Yap. Tokyo agreed for America and the Dutch "to use the island for their own private cable systems." The Four-Power and Five-Power Treaties also finally ended the Anglo-Japanese alliance that had confounded Wilson, even as the British were increasingly turning to the United States for mutual support in the Pacific.[46]

Mandate

Ultimately, the opposition of Senator Lodge would kill Wilson's primary dream for a League of Nations that would include the United States. Still, the issues in seeking a peaceful world for trade after the devastation of a world at war remained; agreement was needed to seal a Pacific status quo. With the Washington Conference, Secretary of State Hughes did not follow up on every concern the Wilson team had monitored, but he did accept the League of Nations mandate for Tokyo to claim Micronesia.[47] The Marshall Islands would be left to the designs of a newly invigorated Japan.

Whatever the expectations of the participants at Versailles, the language of the peace treaty stood. The League's category of Mandate C, under which Japan held the Marshalls, recognized territories in this class as "the most backward, furthest removed from having the ability to determine their own future," and could be administered as "integral portions of its territory." The terms of the Covenant of the League, Article 22, described them as "people not yet able to stand by themselves under the strenuous conditions of the modern world." The "well-being and development of such people form a sacred trust of civilization," Wilson's word again. The purpose of the "trust" was "the material and moral well-being and the social progress of the peoples."[48]

Initially, the Japanese changed little from the German administration of the Marshall Islands, selecting Jabwor in Jaluit Atoll, in the Ralik Chain, as regional headquarters, as had the Germans. In 1922, however, after receiving mandate authority, the Japanese operated under its South Seas Bureau and began to impress upon the islands a Japanese civilian administration.[49] Its director implemented Japanese policy through a complex bureaucracy of direct rule with little input from traditional island leadership.

In the case of the Marshalls, the Japanese appointed a "native administration" consisting of "village chief," usually the *iroij-laplap* (paramount) in each island chain, and a "village headman," a combination of "*iroij, bwirak* (nobility), and *kajur* (commoner) persons." These Marshallese became the "communication link" between the colonialists and the indigenes. Japanese administrators and workers revealed little intent to bring the Marshallese into the process of government. One reporter noted that the only occupation in which Marshallese were employed was in the schools, essentially in the role of translator for Japanese teachers. The Japanese explained this as some locals "who have shown themselves to be sufficiently capable."[50]

In the schools, initial Imperial policy was to use Japanese teachers, offering a limited curriculum of "Japanese language, singing, and arithmetic." Its immediate purpose was to make Japanese the official language of the islands. After 1922, the curriculum gradually expanded somewhat to include Japanese history, geography, nature study, and "morals." Marshallese children attended schools carefully separated from Japanese students. In Jaluit, officials operated its boarding school for the indigenous "exceptional children."[51]

Using the schools to acculturate Micronesians into the Empire, Japanese administrators phased out missionary schools, judging them inferior and suspect since they emphasized retention of traditional culture, the opposite of Japanese policy. Somewhat surprisingly, this same policy allowed the teaching of Christianity, apparently because of the somewhat erroneous perception of a theology of passivity. Aware of Shinto militancy, the Japanese saw Christianity as useful to make the people "meek and pliable."[52] Likewise, the government subsidized the work of the Japanese Congregational Church, which it had requested to locate in the islands. It also supported the Jesuit and Buddhist missions. Gradually squeezed out by the Japanese and lacking support from the Depression-stricken United States, in 1932 the Boston Mission withdrew from the Marshalls. The individual American missionary effort extended until 1951, when Benjamin G. Snow and Luther H. Gulick departed.[53]

The Marshallese remembered the Japanese years with mixed emotions. On the one hand, though it did not involve them directly for the most part, the Japanese economy provided more goods and services to the average citizen. Stores stocked Japanese canned goods, cookies and beer; rice became a food staple. In providing these amenities, however, the unwanted control "destroyed" the "former self-sufficiency of the natives" as it aided economic development for Japan.[54]

One impact that lingered into the decades of the 1970s and 1980s was the loss of fishing skills. Official Japanese policy limited fishing to the shore and lagoon areas of the atolls, while the open sea was left to the commercial fisheries. Traditionally, the Marshallese recognized the reefs, oceanside, as belonging to the *iroij* as personal property, a concept the Japanese negated.[55] In the 1980s, Japan would pay the Marshallese for the right to fish for their valuable tuna catch, while the local people all but lost the art of fishing themselves, excepting a few inhabitants on the outer islands. For the most part, the islanders scarcely ventured into the seas their ancestors once considered home.[56]

In the twenty-first century, Marshallese officials consider regaining fishing skills and trade of first priority for the Republic. Commercial fishing rights and treaties with the Japanese as well as other nations continue to be a significant part of Pacific negotiations. Increasingly, Japan has not only restored cordial relations through official ambassador and embassy in Majuro, but in generous grants and educational exchange programs with Marshallese citizens.[57]

It was in the matter of land tenure, however, that the Japanese made their greatest impact, with carry-over to the American period. Two key concepts allowed maximum government control and both worked to the detriment of the traditional land system of the Marshall Islands: first, state-owned land; and second, separate ownership of land from the trees on that land. The Japanese built upon German foundations in claiming certain lands as government-owned. The South Seas Bureau first placed "all lands and possessions under the jurisdiction of the National Resources Law (kokuyuzaisanho)." Without sanction of its mandate under the League of Nations, the Japanese began with the understanding that the land which was transferred to Japan in its capacity as mandatory was "land which ipso facto belongs to the state by virtue of the principle that all real property without owner belongs to the state."[58]

Clearly, this claim violated every tenet of Marshallese land tenure. Germans had conducted some surveys in Saipan and Ponape (Pohnpei), but no written records existed in the Marshalls. Oral records depended on local witnesses, and, as noted under the German regime, islanders' testimony did not always agree. Further, the opportunity existed for astute locals to claim any disputed acreage as integral to family lineage. As one anthropologist later described the Marshallese, the people were "always plotting to obtain more land."[59]

In 1922, the Japanese put it succinctly. All lands, they wrote in their report to the League, "in accordance with old custom," (Japanese custom), that do not belong to an indigenous citizen or community "are considered as belonging to the State." In the following year, Japan began its land survey designating the "state land."[60]

The additional concept, hopelessly confusing, was the distinction in ownership of trees and land. In the Marshalls, all this was meaningless except in terms of furthering Japanese control. When the United States attempted to complete the future Kwajalein Land Use Agreement, the residue from this policy would be evident. All the animosity felt and consolidated in Marshallese hearts and tradition against this land control by the Japanese continued to be present.

In the areas of health care and economic growth, the Japanese made strong marks over the German effort. Pacific island populations had declined drastically in the first significant contact with European culture. The Japanese worked to reverse that trend by reducing disease and improving hospital and dental facilities for the people.[61]

For the economy, although it never amounted to more than one percent of the Empire's total economic picture, the Japanese developed strong industries in sugar, phosphate mining, and copra production in Micronesia. With characteristic efficiency, the South Seas Bureau set out to increase production of these and other cash crops. By 1932, success would be measurable: two-thirds of all arable land would be under production and the volume of trade would have multiplied "six times over" since 1922.[62]

In the case of copra production, even as the Germans had envisioned, the Japanese moved to make it more efficient, including the design to plant more trees. The new colonialists wasted no time in assembling the Marshallese *iroijs* in Jaluit, challenging them to "decide how many coconut trees each tribe should plant that year." The government encouraged former copra producers to "plant more palms," to "improve old plantations," and to "build better drying facilities." There were two incentives. First, the government subsidized the development. Second, was the onset, in 1922, of a tax system levied on "all male natives sixteen years of age and above," disregarding and oblivious to matrilineage.[63]

In 1921, the Marshall Islands had accounted for more than fifty percent of German copra production. "In 1925, 209.5 tons of copra were collected as tax by thirteen chiefs of the islands." The value of copra export rose from 555,938 yen in 1921 to 1,677,354 yen in 1925. By 1927, the Japanese allowed the Marshallese "the privilege" of paying their "annual poll tax" with copra. The administration eventually took five-to-eight percent of total copra production as taxes. Thus, by 1935, copra production more than doubled from six million tons to fifteen million tons per year.[64] While war in the 1940s would decimate the copra industry, in the twenty-first century, the Tobolar Corporation in the Marshalls revived the copra trade.

Another hard memory from the Japanese period was the obvious racial stigma assigned to various groups. Japan saw the Nippon culture as superior to that of the Micronesians, and Marshallese as inferior to the Chamorro of the Marianas. In reports to the League of Nations, the Japanese compared the islanders unfavorably to "civilized countries." The colonizers forbade the "uncivilized" local practice of tattooing. In 1926, the administration acknowledged a struggle to effect an even-handed treatment policy in the face of this attitude: "It goes without saying," the report stated, that "the Japanese Government does not discriminate" between mandate citizens "in regard to their treatment…." But "this is only relatively true, even Chamorros being very backward as compared with civilized people." The Japanese followed the German system of determining wages based on "levels of skill, length of service, and standard of living." One result was that "distinctions grew between racial groups because of these standards."[65]

In the 1930s, Japanese population expanded in all of Micronesia, growing from 220 in 1915, to 19,835 in 1930, and 51,861 in 1935. Most Japanese settlers were farmers in the sugar plantations in Saipan or in the islands of the Carolines and Marianas. "The major new industries—sugar, alcohol, and dried bonito—employed only Japanese." Most Japanese immigrants settled in Saipan, Palau, and Ponape (Pohnpei), "while very few went to the Marshall Islands or Yap." Only in the eastern Carolines and Marshalls did the Micronesians remain a majority. In the 1920s, the indigenous population in the Marshalls outnumbered the Japanese 9,422 to 217 in 1925, and 9,442 to 215 in 1926.[66] That would change as the Japanese prepared for war and these eastern islands became strategic to the effort.

Researchers disagree as to when Japan moved to fortify the mandate islands. Rumors to that effect abounded even in the 1920s. Some would say "fevered American speculation" was "re-kindled" in the 1930s when the Japanese declined foreign observation in Micronesia. The Japanese denied the charges up until their decision to withdraw from the League of Nations in 1933. More significant perhaps is the question of the status of Micronesia after the withdrawal and loss of legal mandatory authority. The position of the Japanese government was clear that it "had no intention of relinquishing its mandate, yet stopped short of asserting that the islands had now become Japanese territory." Their logic claimed that because Japan had negotiated occupation of the islands "with the principal Allied powers during World War I," the agreement for the mandate was with "its wartime allies" and not with the League at all.[67] Only a second world war would challenge that determination.

In any case, the Japanese invasion of China in 1931 and creation of its "Manchukuo" colony in Manchuria had made clear the ascendancy of

Tokyo's "northern strategy." Then, with the second-stage assault against China in 1937, U.S. officials recalled with trepidation the vow to preserve Chinese territorial integrity, a dilemma to be noted again in the following chapter. Confirming the fears of future conflict, the Japanese began in earnest the move of its population to the Marshall Islands. The mandated islands would serve the dictates of war, while the atolls of Kwajalein, Wotje, and Maloelap soon would act as "forward bases" for long-range bombers. Fortification of the islands was certainly underway, even if not completed, well before the 1940s.[68]

Although the Marshallese had seemed aware of the Japanese attitude toward them as "second-class citizens," the colonial presence had not appeared excessively oppressive until this change toward militarization. After that time, the Marshallese experienced more brutality and more forced labor as the Japanese military populated the Marshall Islands.[69] Ironically, the Japanese attitude of superiority sometimes had worked to the advantage of the indigenous people by allowing them to avoid unsolicited state work. The Japanese official position was that there was no forced labor in the mandated islands, but "should there be any," it would be for "construction and maintenance of roads or for clearing operations"

Japanese ruin: Submarine training facility, Kwajalein Atoll, 1987 (U.S. Army photo).

in the vicinity of local homes. Judging the lack of anything approaching their own work ethic among the Marshallese, the Japanese preferred to carry out the major portion of the work themselves or with immigrants. Tokyo conscripted hundreds of Korean laborers and even Japanese prisoners.[70]

In the pre-war build-up, Kwajalein Island suffered most. The submarine training base created on the island by the Japanese required brutal work and control. The Marshallese were forced into more labor projects, such as building airstrips and military facilities on the island. Kwajalein would serve as launching port for the future attacks on both Wake Island and Pearl Harbor.

In the eyes of many, Japan had violated its League mandate both in fortifying the islands and in using forced labor. Indeed, even before the construction for war began, Japan "neither prepared the natives of Micronesia for freedom nor for a position of equality within the Japanese Empire and in this regard completely failed to live up to the trust ... undertaken."[71] As the world prepared for war, a veil of secrecy dropped over the Marshall Islands.

Four

World War II

The newest chapter in the clash between the United States and Japan only could be understood in the context of previous encounters. The ground had been laid in the nineteenth century with the first migration of Japanese workers to the *haole* plantations in Hawaii; with Americans wresting control of the islands; with the nationalistic competition in World War I; and then Versailles, with the resulting Mandate system in Micronesia.

In retrospect, after chronicling the "simultaneous development" of empires, the confrontation in World War II would seem inevitable.[1]

Many Americans focused on the rise of Hitler and the aggrandizement of Germany seeking control in Europe. After watching and even accommodating aggressive moves of the 1930s, at last England was drawn into the conflict. In 1939, with the invasion of Poland, Great Britain declared war on Germany. While the actual threat of the Nazis to the British at that point was not direct, certainly it was "cumulative," with a direct threat visible on the horizon.[2] Similarly, the ongoing struggle between the United States and Japan presaged the Pacific War, and the theater of conflict in Oceania.

That competition moved in concentric circles around mutually enabling trade and destructive intention in Asia. Though Japan remained a primary trade partner, the U.S. could not ignore its menacing ambition/objective, the "landward pull of the neighboring continent." In September 1931, a component of the Japanese Army in Manchuria manufactured an "accidental" explosion with far-reaching results, providing the pretext for setting up a puppet regime named Manchukuo. The overt "act of rogue policy-making" marked the ascendancy of the military "in national politics and in the cabinet itself."[3] After the League of Nations' examination of the incident, followed by its report of condemnation, Japan withdrew from the League in 1933. The required two-year notice made the withdrawal effective in 1935.

The Japanese militancy in Manchuria would be only the beginning. And what would be the American response? With previous treaties crumpling and China "fragmented and unstable" in the midst of revolution, the administration struggled to formulate a coherent policy. While Secretary of State Henry Stimson denounced the Japanese action, President Herbert Hoover did nothing beyond a verbal rebuke. Damned by his own ideology of trade with no government intervention, Hoover did not have the capability to deal with the crashing domestic economy in the United States, much less that in Asia. The Japanese, hit by the collapse of the silk trade in their own version of Depression and angered by the U.S. refusal to recognize legitimacy in the Manchukuo land venture, revealed no hesitation for continuing their assault in China.[4]

The action, however, did severely challenge stated American foreign policy created by the Open Door Notes back at the turn of the twentieth century under another Republican administration. From the perspective of the 1930s, the pledge made then seemed vastly unrealistic, even as noted at the time, when Secretary of State John Hay added the impossible clause that the U.S. would "preserve Chinese territorial and administrative entity" and "safeguard for the world the principle of equal and impartial trade." The current administration saw no avenue for enforcing that promise. But neither could it allow the Japanese to absorb the raw materials of the continent or ignore the moral obligation towards China. The dilemma created a measure of "paralysis" in the State Department.[5]

It would be the destiny of incoming American president, Franklin Delano Roosevelt (FDR), to confront not only the Great Depression at home, but the entire coming conflagration of world powers. As he began to comprehend the enormity of what lay ahead, and hampered by a strong isolationist contingent in the U.S. Congress, Roosevelt veered between the unseemly probabilities of a naval-superiority race in the Pacific or a land war in Asia. The portent of the latter already had been seen in Japan's bombing of Shanghai in 1932, and then in the aggression of December 1937.

First came what was labeled the "China Incident," the cruel invasion of Nanking, deemed "rape and slaughter" and a "murderous debauch." Then came an unprovoked air attack on the U.S. gunboat *Panay* on patrol in the Yangtze River of China. For the time, the president allowed the Japanese to apologize for the "mistake." Soon after, however, it became clear that he had chosen the challenge of the Pacific arena, his policies "moving down a new path." Working with Congress, FDR signed into law the Naval Act of 1938, which included a huge increase of $1.1 billion over ten years in resources for the U.S. Navy. Inexorably, the United States and Japan were moving toward collision.[6]

In fact, the navies of both governments had been yearning for budgetary increase and spoiling for a fight. Since the "Orange Plan" early in the century, the U.S. Navy had anticipated possible Japanese aggression and enacted numerous "war plans" to deal with the threat. Some feared the U.S. would be unable to successfully defend the vast Pacific; others proceeded aggressively. While Orange was never "formally abandoned," a new "Rainbow" series considered other options, including strategy to face a combined Japanese-German alliance.[7]

One would include offense rather than defense, not waiting for Japanese attack. The American Navy would seek to capture eastward-reaching islands, possibly Kwajalein in the Marshalls, recognized as the Empire's significant forward-basing center. With ominous sameness, the Japanese Naval Commander, Admiral Yamamoto Isoroku "bleakly contemplated" war with the United States and realized the vulnerability of Japan's "poorly defended" mandates in the central Pacific.[8]

Yamamoto provided a fascinating adversary to contemplate. Having studied at Harvard in the 1920s, served as a Naval attaché in Washington, and attended Naval conferences, he was well aware of America's potential power, still latent in military might. Though "apprehensive" of war, as a "moderate nationalist," he believed that Japan "should build an empire" to rival the U.S., but not before it had adequate military might and "naval parity."[9]

While he feared the confrontation, his cautious strategy was sneak attack, well accepted as defensive in the samurai culture and already employed by Japan in recent history with the surprise bombing of Port Arthur in 1904. Yamamoto's scheme was to cripple the American Pacific fleet—for six months at least before it could rebuild—to allow time for the military to move south unopposed, toward the oil reserves in the Netherlands East Indies (Indonesia). While he wavered on the timing and considered a strike first in the Philippines, he saw as essential an initial offensive aggression, of course justified as defensive. Yamamoto chose the surprise air attack on the equally unprotected Pearl Harbor, "no matter what the cost," to retard the U.S. Navy's effort to confront his nation. Other planners disagreed, seeing it as a "gamble," a project "fraught with risk," as it was. And after the first attack, the decision to forego a second, follow-up strike in Hawaii would deprive Japan of the desired six-month reprieve.[10]

Further omen for America's role came in September 1940, when Japan joined Germany and Italy in the Tripartite Pact. These partners saw benefit for each in confronting a potential U.S. enemy. Though Yamamoto was an

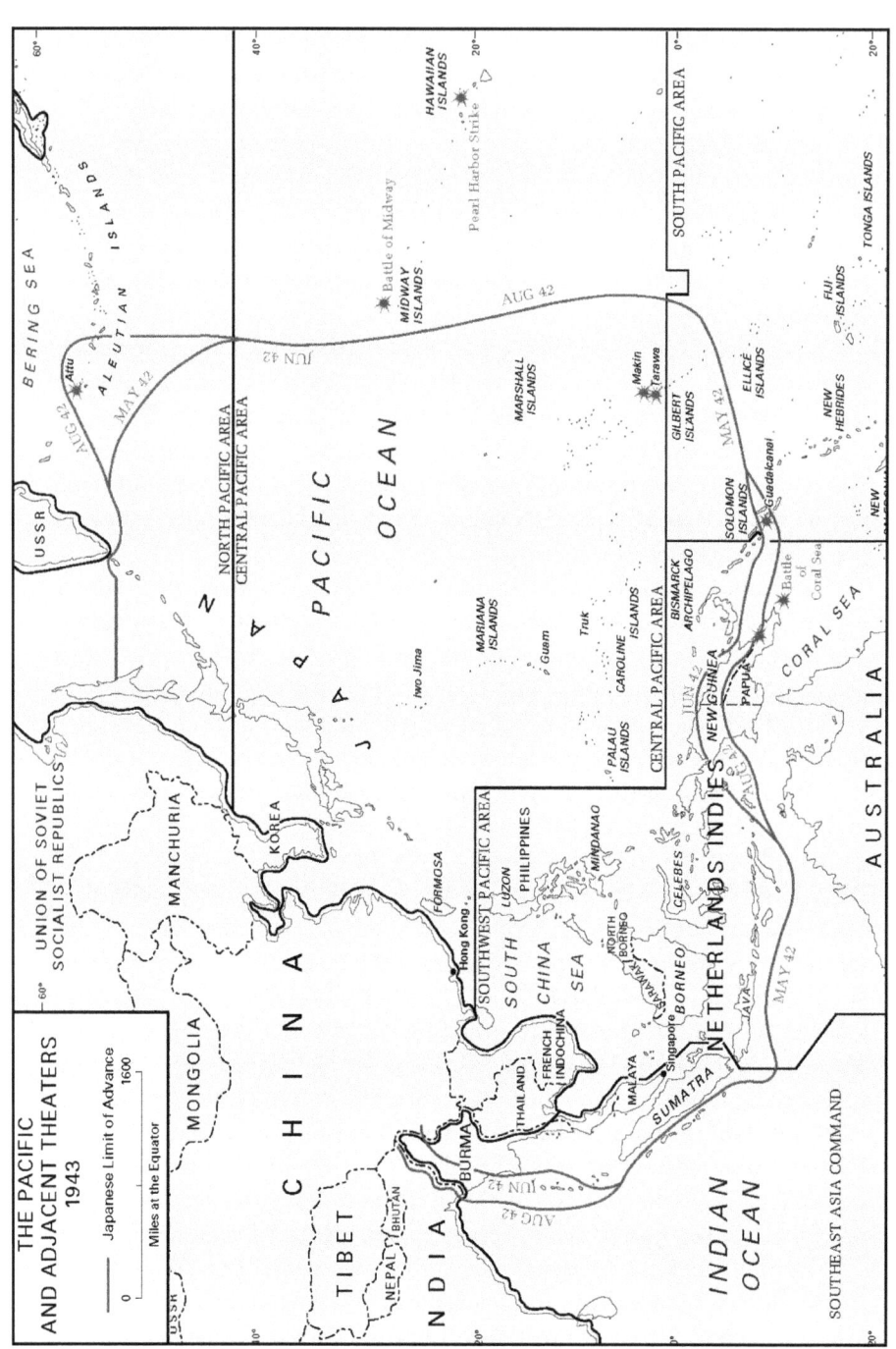

"outspoken critic" of the deal, the Japanese purpose was to intimidate the U.S. with the promise of the signers for mutual military aid, while Hitler wanted America occupied in the Pacific. The plan would achieve the desired result for neither.[11]

America had been stunned by the German blitz against western Europe in the spring of 1940, the fall of Paris; only England still stood "between the United States and the Axis," and its "survival appeared doubtful," as some saw it. But Roosevelt refused to "write off Great Britain" and had no intention of abandoning this ally, well aware that the British Navy was the barrier for America against German control in the Atlantic.[12] The Atlantic Charter would be signed by Churchill and Roosevelt in August 1941, and would underline American commitment to the British. The significance of that charter will be discussed in the next chapter.

After the English declaration of war against Germany, FDR quickly penned a message to Winston Churchill, First Lord of the Admiralty, suggesting what became a significant and secret correspondence: "I shall at all times welcome it if you will keep me in touch personally...." The two leaders had been aware of each other since the days of Roosevelt's term as Assistant Secretary of the Navy and Churchill's first stint as Lord of the British Admiralty. After Churchill became the British Prime Minister in 1940, and during the war years, the two would hold many personal conferences, as well as continue the confidential messages. Despite differences in style, temperament, and character, despite well-rumored tensions and arguments over the years, they not only came to respect each other but share affection. They would develop a "remarkable closeness," a formidable alliance "forged in war."[13]

The Tripartite Agreement fueled Roosevelt's determination to strengthen U.S. forces in the Pacific. Then, in September 1940, when Japan moved into northern French Indochina, FDR shocked Tokyo by throwing down the gauntlet of freezing Japanese assets in the U.S. This was followed by cutting off iron and steel exports to Japan—and then oil—an action "certain to drive the Japanese further into Asia in quest of these resources." The challenge was accepted—in July 1941 the Empire pushed on, south into French Indochina.[14]

Then, it came, with consequence not yet envisioned. The surprise on Sunday morning, 7 December 1941, gave the American public a patriotic reason for a "righteous crusade" to retaliate against the perpetrators. In hindsight, the "great mistake" was not so much to attack Pearl Harbor, but "to attack the United States at all."[15] With the president's stirring

Opposite: **Pacific and Adjacent Theaters, 1943 (U.S. Army, Center of Military History).**

description of the day as "a date which will live in infamy" and the declaration of war against Japan, the United States was thrust into world conflict on two fronts, as Germany quickly declared war on the U.S.

While hailed at home for daring and success at Pearl Harbor, Yamamoto later bemoaned the decision to forego additional strikes, believing they "should have delivered a final knockout blow." From the military perspective, the attack had been not only a "political blunder," but also a strategic one, for the assault failed to destroy the U.S. "most lethal weapons," its aircraft carriers. In a defiant gesture to illustrate resiliency, in February 1942, the American admirals dared a "nuisance raid" on the Marshalls, including a bombing hit-and-run on Kwajalein.[16]

The future for Kwajalein Atoll as well as the fate of all Japanese mandates was at stake. Further, after the attack on Pearl Harbor, the Japanese had quickly followed with a devastating raid on the Philippines. Inexplicably, even with ten hours' warning, General Douglas MacArthur, commander of U.S. forces in the Far East, had left his force of new B-17 bombers exposed to attack on the airfield. Next he subjected his troops to the overwhelming ground force of the enemy. The result was the shocking "Bataan Death March" of survivors, while he retreated to safety. The Japanese onslaught then overtook American resistance on Guam and Wake Islands, moved into Burma, and as far south as the Dutch East Indies.[17]

Whatever the pre-planning, the U.S. Navy now faced the eastward movement of the "Japanese juggernaut," as well as rebuilding a damaged fleet. Even while realizing it would take months to fully "arm and equip" the force, American military planners collaborated on various strategies for future campaigns. Army Chief of Staff General George C. Marshall would advise for the European arena, while Admiral Ernest J. King had become Chief of Naval Operations after Pearl Harbor. Even after stopping the advance of the Japanese at Guadalcanal in the Solomons, it was not until June 1942, in arresting their forward drive in the battle for Midway Island, that the U.S. would be confident of how the war could be won.

From the time of the Casablanca Conference in January 1943, Roosevelt and Churchill had agreed on two objectives. For Churchill, the priority was "Germany first," to defeat Hitler in Europe. FDR agreed, but surprised some by also exacting "unconditional surrender" of the Japanese, insisting that simple defeat in "battle at sea" would never be sufficient. This demand would require rigorous new thinking. At the conference, the proposal of Admiral Ernest J. King, Commander in Chief, U.S. Fleet, and Chief of Naval Operations, was to take first the central Pacific.[18]

General MacArthur, who in the minds of many had been "doubly responsible for the debacle on the Philippines," still wanted to prepare for immediate battle to retake those islands. This idea was deemed "tenuous at best" at the outset and in hindsight an "utterly unrealistic" option. America's colony must be written off for the present, officials long having realized that the islands lay "clearly vulnerable to any Japanese expansion southward." While retaking the Philippines would surely be a significant objective, for the time, they "would simply be sacrificed."[19]

The result of the decision was a divided Pacific Command. For the time given an unwanted secondary role, MacArthur was made Supreme Commander, Southwest Pacific Area, including Australia, New Guinea, the Solomons, and the Philippines. Admiral Chester W. Nimitz became Commander-in-Chief, Pacific Ocean Areas, which included New Zealand, Samoa, Fiji in the South Pacific, and in the Central Pacific Area the Eastern Mandates, including the Marshall Islands.[20]

Building on Admiral King's model, Admiral Nimitz developed an operational concept that would move west from Hawaii, "using sea power and carrier-based aircraft to seize isolated Japanese islands that could not be easily reinforced by the enemy," reminiscent of the pre-war "Rainbow" series and the resiliency raid shortly after Pearl Harbor. In March 1943, Joint Chiefs and Joint Staff Planners met in sessions known as the Pacific Military Conference to discuss estimates of forces required for "amphibious" warfare. This would entail the "landing and supply of troops in combat," as well as required "air and naval support."[21]

By May 1943, at the Anglo-American Washington (Trident) Conference, the Nimitz design became the "Strategic Plan for the Defeat of Japan," setting the "pattern of strategy for the duration of the war...." This formula came to be known as "island hopping," seizing one island chain to support operations in the next. The purpose was to "keep pressure on the Japanese across a wide expanse of territory."[22] Thus was unveiled the campaign to take the Marshall Islands, and blueprint for the Battle of Kwajalein, Operation Flintlock.

Battle of Kwajalein

As Commander, Admiral Nimitz would also determine the plan for combat. Cautious not to target the Marshalls before guaranteeing support operations, the American force would first invade the Gilberts, British-mandate islands seized by the Japanese just three days after Pearl Harbor.[23] In the Gilberts, the first objective would be the northern outermost atoll of Makin, followed by attack on Tarawa Atoll.

Beginning the strike in November 1943, the U.S. Army 27th Infantry Division took Makin Atoll with "relative ease," finding it only lightly guarded. In the first landings, fewer troops of the enemy were engaged than had been expected, while defenses seemed to have been "abandoned." The final assessment, however, was less sanguine. Even with the superior attack force and the "comparatively weak state" of defense, while the total of 128 was relatively low, the ratio of combat casualties, two Americans to every three Japanese, was "remarkably high." Further, the loss of a valuable escort carrier to torpedoes from a lurking enemy submarine made some judge that the taking of Makin was consequential.[24]

In the taking of Tarawa, the cost would be even higher, as the Americans faced a "numerically stronger" and "far better prepared enemy." The U.S. 2d Marine Division found this atoll "strongly fortified and defended." A horrific battle resulting in more than three thousand American casualties, one Marine historian would call it "utmost savagery." It would be a "wake-up call" to the "ferocity of the war that lay ahead."[25]

In post-battle assessment, the commanding admirals agreed the "chief strategic significance" of the fight for the Gilberts was that it was the onset of the Central Pacific drive, not at the "geographic center" of Japanese power, but "against the perimeter." Further, it was the "first instance" in the Pacific war that an American force had attempted a "large-scale amphibious assault" against a heavily fortified enemy beachhead. The win proved the capability of the U.S. Navy to secure an "isolated outpost," controlling air and sea "long enough to support a successful landing." The capture of Tarawa and Makin was "necessary prelude" to invasion of the Marshalls. Moreover, the manifold lessons learned would serve as practice run for the upcoming Battle for Kwajalein Atoll.[26]

Corrections were needed, of course, one of which was that the preliminary naval bombardment would require more than the three hours allotted for Tarawa. Another lesson learned was the need for adequate air support, after a disappointing showing. The shared blame for this lay in "poor communications, poor coordination, and the poor training of the carrier pilots." For the upcoming battles, improved communication between water and land, and cooperation between services would reflect the prior experience at Tarawa.[27]

Reasoning by both the Japanese and Nimitz's own staff was that the American attack of the Marshalls should begin with the southern outer islands. With the advantage of recent intelligence, however, the Admiral insisted on taking first the Kwajalein Atoll, which lies in the geographical center of the Marshalls. In the crucial Battle of Midway, Nimitz had been aided by the "sophisticated decrypting technique" military intelligence had developed after Pearl Harbor. Similarly in the current campaign, reports garnered from cracking the enemy's military code, dubbed Ultra, revealed that the outer islands would be heavily fortified, in anticipation of "an attack on the periphery." The first surprise for defenders would be the initial thrust.[28]

Still concerned about circumventing the "outer bases," Vice-Admiral Raymond A. Spruance, who commanded the Fifth Fleet, requested that at least Majuro Atoll, in the Ratak chain and only 190 miles southeast of Kwajalein, be secured first to provide airfields and fleet anchorage. Thus granted, the battle of Majuro was considered a "second phase" of Flintlock and accomplished the same day as the first landings on Kwajalein. Finding that the Japanese had nearly abandoned Majuro, the Second Battalion of the 106th Infantry quickly secured that atoll before moving on to the primary assault target. Majuro Atoll would become the U.S. headquarters in the Marshalls.[29]

Kwajalein, the world's largest low-coral atoll, measured sixty-six miles in length and twenty miles across. Within the atoll, there were ninety-three islands and islets, thirty-eight of which planners saw as of "significant size." In the northern part of the atoll, the Japanese had conjoined the small islands of Roi and Namur with a concrete causeway along the sandpit on the lagoon side. These islands had roads, airfield, barracks, and provided headquarters for the Japanese 6th Base Force, which commanded all Japanese air forces in the Marshalls and Gilberts. Kwajalein, the largest island in the atoll and located in its farthermost southern part, formed a graceful crescent shape, more than two miles in length. The main body of the force was stationed here. As the crescent turned north, the center inland section housed a building complex "known as the Admiralty Area," the island headquarters.[30]

"D-plus-1" would be 1 February 1944. Again remembering Tarawa, with increase in both "quantity and accuracy of fire power," preliminary bombing in the outer islands began in November 1943, and accelerated in late January 1944, together "literally overwhelming." Then, on Day One, 31 January, pre-invasion bombing of Kwajalein Island began. Simultaneous bombing on the atoll's northernmost islands of Roi-Namur meant the Americans would gain "absolute air superiority." At first light on 1 February, battleships and heavy cruisers joined the onslaught that destroyed all beach defenses of anti-aircraft batteries. The principal landing force would be Marines of the Fifth Fleet, while the Army's 7th Infantry Division handled land operations.[31]

Japanese ruin: Defense fortification, Kwajalein Island, east seaside, 1987 (U.S. Army photo).

The second surprise for the Japanese was the direction American forces would employ in reaching Kwajalein. Expecting assault from the sea, Japanese defenses were employed at the northern tip and the west of the island. On the eastern side, they had built huge earthwork/concrete fortifications with guns open to the ocean expanse. The contour of the island provided a deep 380-square-mile lagoon, naturally protected by the coral reef, with the exception of several entry points. Islets in the atoll just to northwest of Kwajalein Island itself—Gea and Ninni—the Americans dubbed "Carter" and "Cecil." Initial landings would target these islets; hence, the marines would enter through the Cecil Pass and attack from the lagoon side of the island. The islets of Ennylabegon, "Carlos," and Enubuj, "Carlson," would serve as artillery bases for support. The Americans again confounded defenders by avoiding a frontal assault even on the lagoon side of the island. This tactic achieved surprise needed for an entry, where "reef and surf conditions were more favorable" and where it was only lightly defended.[32]

Another first was the use of combined Army-Navy underwater demolition teams to discover any mines or obstacles, though they found none

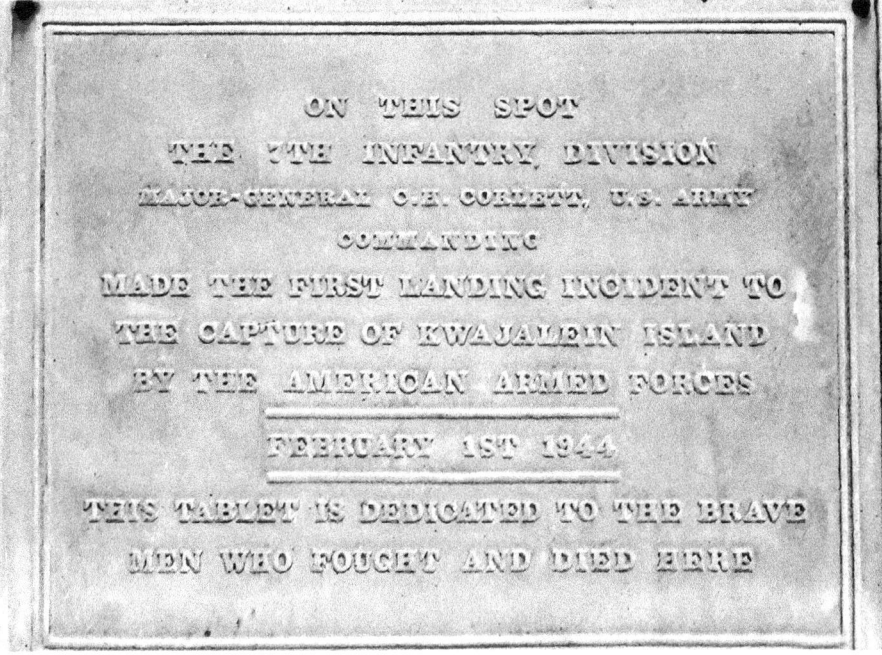

U.S. Army 7th Infantry Division Plaque, Battle of Kwajalein, 1944. Taken on Kwajalein Island, east seaside in 1987 (U.S. Army photo).

in the Kwajalein lagoon. New amphibious trucks carried troops and equipment to shore. As the men moved inland, armored amphibian tractors with guns and flamethrowers supported their progress. While initial bombing had reduced the Japanese defenses, intense fighting followed the invasion, especially on the first of the three days needed to take the entire island, which was covered in large sections by thick vegetation. On the third day, the infantry took nearby Ebeye Island. On 4 February, "mopping up" was the order.

Battle casualties for the 7th Infantry Division were 176 killed and 1,000 wounded. Thanks to the prior bombardment, estimates held that only 1,500 defenders were actually still alive when fighting began. The Japanese defenders of Kwaj and nearby islands had numbered 5,000, another 4,000 on Roi-Namur, but only half of these were combat troops. The 5,000 Japanese and 3,000 Korean laborers defending Kwajalein Atoll sustained major loss, with only 125 Korean and 49 Japanese survivors.[33]

With the capture of Kwajalein, Roi-Namur, and Majuro, and with new resources available to the U.S. Navy, Admiral Spruance "accelerated the pace of operations" in the Marshalls, making the next target Eniwetok, northwest of Kwajalein and one of the outer atolls. Having previously planned for the battle in May 1944, American forces now went there directly and secured the atoll in battle on 18–23 February. But divining the new direction of American intent, the Japanese had hastily strengthened the defenses of Eniwetok, making it more resistant than expected. American casualties mounted to 262 killed, 757 wounded, and 77 missing, while the Japanese suffered more than 2,000 fatalities. Securing the remaining islands of the Marshalls continued in March and April 1944. Three tasks remained: first, occupying lightly or undefended atolls; second, building air and naval bases to support the continuing drive; and third, aerial bombardment continuing against bypassed Japanese strongholds such as Jaluit.[34] The conquest of the Marshalls had proven the "soundness" of the "amphibious doctrine" and the Central Pacific strategy. The next target became Japanese control of the Marianas.

After the Battle of Kwajalein

Americans assessed Flintlock a successful operation; some in the press would say "brilliant." After the battle, Admiral Nimitz himself arrived on 5 February to survey the damage and relish his sound decision making. Together with his Commanding Admirals Spruance and Turner, Marine Corps Major General Smith, and Army Major General Corlett, he toured the "battle-scarred islands" of the atoll and Kwajalein Island, where "fires were still burning."[35] The devastation was major. With thousands of enemy casualties and close to 200 prisoners, the issues immediately became those of logistics. After the battles for "these destroyed atolls," noted Lieutenant General Robert Richardson, "the problem becomes one of engineering for at least six weeks."[36]

Officers in charge gave the wounded and dead priority treatment. American personnel took the bodies to Carlson Island, "a dignified setting for the burial of our men," in a site Major General Corbett had declared a "national cemetery." The victors treated the former-enemy dead somewhat less ceremoniously, picking up bodies in trucks, spraying them with sodium arsenate, and using Marshallese volunteers to carry out the burial assignment.[37]

In addition to concern for the stench from rotting bodies, the difficulties involved with bivouacking so many servicemen became an immediate problem. As noted, Kwajalein Island was crescent shaped, more than two miles long. At the time, its maximum width was 2000 feet; total area was approximately 480 acres, 280 acres of which was taken with "airfield landing strip taxiways and plane parking, and by ammunition and fuel storage." In future years, with landfills, Americans would add additional surface, making the size of the island 741 acres by 1964.[38]

In such a small area, the problems associated with disposal of human waste, wash water waste, kitchen waste, as well as fly control and finding clean drinking water were compelling. By April 1944, the Corps of Engineers ruled that emergency facilities of "pit latrines" were "unsatisfactory" and represented a "menace to the health of the command." The Sanitary Corps recommended the construction of "concrete vault latrines," and the "disposal of sewage by hauling out to the sea," estimating a cost of $32,000 to accomplish the work. According to the corps, saltwater wells provided a "raw water source definitely superior to the ocean or lagoon." Presumably, these guidelines were followed, for by the summer of 1944, reports showed the organization was "running smoothly."[39]

Essential for this assessment would be cooperation of the Marshallese. The war had brought mixed treatment by the Japanese. With forced labor, brutal treatment, and disregard for civil rights, relations with the islanders had deteriorated. After Pearl Harbor, the Japanese had suspected espionage of those who knew English. Agents had searched the homes and interrogated suspects; execution by beheading was not uncommon. On the Island of Milo, the locals reacted to Japanese mistreatment and shortages with active resistance.[40] Then, when fighting began in the islands, Marshallese suffered as much as Japanese.

After the Battle of Kwajalein, initially there was little concern for the issues that eventually would trouble contact between Americans and the Marshallese. In the first place, success on Kwajalein did not mean that the war was over. Servicemen occupied the Kwajalein Atoll, and would other atolls, by the international law of "belligerent occupation." Also, the Japanese did not leave the area with no afterthought; both islands of Roi and Kwajalein were subject to air attack in coming weeks. Beyond the Marshalls, the battle for the Pacific would continue long after this first offensive turn toward total victory.

In the second place, by all accounts, and confirmed in photos, the survivors were "a bedraggled lot. Many of them were wounded and they were all frightened and hungry." Welcoming the victors, many saw Americans as liberators, who were "very generous and very good in providing food." To some it seemed as though the newcomers "were magicians, capable of producing anything out of the holds of their ships."[41]

Because of the heavy battle, Kwajalein Atoll had suffered the most

Japanese Memorial, Roi-Namur Island (U.S. Army photo).

damage in the entire Marshalls, contrasting Majuro where destruction was light. On the outlying islands, the physical condition of the people "varied from fair to poor." Hunger and disease were common. On some islands, "yaws had infected about 45 percent of the people, skin ulcers and sores were common...." In February 1944, body counts showed fifty-five Marshallese dead in the entire atoll; officers judged that the total indigenous population for the atoll was "approximately 625," ninety-six of these on Kwajalein Island itself. The Japanese had displaced the islanders mostly for labor needs. By late spring of 1944, when it was clear that the war finally had bypassed the Marshalls, Americans began to sort out claims and allow them to return to home islands in some cases.[42]

Administration

The exemplary cooperation between American military services during the Battle of Kwajalein continued in the first phase of occupation. Commander of the Central Pacific Force, Lieutenant L. C. Bergquist, and Lieutenant G. H. Sturgeon aboard the USS *Pennsylvania* prepared "final instructions" for the jurisdiction of military personnel. For Kwajalein Atoll, they established joint command with an island commander for Roi-Namur (Navy); West Sector Ground Defense Force (Marine); and Kwajalein Island (Army). Soon after the battle, officers combined the latter two—and naval officers replaced the Marines.[43] The inter-service rivalry experienced during the war, however, was not far beneath the surface and would continue. In addition, inter-departmental competition would mar administration of the islands for the next thirty-five years, as will be seen.

In November 1942, after success with the Battle of Midway in June, but well before the end of war could be guaranteed, the State Department had planned for victory and raised the question of what agency would be given responsibility for areas potentially to be brought under U.S. control. Interest groups from Departments of State, Interior, and War; Boards of Economic Warfare, Foreign Relief and Rehabilitation Agency; and the Food Administration all stepped up and vied for the honor.[44] Army and Navy personnel worked furiously to appear worthy of gaining jurisdiction in the territory that might be seized by the Allies. Both established training schools and promised the White House they would provide seasoned, trained officers from civilian administration.

The Navy seemed to have the stronger case and put the best face on "the administration of liberated peoples." To bolster its credentials, Navy personnel dusted off President McKinley's Executive Order in 1898 making the Navy administrative agency for the Philippine Islands.[45] With that expertise, the Navy claimed both the "right and an obligation" to assist the "military objective" by suspending the enemy's former civil government. Further, it boasted its first responsibility for "dependent peoples" among indigenous Alaskans in 1867, and its most recent experience in Guam and American Samoa. As it became apparent that the Marshall Islands would be the first "prewar Japanese-held" territory to be occupied, it was doubly important to the Navy, because it was the service's first effort in World War II civil administration, as European efforts had been under Army's command.[46]

In January 1943, the Navy hastily pulled together a team at Columbia University in New York, barely in time to influence and gain success for the March 1943 decision by the War Department that the Navy would be "primary agent to plan for handling of civil affairs" and "coordinate activities of civilian agencies" for the anticipated occupation of islands. Then, by December 1943, the Navy established a Civil Affairs (Military Government) Section at Pearl Harbor to plan and prepare for governing the Marshall Islands. Lieutenant Bryan Hunt, USNR, first officer in charge, wanted the cream of naval and civilian personnel for the assignment, but he was faced with a pressing schedule and limited training program. Consultants and planners came up with an acceptable goal of "a government paternalistic in character," but one that "ruled as indirectly as possible." Candidates took on a quick study in Marshallese culture, history, mores, and language. Pressure to "get it right" would be intense. It was not until January 1944, just before the invasion of Kwajalein, that the Navy assigned its first Supply Corps Officer, a lieutenant, for supply and finance matters. For the Marshalls, supply planning and implementation in the field was handled by CinCPac/CinCPOA Supply Section.[47]

Once occupation began, the Navy called on the graduates of the Officers Training School in Civil Affairs, but these newcomers could have little idea of the extent of destruction of the islands and needs of the people in a post-battle environment. Naval officers would go ashore "to jobs that few people could perform in the manner the book directed." Still, observers would remember the "Columbia graduates" as "self-sacrificing, unrecognized martyrs," "impractical visionaries," and "some with horse sense." In the view of the Navy, the latter type "prevailed," and despite limitations and inadequate training, the effort marked a "success" for the service.[48] In future years, Monday-morning quarterbacks would disagree and argue against Naval Administration.

Whatever the later assessment of the overall effort, the military involved in the battle obviously made the first effort at benign imperialism. Not many days after fighting ceased, one marine correspondent highlighted the reciprocal good will as he sketched a scene in Kwajalein Atoll with Americans "stretched out in a lazy semi-circle on a white coral beach singing with the natives." Temporarily forgotten was the destruction; it was the fantasy of exotic Polynesian islands played out. The writer exuded vintage Western paternalism: "In some ways the native people behave much as we do. They marry and raise families and divorce their wives...." Although he did allow that some might "wait to see how they like Americans before they decide how they like the Japanese," most "show their gratitude for American generosity by honest smiles and gifts of their own labor." As for the Americans, the writer was certain that the American troops "do not know how to think in terms of racial condescension."[49]

In the mellow post-victory atmosphere, perhaps it seemed so, but not far below the surface lurked the same faith in Anglo-Saxon superiority that had plagued Americans at home and in foreign policy throughout the nation's history. Moreover, officers soon saw the dangers of too much fraternizing and the "normal existence" of the Marshallese being "immediately compromised" by the "intermingling of natives and greatly superior numbers of military personnel."⁵⁰ That realization curtailed the initial easy atmosphere described by the Marine correspondent.

The Navy attempted to work through Marshallese representatives, recognizing the *iroij laplap* (paramount chiefs) and allowing them to occupy respectful "ex-officio" positions in the village and atoll "council," constructed, of course, by Western concepts of government. Department and military governors maintained overriding authority, but encouraged "self-government" through atoll and island councils. The Marshallese were cooperative and took seriously the responsibilities of passing on military policy to the people. Expecting male leadership, it is unlikely that the Americans suffered any input from the traditional place of women or even understood a matrilineal culture, as they clearly designated women for only subordinate roles.⁵¹

As they restored order, the Americans made "initial contact" with Marshallese *iroij*, but also left little doubt as to who was in charge. Proclamation Number One explained "To the People of the Marshall Islands," that "to preserve law and order and provide for the safety and welfare" of U.S. forces and the islanders, it was "necessary to establish Military Government in the islands occupied by United States Forces." Admiral Nimitz, as Naval Commander and now also Military Governor, would exercise his authority through subordinate commanders. The proclamation expected prompt obedience, cooperation, and peaceful adherence to new regulations. From the outset, it noted that the U.S. "dollar currency, overprinted 'Hawaii' and United States coins" would be legal tender in the occupied territory, and promised that "existing personal and property rights" would be "respected." Also, "existing laws and customs" would remain "in force and effect," with one telling caveat: except "to the extent that it is necessary for me in the exercise of my powers and duties to change them."⁵² A significant exception, and pertinent to this study was the clause "existing personal and property rights," to be examined below.

The Navy was determined that regulations would be "rigidly enforced" and "strictly adhered to." Well aware of the dilemma, the Service made expectations clear: "The treatment of natives in the conquered Marshall Islands will receive world-wide attention. It is the responsibility of each member of the armed forces of the United States to exemplify the conduct of civilized warfare." General Order Number Seven added the restriction that "only authorized and recognizably uniformed members of the Provost Guard shall enter the native compounds without specific written authority...." Further, it continued, no member of the military authority will address himself to a native by voice signals, signs, gestures or other means unless specifically authorized by proper authority. However, the return of a commonly recognizable friendly salutation of native males which is customary to all civilized peoples, is not only permitted, but is considered highly desirable for the general furtherance of amicable relations."[53]

More proclamations detailed restrictions against potential disorder. Proclamation Number Two dealt with "war crimes," while Proclamation Number Four dealt with "military courts." The officers worked many hours "carefully and patiently explaining the provisions" of each ordinance. The voluminous military legalese was, even by the Navy's admission, "an immense amount of law for simple, law-abiding people." In fact, though slapped with stringent edicts, curfews, and courts, there "were simply no charges of military infractions to be brought" against the Marshallese. For military personnel and civilian contractors, on the other hand, it was a different story. Some engaged in illegal barter among other infractions, as well as illicit sex, having "been known to walk the three-mile reef between Ebeye and Kwajalein in order to seekout [sic] women."[54]

Labor and Land

Ironically, with all of the regulations for crime, law and order, and procedure, the Navy underestimated the one thing most needful to the islanders, the restoration of their land. Instead, the Service focused on the need to find additional laborers to fulfill its mission. The unfortunate confluence of the two perspectives would be in labor camps and the designation of land for military use. While the Americans looked to the islanders to be workers, the desire to be perceived as benevolent liberators required a volunteer labor force. Special Order Number One, issued in Majuro, had been specific: "For our purposes, it is important to enlist native goodwill. We *need* labor—*all* that can be made available. It must be volunteer labor, and to secure it must promote a friendly spirit of cooperation with the native population."[55] Not appreciating their number-one concern, that of restoring the land, the Americans naively thought first of capitalism as a means of motivating Marshallese to work. They were quick to introduce wage standards and to authorize "laborer chits showing the number of hours worked." As noted, the first proclamation established American currency as legal tender; thus, these chits could be redeemed "in trade goods and food at a fair value."[56]

Captured Japanese food and supplies became the first stock for a general store. Since the military did not want to "distribute [the goods] indiscriminately," they appointed *Iroij* Laminini as storekeeper. Once they had distributed laborer chits, the store flourished. By 1 March 1944, the Majuro Atoll Commander had set the wage scale, presumably for the entire Marshall Islands, at $.40 per day for laborers, $.60 per day for skilled workers, including pilots and carpenters. Unified military government in the Marshall Islands resulted in standard rates for wages, purchase price, and trade goods.[57]

Betraying another level of paternalism, the Navy believed that handicrafts were the key to Marshallese self-sufficiency. By 11 March 1944, the Atoll Commander for Majuro had set regulations for "articles of native handiwork." Included were: cigarette cases—$.25–.50; shell necklaces—$.15–.25; hats—$.25–2.00; baskets; and $.10 per-inch of length for belts, mats, and fans. For shells, the "Navy buyer" could "fix price at time of purchase." Recalling the order against unauthorized contact with indigenes, this Majuro order directed that all purchasing should be done through "the headman on each community by an officer authorized to handle such transaction."[58]

The command also set the price for local trade goods, emphasizing that such barter also helped to establish self-sufficiency, in some cases by the summer of 1944. By October 1944, the Navy optimistically reported that the "money economy" had taken hold. Trade goods ranged from those called "essentials," such as tobacco, pipes, fishhooks and lines, twine, calico, thread, knives, and laundry soap; to "desirables," such as redwood (canoe timber), pocket combs, toilet soap, cooking pots, and kerosene.[59]

With the islanders hopefully motivated, the ongoing dilemma was to organize the labor force. But problems remained. The careful restrictions on fraternizing required enforced segregation between GIs and Marshallese necessitating "labor camps," which the military established at Majuro, Kwajalein, and Roi. Sensitive to comparisons with Japanese policy, the Americans held "interisland competition" for jobs and invoked an "enlistment period" of six months. After this period, a month's "leave" at home made workers eligible for rehire. Rules required that women be employed only as nurses or nurse's aides. The U.S. used male workers to reconstruct airstrips, to build hangars, warehouses, barracks, etc. "After the initial phase of rehabilitations," families, including children, were rejoined on Kwajalein.[60]

Assigned tasks for the military determined the labor pattern. Initially, the Americans had seen handicrafts as the means for self-sufficiency, but hiring of Marshallese workers overwhelmed any local industry, as well as the supposed souvenir market, which became inflationary in any case. American military personnel classified the workers as skilled (interpreters, storekeepers, etc.) and unskilled, with clear wage differentiation between the two. Laborers worked eight hours each day, six days per week. At the outset, their living quarters were tents, but were later replaced by wooden structures of Quonset huts. Workers ate distributed K-rations or "that provided for the general mess." Marshallese *Iroij* Laminini also served as military liaison in handling the rotation of workers, as he did in managing the store.[61]

In Kwajalein Atoll, the Army ran the labor camp on Kwajalein Island, while the Navy had responsibility for the one on Roi. For the two, the combined indigenous work force was around 400, with about sixty additional men "employed on a casual basis." The interaction of Americans and Marshallese through work began a pattern that would continue with the Americanization of the occupation. As demonstrated in the missionary effort of the nineteenth century, the Marshallese were cooperative and eager to learn, not burdened with negative memories of Americans as previous colonizers. The result would be seen in Naval observation that the work in "offices, hospitals, and schools" later enabled islanders "to assume greater responsibility in the postwar period when the numbers of Naval administrators were decimated by demobilization."[62]

A less favorable view of the labor camps, and less official, saw the camps as having "squalid, shantytown appearance," contrasting sharply with the "spick and span buildings of the adjacent military establishment" the workers helped construct. By January 1950, the population of the camp had risen to 559, including 258 workers, of whom 188 were married, almost 100 children, and over 100 transients.[63]

The Navy clearly faced a new problem of logistics as well as a social problem of some dimension. Also, as the post-war period continued, the claim of "belligerent occupation" grew stale; official policy in Washington would determine a new status for the Marshalls. In that wake, the Navy would face loss of control in administering the islands, all to be discussed in following chapters.

In February 1950, to deal with the "turbulent conditions that existed on Kwajalein," the Navy acted to relocate the Kwajalein labor camp to the island of Ebeye, three miles to the north. This tiny island of seventy-six acres lay on the eastern arm of the atoll, conveniently close for labor purposes, but removed from the expanding installations on Kwajalein.[64] Thus, officials moved the camp, thereby creating another dilemma with its own vast proportions for the years ahead: "the Ebeye problem."

Whatever the employment issue, for the Marshallese, land claims remained their first priority. Little anticipating what lay ahead, the Navy's Proclamation Number One had blithely promised that "existing personal and property rights" would be "respected...." Proclamation Number Five went further, outlining the plan for "control of enemy property" and declaring that former Japanese claims were "hereby abrogated." Provisions for wartime claims, in any case, were wasted effort at the outset. While this later changed, during the war no Marshallese had come forward to claim private land, not surprising considering the devastation and dislocation.[65] Further, the local disposition toward accommodation so soon after battle would make such action unlikely. Even in 1944, Americans had allowed several Marshallese families to return to home islands, including Roi-Namur, where the Navy began a "large-scale" tree-planting effort.

Unfortunately, in view of no overt war claims by the Marshallese, the Navy had moved almost by happenstance to use land as it saw the need and simply to take a certain amount of land that the Japanese had purchased or seized in the late 1930s or early 1940s. U.S. authorities assumed the view that Japanese "public land" was "alien property" to be controlled by the U.S. as the "successor sovereign." Marshallese and independent courts alike would later question this interpretation.[66]

The new "sovereign" found few records concerning land ownership. The Japanese had removed all of value, while precious few had existed regarding the Marshall Islands. The islanders kept no written records, of course, but knew the land and traditional ownership. Americans faced an immense and complex enigma that would bring complications beyond their imagining. The settlement of the Kwajalein Land Use Agreement was well into the future. One observer reported that the Marshallese "viewed with silent amusement the administration's attempt to settle 'the land question.'"[67]

Five

Truman, the United Nations and U.S. Control

In his memoirs, U.S. President Harry Truman named 1945 the "year of decisions." So it would be. Though he had not participated in and had little knowledge of wartime strategies, the new Commander in Chief faced the responsibility for charting America's future. In April 1945, with the conclusion of the Pacific war still before him, the Marshall Islands, along with other former Japanese claims were surely a part of his thinking. And surely, it was with relief he learned that planning for future disposition of the mandates was well along.

In fact, the stratagem for the islands must be a part of a larger design. Truman's predecessor Franklin Roosevelt had dealt with a nation reluctant to enter the European war. The crucial public awareness came in August 1941, when the president met with the British Prime Minister Winston Churchill off the coast of Newfoundland. It would be their first meeting in person, but FDR had corresponded privately with Churchill and fostered their shared commitment to confront the Nazi menace. While without promises of military aid, the hugely significant Atlantic Charter publicly acknowledged American involvement in the fight against the Tripartite Pact, solemnized in September 1940.

With skillful diplomatic camouflage, the language of the Charter offered the expectation of "certain common principles" on which to base "hopes for a better future for the world." Roosevelt imagined the end of "the system of unilateral action, the exclusive alliances, the spheres of influence, the balances of power, and all the other expedients that have been tried for centuries—and have always failed." FDR may have fashioned himself the champion of the islanders to be liberated from colonial and mandated control, but the real world before the war included vast claims of empire. Undeterred, he continued with the vision for a world peace organization on the model of Woodrow Wilson's League of Nations.

Skeletons remained in all closets. In light of U.S. claims in the Pacific and its own hemispheric control, America's antipathy to "spheres of interest" struck some as rather ironic. "As if there was ever such a sphere-of-influence agreement as the Monroe Doctrine!' complained one London official."[1] And how could Wilson's principle of "self-determination" remain a part? Churchill would make the boisterous claim that he "had not become the King's First Minister in order to preside over the liquidation of the British Empire." Nevertheless, with the alliance at stake, and Wilsonian rhetoric intact, the two leaders signed the Atlantic Charter, proposing "a set of principles for international collaboration in maintaining peace and security." The following year, FDR coined the name that would embody the dream. In January 1942, representatives of twenty-six Allied nations met in Washington, D.C., and pledged support in a "Declaration by United Nations."[2]

Diplomatic efforts throughout the entire war would require the same careful negotiations. Once the Allies included the Soviet Union, the planning for the postwar world became even more delicate. Further, Roosevelt struggled with the competing military concerns of Churchill, Stalin, and Chiang Kai-shek.[3] Still, in a series of wartime conferences, including at Moscow in October 1943, Cairo in November 1943, and Teheran in December 1943, he balanced support for Allies to conclude the fighting with the concept of a postwar international organization.

On-the-ground issues remained. What would be the means of dealing with the land taken in combat? If not sphere of influence, what would be the U.S. claim for the territories of defeated Japan? In his memoir, former Secretary of State Hull recalled that the seed of Roosevelt's concept of "trusteeship" was born in March 1943, but clearly based on the League's "mandate" system.[4] In 1913, in his State of the Union speech before Congress, Wilson had evoked the need for "public conscience" in dealing with America's own territories, where we are "trustees" with "responsibility" for the "performance of our duty."

As yet, however, the Americans chose not to discuss such a potentially controversial claim for the Pacific islands. The talks at Dumbarton Oaks, D.C., 21 August–7 October 1944, included in one conference not only the U.S., Britain, and the USSR, but also China. Beforehand, even that late in the campaign, the War Department had advised delaying discussion of the "territorial trusteeship" until "after the defeat of Japan," in light of the potential to disrupt the wartime alliance, "particularly as they may adversely affect our relations with Russia...." The U.S. delegation steered clear of anything more than the "machinery and principles of trusteeship," vaguely described and limited to: (1) existing mandates; (2) territories detached; and (3) any other territory.[5]

Also brewing was the dispute in the Roosevelt Administration between the Military and the State Department. Even during the war years, under Admiral Harry Yarnell, who headed a Special Planning Section, the Navy had sought a way for postwar hegemony in the Pacific and contemplated various means of control of the Japanese mandate islands. Yarnell reportedly thought the islands were mostly economically "worthless" anyway, so any means of control could be allowed without a charge of imperialism.[6]

The State Department would have a different view. Soon after U.S. success against the Japanese with the Battle of Midway in June 1942, the State Department had questioned what agency would gain responsibility for administering any potential territory gained. And, as noted, in March 1943, with the hastily drawn "Columbia graduates" in place, the War Department had assigned administration of the Marshall Islands to the U.S. Navy. After February 1944, the Battle of Kwajalein and initial success of the Central Pacific strategy, it became clear that new planning was needed. In December 1944, the administration formed a new Coordinating Committee "to reconcile and coordinate the views of the State, War, and Navy Departments in matters of common interest and to establish policies for the Departments," thus to avoid any disruption in a united effort to secure the islands.[7]

By February 1945, at the Yalta Conference in Soviet Crimea, the subject of "territorial trusteeship and dependent areas" would be on the table. At that juncture, American advisers were convinced the time had come to focus on the Pacific and causes the nations had previously sacrificed to other concerns. Stalin was now a willing supporter of the template for "the mandates," even though the Foreign Ministers still danced around the specifics.[8]

The Yalta Conference would prove to be a temporary consolidation of unified purpose that only lasted until the victory was assured. Roosevelt achieved Stalin's promise of entry into the war against Japan to secure Manchuria for Nationalist China's control, promise kept. But the issues related to Poland and Eastern Europe proved to be a loose agreement for cooperation and "free elections" that would not be achieved in the postwar military realities. Despite later critics of the Yalta accord from both the right that FDR "gave away" too much, and from the left that the U.S. sought to "dominate" the world, at the time, both Roosevelt and Churchill appeared satisfied. FDR "knew that Americans believed they were fighting for self-determination and the Atlantic Charter principles."[9]

Each leader saw the world through his own unique lens. Certainly, Stalin would eschew any condemnation of "sphere of influence." Remembering the Nazi invasion of its homeland, the Soviet Union's plan for future security was grounded in control of neighboring territories. While still skeptical, Stalin did agree to the proposal for a United Nations organization, qualified by the stipulation that in addition to the Soviet seat, the General Assembly would include additional separate membership for the Ukraine and Byelorussia. The Big Three agreed that a conference would be held in San Francisco in April 1945 for the purpose of writing the establishing charter.

In the weeks following Yalta, the newly established Coordinating Committee delayed specifics and worked with "general principles." The major focus would be "future defense needs" with no "direct or indirect discussion" of disposition, or any agreement "that may eventually give any foreign nation claim to any control of the 'Japanese Mandated Islands' north of the Equator."[10] Still, biases were evident. While preferring outright annexation of island groups including the Marshalls, Marianas, and Carolines, the military also knew such preemption would violate the Atlantic Charter and Cairo Declaration.[11]

This time the President wanted no slip-ups. Roosevelt himself had approved the position of the War Department that all "Japanese Mandated Islands lie in the 'Blue Area' described as 'Required for the direct defense of the United States....'" The final appellation of "strategic trust" for the islands, including the Marshalls, would come later, but that intent was already in the military mind to "assure the security interest" of the "agreeing nations."[12]

With the San Francisco Conference on the calendar for April 1945, all parties well understood the purpose. Soon after Yalta, the president had appointed the seven who would represent the United States; then, the eighth as advisor, Former Secretary of State Cordell Hull, who had resigned his cabinet post for health reasons after Roosevelt's reelection in November 1944. Remembering the sabotage of the League of Nations by Republican opposition in the person of Senator Henry Cabot Lodge, whom President Wilson had excluded in negotiations for the League, FDR made sure to include Senator Arthur Vandenberg, Jr. (R-MI), a former isolationist and conservative member of the Senate Foreign Relations Committee. His participation would be essential in building bipartisan support.[13]

Less than a week after Roosevelt's death on 12 April, Secretary of

State Edward Stettinius gathered in "Executive Session" the eleventh meeting of the Coordinating Committee to discuss "the question of trusteeship." The issue before them was on how to advise a new president regarding the desired policy going forward. In his fateful "year of decisions," and overwhelmed by a myriad of crucial issues, Truman was in no position to receive various viewpoints for his consideration. Astutely, he had decreed that he wished a clear consensus.[14]

All agreed that a unified plan was imperative, but each part of the committee claimed a valid requirement for its interest and from its viewpoint. The State Department feared the international charge of power grabbing, seizing territory or annexation. Stettinius was firm that an "annexation policy would be contrary to a policy consistently followed by the late President Roosevelt."[15] The dilemma was how to secure control, deemed necessary by the military. Secretary of War Henry Stimson seemed uninterested in previous questions such as colonies and resources, and now focused only on future bases.

The seventy-eight-year-old Stimson, senior diplomat par excellence, had been Secretary of State from 1928 to 1932, as the Japanese had executed its northern strategy of aggression in Manchuria. Secretary of War since 1940, he now carried the memories and the scars of previous mistakes in American judgment. He warned it was:

> necessary to avoid the paths of danger for possible aggressive nations. He called attention to the error of our ways after the last war, and this, he said, had been burnt into his soul. After the last war, when the question of the disposition of the mandates to Japan was up for consideration, Mr. Wilson had been approached on the effect it would have on the Philippines.[16]

Despite the agony of Wilson's decision at that time, the results had only opened doors for Japan. Stimson's memory was correct. The group agreed that the U.S. must have "full power over necessary protective bases...." Secretary of the Navy James Forrestal wished to avoid such a limited approach as considering isolated naval bases. Rather, he would add more specific routes in the Pacific to be protected and "a system of defense."[17]

The committee members were moving to the consensus the president needed. Not surprisingly, the "Blue Area" identified in November 1943 by Roosevelt, which included all the Japanese-Mandate islands, and "required for the direct defense of the United States" would be the key: "we must have an entire chain of island bases." The language led to the "distinction in the degree or in the terms of the trusteeship in the strategic areas on the basis of military requirements."[18]

Thus, President Truman received a report reflecting State's fear of "the question of annexation," combined with the military's "necessity of control," essentially a "dual mandate," with the essence of the two contradictory. The summary he approved would go forward for the San Francisco assignment. He gratefully accepted the conclusion of his predecessor: America needed "strategic bases in the Pacific," but "at the same time" did not wish to be "charged with annexation and expansionist policies." Truman thanked the committee, saying he "thought it gave him a clear understanding of the subject." The new president was reassured. Ready to move forward, and "with this matter off my hands," he went on to face other great decisions.[19]

The United Nations and Trusteeship

Clearly, the concept of trusteeship was a direct descendant of the Mandate system of the Versailles Conference. Just as the spoils of World War I went to Germany's conquerors under the guise of protection, so the victors of World War II would strip Japan of the mandated islands of the Pacific. Trusteeship, of course, would go "considerably farther" than the old Mandate system; the American delegation attempted its sell as a "daring venture," "bold and broad-visioned." High expectations accompanied the optimistic terms of: (1) furthering "international peace and security"; (2) promoting political, economic, social, and educational advancement as inhabitants moved to self-government; (3) encouragement for human rights; and (4) equal treatment, equal justice.[20]

As the climax of the San Francisco Conference, on 25 June 1945, the fifty nations represented unanimously adopted the establishing Charter of the United Nations. In October of that year the five permanent members of the Security Council and a majority of the signatories would ratify. The Charter allowed for two categories of dependent peoples. Earliest drafts of the documents planned for "all dependent areas" to be under the trusteeship system, with "'full independence' as the goal."[21] Neither the French nor British, however, wanted to see their colonial empires destroyed. As noted, Churchill blasted the idea:

> He "did not agree with one single word of this report on trusteeships.... As long as he was Minister, he would never yield one scrap of their heritage." Being assured that the subject did not affect their colonies, but "the Japanese islands in the Pacific," the British would consider the islands expendable. "If the Americans want to take Japanese islands which they have conquered," Churchill informed his Foreign Secretary Anthony Eden, "let them do so with our blessing and any form of words that may be agreeable to them. But 'Hands Off the British Empire' is our maxim."[22]

The result of their opposition was a two-tier system. The first tier was the group already under the sovereignty of UN member nations, i.e., existing colonial holdings, termed "non-self-governing territories." A second tier created an "international trusteeship system" with the designation of "trust territories," including those: (1) "now held under mandate"; (2) those "detached from enemy states" by the war; and (3) those "voluntarily placed under the system" by responsible states.[23] The basic understanding for both was that "due respect for the culture of the peoples" would lead them to "develop self-government," with the four basic areas of development being political, economic, social, and educational.[24] Negotiators ignored efforts by China and the USSR to add specifics in the goal toward autonomy. That lack of specificity would provide an easy out for colonialists and would delay any real "self-determination" for decades in some cases.

For the United States, with the category of those "detached from enemy states," Micronesia was of primary concern. Certainly, in the long conflict and war, the Japanese had successfully made the argument, if any needed, that the islands had strategic importance.[25] The challenge for the victors would be to allow any previously held peoples to "develop self-government" and attain real independence from their "protection." Thus, after the definition of trusts, the question of oversight remained.

To meet this challenge, the UN Charter established a Trusteeship Council to be composed of representatives from the permanent members of the Security Council, those administering trust territories, and elected members to three-year terms. This Trusteeship Council would monitor the progress of the various trusts granted, visit the territories, and regularly report to the General Assembly.[26]

Fearful of unwanted oversight or interference, the Americans argued for special consideration. The Draft Statement of the Trusteeship Agreement spelled out U.S. apprehension on this point:

> a "major part" of the Japanese attack "staged through Kwajalein…"; the Japanese continued "extensive operations against the U.S. shipping in the eastern half of the Pacific Ocean for years"; "Air bases and amphibious staging points in the Marianas facilitated the capture of Guam in December 1941"; "Air Forces and naval forces operating from the Marshalls were used in the capture of Wake Islands"; The Japanese "naval and air forces and shore defenses" "served to screen and protect" Japanese marches on the Philippines and British, U.S. and Dutch possessions; the "Palau group in the Western Carolines" served as "forward support base" for attack of the East Indies; the Japanese used "atoll of Truk" as naval and air base used against the Solomons; from Truk, the Japanese threatened "the Allied lines of communication between the U.S., Australia, and New Zealand"; and on and on the "lessons learned" continued.[27]

The American people, the draft asserted, "are firmly resolved that this area shall never again be used as a springboard for aggression against the United States or any other member of the United Nations."[28]

With this insistence, the United States conceived the concept of "strategic trust," combining military concern for "strategic defense" with absolute command by the U.S., thus limiting UN oversight. Such a brilliant image, with great potential for control, had multiple claims of authorship. Some would credit Congressman, later Senator, Mike Mansfield (D-MO) with the idea of "strategic trust." Others would maintain that Under Secretary of the Interior Abe Fortas had been the architect.[29]

Whoever the originator, the crucial question remained: what did "strategic trust" mean? The first meaning was that the U.S. would have almost a free hand in administering it. The other trust regions fell under jurisdiction of the Trusteeship Council of the General Assembly, while the strategic trust would come under the supervision of the Security Council. Not lost in that adjuration was the knowledge that the United States would hold a permanent seat on the Security Council, where its "concurring vote" would be needed for any action, essentially a veto power.

In 1949, except in security matters claimed only in nuclear testing, the Security Council delegated supervision to the Trusteeship Council. The means of reporting to the Trusteeship Council was to be an annual report written with guidance from a questionnaire that followed the four major categories of social, education, political, and economic development. According to one judgment in 1975, "reports of the Trusteeship Council to the Security Council [were] perfunctory."[30] For the time, this approach to oversight made supervision practically nonexistent.

The second implication for strategic trust lay in the military aspect. One rather cynical view was: "As long as its military interests were served, the U.S. had no other particular concerns for the area."[31] Ironically, in creating the strategic trust concept, the U.S. claimed autonomy for military operations and facilities, a "radical departure" from the League of Nations Mandate system. The League had "prohibited fortifications or bases in mandated territories," violations for which America had roundly criticized the Japanese Empire.[32]

On the one hand, the allowance for fortifications gave the U.S. the guarantee of security it sought; while on the other, the winning justification was in motive: security needed "in the maintenance of international peace and security." The official view was that the U.S. had "not only the right to establish defense installations in the Trust Territory of the Pacific Islands, it [had] the responsibility." Or as stated in a 1950 letter, the provision to establish bases and station armed forces was "a right and a duty."³³ Under this broad umbrella, the U.S. would be "entitled" to:

(1) ... establish naval, military, and air bases and to erect fortifications in the trust territory;
(2) ... station and employ armed forces in the territory; and
(3) ... make use of volunteer forces, facilities, and assistance from the trust territory ... as well as for local defense and the maintenance of law and order within the trust territory.³⁴

It was as blank a check as any militarist might desire. Although, at the suggestion of the USSR, the U.S. deleted the phrase "that the territory could be administered 'as an integral part of the United States.'" The omission did not diminish the complete authority the U.S. had won.³⁵ Strategic equals security equals U.S. control.

Thus, the UN Charter created eleven trusts, but only one "strategic trust," with that one alone reporting to the Security Council.³⁶ The Coordinating Committee, "as a matter of priority," had requested that the War Department would consider the merit of trusteeship "from a military point of view" and define the "strategic control" required.³⁷ Truman, therefore, accepted that the "considerations of security are so overwhelming that the United States will find it necessary to become the sole administering authority, at least for the majority of the [Japanese] islands." He had achieved his seemingly contradictory dual mandates, the fear of annexation versus the necessity of control, all under the palatable banner of benevolent protection. In his report to the U.S. Congress in March 1946 the president claimed that the U.S. had taken "a leading part" in "establishment of the Trusteeship System...."³⁸

On 2 April 1947, the UN Security Council approved the trustee agreement creating the "Territory of the Pacific Islands, consisting of the islands formerly held by Japan under mandate..." specifically the Marianas, except Guam, the Marshalls, and the Carolines. The Security Council designated this "a strategic area and placed under the trusteeship system established in the Charter of the United Nations." On 18 July 1947, the United States ratified the agreement by Congressional Joint Resolution.³⁹

On that same day, Truman issued his Executive Order 9875, granting Interim Administration authority to the Secretary of the Navy, "subject to subsequent modification." Also, the order recognized that under the UN Charter, "the agreement to close any areas for security reasons and to determine the extent" to which "such closed areas shall be exercised jointly by the Secretary of the Navy and the Secretary of State" in dealing with the authority of the Trusteeship Council.⁴⁰

Interior Takeover

In recognizing these overlapping missions, President Truman faced the old inter-agency competition and question of which department would administer the Trust Territory of the Pacific Islands (TTPI). One official would later judge that "Defense and Interior were natural enemies," while State displayed "arrogance" and "seemed incapable of a straightforward and unclassified answer."⁴¹ Eager for the most acceptable face for U.S. occupation, the president was open to the advice not only from the State Department, but from two influential political leaders who saw the preferred international image as civilian, not military control. Longtime Secretary of the Interior, Harold L. Ickes, and U.S. Representative Mike Mansfield (D–MO) offered the way of resolution by another task force. With their suggestion, back on 20 October 1945, the president had created a committee composed of representatives of the usual adversaries of State, War, Navy, and Interior.⁴²

Secretary Ickes had only one goal: moving administration of the trust to the Interior Department and away from the U.S. Navy. In addition to his confidential advice to the president, he even built his case using public pressure, publishing articles of opinion in the popular *Colliers* magazine. In February 1946, in a seeming innocuous effort to tout Interior's role in environmental concerns, he raised the matter of "Underwater Wealth," or "mineral or fishery resources" that "might exist" under the continental shelves of U.S. boundaries—and surely under the "high seas contiguous to the Hawaiian Islands, to Guam, to Wake, to Midway, and to those former Japanese islands which we may use for bases. How valuable this assertion of jurisdiction over fisheries in the high seas may become...." In the subtlety, one could hear: especially if Interior had jurisdiction.

More specific was the article in August 1946, entitled "The Navy at Its Worst," in which Ickes excoriated the Navy's administration, charging "a policy of tyranny in Guam and Samoa," and now "planning the same harsh treatment for the islands won from Japan in World War II." In all-out warfare, he claimed it "is the Navy which has largely been responsible for our undeclared moratorium on democracy...." The "American Navy controls its subject populations by direct and autocratic methods," an "absolutism" that "sneers at every constitutional guarantee." He reserved some of the most severe criticism for the "inferior" and "segregated" schools and "wage discrimination" practiced on these islands.[43]

Under such a barrage of condemnation, Truman could hardly allow the Navy to extend its jurisdiction. Ironically, Ickes' Interior Department later would be charged with worse. Islanders would remember the "good ole" Navy days, after Interior's mismanagement and inefficiency.[44] For Ickes, there was little sympathy for the challenges the Navy had faced after the battle, but some later saw it differently.

One high-ranking official, Fred M. Zeder, who was Director of Territories in the Department of the Interior, 1975–1977, would recall the claim that the "only time there was ever any efficiency in Micronesia itself from the trust territory was right after the war when the Navy was running it." He concluded, "I can believe that." Interior brought with it no experience with islanders, little interest in understanding their cultures, but a long history of "reservation mentality" and prejudice against indigenous peoples. Certainly, "economic development has certainly never been a long suit of very many people in Washington and certainly not the Department of Interior."[45]

Unfortunately, it appeared that the effort at "research into the local social and political organization," needed "as a basis for working out with the islanders community," would be started from square one. The first civilian High Commissioner ordered a paper, "Basic Information" that literally began with basics for the staff.[46] Interior's effort "to enlist the assistance of social scientists in this research" apparently did not make use of the Navy's extensive anthropological work in the early years of its administration, but sought Interior's own expertise, or lack thereof. Interior's takeover ended the nascent efforts begun by the Navy for islanders' representative government, to be followed below.[47]

In addition to the attitude barrier was the budgetary one. The Congress gave Interior the same budget for the Trust Territory allotted to the Navy, but without the Navy's experience, training, and equipment, Interior's effort suffered by comparison. Despite the Navy's "cooperative attitude," Deputy High Commissioner Admiral Carlton H. Wright reported a loss of morale and some difficulty getting Navy officers to take a trust territory assignment. The Navy expertise evidenced in the enthusiasm of early years apparently waned before the hand-off to Interior. The department's first, crucial decade would be spent learning lessons the hard way in a morass of gradualism and what would later be called benign neglect by the UN, to some a "rust territory." Ickes resigned as secretary in March 1946, but continued on the lecture circuit.[48]

On 18 June 1947, his Task Force's recommendation to the president was to transfer administration of Guam, American Samoa, and the TTPI to a civilian agency "at the earliest practicable date and that the Congress be urged to adopt an organic act establishing the framework of government and the status of the inhabitants of these areas." The following month, the president had issued his Executive Order 9875, noted above, with the caveat that the Navy's Interim Administration would be "subject to subsequent modification." On 14 May 1949, Truman would follow the committee's recommendation, directing the Secretary and the Navy to submit plans for such a transfer.[49]

Acting as the new, if interim, "civil authority," the Navy's Commander-in-Chief Pacific and United States Pacific Fleet, Admiral I. Louis Denfeld, took office as the Trust Territory of the Pacific Islands' first High Commissioner on 18 July 1947, the same day as Truman's Executive Order. With no little irony and reminiscent of the Navy's Proclamation Number One back in 1944 after the Battle of Kwajalein, he proclaimed that the "existing customs, religious beliefs and property rights" of the islands' inhabitants would "be respected...." Further, "existing local laws" as well as previous military regulations would remain in effect "except insofar as they are not in consonance" with the trusteeship agreement and the President's executive order, and "insofar as it may be necessary for me in the exercise or my powers and duties to change them." Some would judge that "the aims of the naval government and the training given at the School of Naval Administration had been aimed from the first at government of civil rather than military type."[50] The Navy had kept its headquarters in Honolulu.

In retrospect, it appears that there was blame to go around and each agency could take a share in the inter-agency warfare. Both suffered from the Western version of paternalism, working "to justify America's position of global primacy and to obscure the disruptive, even destructive consequences of that exercise of power over others." Later, some would eschew even efforts toward forms of economic "development" for indigenous peoples.[51] In the Marshalls, the military demands of "strategic trust" would need its own definition. In either case, the islanders had their own vision for self-determination and would challenge any category for their future forced upon them, as will be seen.[52]

Delivering authority to the Department of the Interior, one could predict, would further complicate a hopelessly convoluted chain of command. The High Commissioner operated under Interior, but the oversight of the UN Trusteeship Council was exercised through the State Department. In addition, State's responsibility for U.S. diplomatic relations with other countries came through the United Nations. Of course, under the Constitution, the Congress had authority for the territories, which would mean any policy executed by Interior would bear scrutiny from the legislative branch of government.

The U.S. Senate confirmed Elvert D. Thomas, the president's appointment of civilian High Commissioner of the TTPI, as the "principal United States government official in Micronesia." For administrative purposes, the U.S. divided the Trust Territory into six districts: Palau, Ponape (Pohnpei), Truk (Chuuk) and Yap in the Carolines; the Marshall Islands; and the Marianas, excluding Guam. These divisions would change slightly with future negotiations, as would district spellings. In 1977, Kusaie, originally part of the Ponape (Pohnpei) district, became a separate district. Population in the districts varied from Truk (Chuuk), whose population numbered 32,732 in 1976, or twenty-eight percent of the total; to Yap, population 7,536 in 1976, or sixty-seven percent of the total. Palau and the Marianas were about the same size, around 13,000. The Marshalls and Ponape (Pohnpei) were similar with 24,248 and 23,723, respectively.[53]

On 1 July 1951, the U.S. Navy's four-year interim as "civil authority" ended. President Truman's Executive Order transferred "Administration of the Trust Territory of the Pacific Islands from the Secretary of the Navy to the Secretary of the Interior," rather dubiously adding that this "appears to be in the public interest."[54] By that date, with the onset of what became the Cold War between the United States and the Soviet Union, new political and military realities were in place that made the decision to move from military to civilian control somewhat counter intuitive.

Another of the momentous "great decisions" of 1945 facing President Truman was deployment of a new, horrific weapon, developed in the secret Manhattan Project, another of the wartime strategies of which he had zero knowledge when becoming the new Commander in Chief. Some suggested using the bomb merely as display and threat, to forego dropping it on any civilian population. But the U.S. possessed only two bombs in its arsenal at the time. The possibility of using one only for a demonstration of American military power was not convincing for Truman. Authorizing the full, awesome use of the destructive atomic bombs forced the end of war in the Pacific, satisfying Roosevelt's insistence on unconditional surrender from the Japanese. The other, even more horrific ramification for the future of humanity was the dawn of the Atomic Age. Albert Einstein himself had feared, "thus we drift toward unparalleled catastrophe."[55]

The decision to continue testing the bomb would have profound impact for the Marshall Islands. U.S. control of the Marshalls as part of its "strategic trust," would offer exactly the ideal "remote" location, "such as over a deserted island," about which the president had mused. The choice would seem remote to planners in Washington perhaps, but not to the Marshallese. The first two tests at Bikini Atoll, Operation Crossroads, occurred on 1 July 1946. Blithely naïve and ignorant of any danger, congressmen who at the time were negotiating sensitive atomic legislation, made time to view the test in person, along with reporters, military personnel, and UN observers. The second, on 25 July, would bring even more radioactive damage to spectators than the first.

For legislators, again the argument was primarily about the wisdom of civilian versus military control of the nation's new "secrets." The Atomic Energy Act, which became law the next month, on 1 August 1946, betrayed the hopeful optimism of some for international cooperation in controlling atomic energy. The Congress gave "extraordinary power" to a civilian United States Energy Commission, and provided for three major advisory committees, composed of members from the Congress, the military, and the scientific community. It would guarantee ongoing competition between military branches, departments, agencies, as well as both allies and potential enemies. In 1949, the Soviet Union tested its own atomic bomb.[56]

Faced with the competition of the Soviets, President Truman's next crucial decision came on 31 January 1950 with the resolve to go beyond the fission of atomic energy to an even more devastating thermonuclear bomb of nuclear fusion, brainchild of scientist Edward Teller. The president directed the Commission "to continue work on all forms of weapons, including the so-called hydrogen or super-bomb." Some would say the president had no option, it was "absolutely essential" for national security. Others were shocked that he acted so quickly. David Lilienthal, Chairman of the Commission, resigned on 15 February 1950, his goal for "the peaceful atom" now unrealistic.[57]

The Marshalls thus became the essential location for sixty-seven tests from 1946 to 1958. The next series had already begun at Eniwetok Atoll in 1948. Between 1954 and 1958, the deadly Bravo series unleashed more than twice the anticipated powerful explosion in massive, fifteen-megaton nuclear bombs, "1000 times that of the weapon that destroyed Hiroshima." This display frightened even previous supporters enough to terminate atmospheric nuclear testing, though the U.S. continued sixteen more tests even after Bravo. Tests in the Marshalls represented only seven percent of total testing, but eighty percent of the "atmospheric megatonnage detonated." Overall testing would continue until 1988.[58]

The Cold War with the Soviet Union transformed the world and the future of American defense needs. Unveiled in May 1947, the Truman Doctrine assured American resistance to Stalin's design on Europe. Also in 1947, the National Security Act would remodel the reporting structure in the executive branch. Rather than relying on the reoccurring Task Force approach, a new National Security Council would advise the president. The council would include not only a National Security Advisor, but also the Secretary of State and the Secretary of Defense, who would head the Department of Defense (DOD). The Act would terminate the War Department, creating instead the Joint Chiefs of Staff. All the new organization, however, did not end the inter-service rivalry. The next chapter will recount the strategy that would bring the struggle for control of Kwajalein to one between the Navy and the U.S. Army.

Six

The Trust Territory of the Pacific Islands

In the 1950s and 1960s, the dilemma of military use versus landownership rights in the Marshalls continued to plague the United States. Creation of the Trust Territory of the Pacific Islands (TTPI) with its own bureaucracy did not ease the difficulty of sorting out the concept of "strategic trust." President Truman's handoff of administration to the Department of the Interior created a nightmare of multiple levels in decision making, as well as potential for pitting the Department of the Interior against the Department of Defense. As the Navy continued its earlier "use as needed" modus operandi for land, sign-off now would be required from the Interior Department as well. Kwajalein Atoll in general and Kwajalein Island in particular would provide the locus for an emerging and growing disputation.

Meanwhile, the "Ebeye problem," mentioned over and over again in Trust Territory and U.S. documents, festered and grew worse. In February 1950, as a response to the conditions on Kwajalein Island, the Navy had relocated the workers labor camp to the island of Ebeye, some three miles to the north on the eastern arm of the atoll. In 1951, despite protests from Ebeye landowners, the representatives of the "Ebeye Village Council" allowed the Navy's use of the island "under a purchase or lease agreement." The signers, however, postponed clarifying the exact meaning of this phrase, and what "agreement" they meant.

At the time, no compensation was made to the owners of Ebeye for land occupation and there was no resolution of how that would be accomplished. The paper did state that the Trust Territory would acquire land "either by purchase in fee or by a long term lease" and instructed landowners to "file claims" for rent and damage restitution, but it thereby postponed settlement. One observer would later speculate that this philosophy, the "idea of taking the land and paying later, as we have done, is contrary to Anglo-American theories of law."[1] The Navy would have a difficult time producing documents to justify its actions.

What may have seemed an ideal solution instead created a new headache with increasing overcrowding of the tiny island of Ebeye's 76.754 acres. Reports revealed a grim picture with unsatisfactory standards of health and sanitation, housing of small wooden structures built by the Navy, and unpaved streets.[2] The "wage economy" at Ebeye primarily derived from the income directly or indirectly gained by working for the military on Kwajalein Island. Further, economic opportunity available in taking American jobs served as a magnet to other Marshallese, some transient workers, and some extended family of Ebeye landowners.

The Marshallese quickly saw ways to manipulate the pseudo-government structure imposed by Americans. With authority over land usurped from the traditional *iroij laplap*, artificial offices created for and held by islanders became the avenue for control. Complaints reported by the so-called "public relations manager" to the commanding officer would include some "mistreatment" by the Americans. The sailors did not beat the workers as the Japanese had done, but they did "ruffle some feathers" and were remembered as being "tough." Incidents were usually minor, but "everyday little complaints ... if they were not answered would turn into big ones."[3]

Understandably, Marshallese from outlying atolls made every attempt to get a part of the American action. By the mid-fifties, one observer estimated that easily ten percent of "able-bodied Marshallese" were concentrated on Ebeye doing "mop jobs mostly for the Navy." Census figures showed a jump from 216 residents in January 1953 to 1,198 in November 1955. There was "constant dispute between landowners and the Navy labor force who do not come from Kwajalein Atoll." This has led, he continued, to "bitterness between the outsiders and the Kwajalein people."[4]

One irritant was the role of the "Ebeye Council," racked with factions between Ebeye citizens and the "out-islanders," who sometimes gained a majority on the council. As the liaison with TTPI officials, council offices of the "magistrate" and "scribe" held a great deal of power in issuing permits and licenses. According to one report, before the 1953 election, an incumbent magistrate "sailed his schooner around in Kwaj Atoll picking up all his friends and relatives." After a "big feast" and stay during which they "were taken care of," the visitors voted in the Ebeye contest, thereby guaranteeing the reelection of their candidate. Marshallese frequently accused the Navy interests of siding with one or another faction of the council.[5]

Ebeye also became the location for competing economic ventures. Stores, bakeries, "and one restaurant" depended on "Navy employees" and transient Marshallese. Out-islanders and Kwajalein Atoll residents, including those from Ebeye, vied for "import-export" trade, as the Marshallese became more and more dependent on imported food. Traditional foods were rare, while "rice, sardines, and corned beef" became staples. Some Marshallese kept small numbers of "swine and poultry," while they engaged in only limited fishing for food. In 1960, Americans would lament wryly that the people of Ebeye had developed "expensive tastes," listing such "exotic foods" as potatoes, onions, oranges, and apples.[6] By the twenty-first century, the compounded effect of processed food over decades would create a massive problem of obesity and diabetes among the people, leading to an "Emergency Health Crisis" proclamation in 2013.[7]

Land

Administrators for the Trust Territory reeled with the difficulties of sorting out the needs of the Navy from conflicting Marshallese land claims, complicated by the Japanese practice of assessing ownership of land versus trees: land owned by *iroij* (chief), but trees owned by *kajur* (worker). District Anthropologist Jack Tobin provided what would become the best documentation the military could muster for American use of land in Kwajalein Atoll. The list showed the islands occupied by U.S. forces, some taken over from Japanese "public lands" category. Tobin's descriptions for acreage and methods acquired was inadequate but the only "evidence" that confronted the barrage of Marshallese claims of ownership. In their cases, Marshallese began to count trees cut: $25/coconut, $20/breadfruit. With frustration, the Navy would estimate that over 100 people possessed some manner of "land rights" on the island.[8]

In May 1954, one visiting Trust Territory official acted after noticing the laxity of old Naval standards, with Marshallese living on "Navy land." But that was the problem. Whose land was Ebeye? The Marshallese answer was clear: remove the Navy entirely from their island. For the military, on the other hand, Ebeye was now "second in importance only to Kwaj," because it served as a "bedroom island" available for Marshallese labor.[9] With shades of former German answers, one U.S. official suggested removing all the indigenous citizens from the island. One solution less drastic than evacuating the Marshallese was to segregate Ebeye into "worker camp areas" with the Navy then returning unused land to Marshallese landowners, negotiating new working agreements, and restricting further building on Ebeye.[10]

Rather than ending further building, and only intensifying the problem, Navy planners instead initiated an effort to build a Navy transmitter on Ebeye. Trust Territory officials reacted with unusual vehemence. The Navy "already has" Kwajalein, Roi-Namur, and South Loi Islands, the district administrators stormed to the High Command. Though Marshallese landowners had "tolerated with equanimity" U.S. actions, further usurpations on Ebeye "might disrupt" their "evenness of temper."[11]

With the land issue in dire need of settlement, 1957 became the pivotal year for the coming reckoning. "As a result of the continued use without agreement or compensation," one writer stated, "there has arisen an air of resentment and distrust toward the Administration in the Marshall Island District that is becoming manifestly more evident."[12] Additionally, in that same year, the U.S. Army would assert its new mission and need for land, discussed below.

Optimistically hoping that the Marshallese had filed "nearly all claims," Trust Territory officials assessed acres and needs and determined that currently the U.S. claimed "150.164 acres" occupied in the Marshalls. Looking for a one-payment solution, they offered Kwajalein landowners $500 per acre for the land used by the Kwajalein Naval Station, covering use and future use for an "indefinite" time. For land previously used, the department offered $25 per acre, per year of use. At $500 per acre, total payment would be $75,082.[13]

Officials were only beginning to realize the depth of islanders' passion for their land. They had no intention of settling that cheaply; most assuredly, they were "not satisfied." Legal counsel for the Trust Territory reported that the Marshallese were increasingly discontent. Already sensitized by the Ebeye resident claims, District Administrator Maynard Neas wrote to the Deputy High Commissioner in July 1957 of several individual claims in Majuro as well. He noted that with no overall policy, the U.S. was more and more in an "embarrassing position." With no settlement in sight things were at a "highly critical stage." The problem was that "very little" remained in the way of records to show any payment for land.[14]

By December 1957, the crisis eased somewhat when the Navy agreed to cut from its budget the ill-considered transmitter and further construction on Ebeye. With this welcomed breather, the Trust Territory government attempted some damage control. In February 1958, Thomas Gilliland, Land Law Examiner, issued an official notice: Whereas, on 22 February 1944 the U.S. entered the Marshall Islands; whereas, on 1 July 1951 the

Department of the Interior took responsibility for the islands; whereas, the Marshallese people would be allowed to file claims for the period of 22 February 1958–1 July 1959 for only a limited time; "therefore, after 30 June 1959, no more claims, damage, or rent due will be accepted."[15]

As the deadline for claims passed, officials could assess the routes to settlement. First was the matter of Ebeye claims and the Naval needs. Having cancelled the transmitter and further construction, the Navy began a conciliatory gesture in land return of thirty-nine acres on Ebeye. Still under the illusion that any effort would suffice, however, the offer included the barb that return would be on a "temporary" basis, contingent on use "until needed by the Navy." This, of course, did little to restore good will, since, as one observer noted, it was "useless" because the owners could not "build homes" or "plant trees" on a temporary basis.[16]

Eventually, the Navy recognized the logic and intended "complete release of the land," even "immediately upon demand," with "no strings attached." Trust Territory officials grumbled that the land retrieved was "covered with rusting equipment." They felt, nevertheless, that the return "shows muscle" of Trust Territory over the Navy and resulted in "two good effects": the "rightful" return of Marshallese land; and "prestige" for the Trust Territory administration.[17]

Ebeye was only the beginning. Next was the matter of additional claims. After the Kwajalein landowners refused the initial offer for Kwaj, one official noted that this would not be easy. He darkly reminded the High Commissioner, "we still have pre–1951 to negotiate."[18] Dissatisfaction among the Marshallese had led them to seek legal assistance in dealing with the Americans. Attorneys in Hawaii, E.E. Wiles, and in Washington, D.C., Paul C. Aiken & Smith, came to their assistance.

What followed were many surveys and hearings to determine lands, lease, and payment values. After over 150 hearings, in August 1959, the Trust Territory paid $20,000 for sixty-two-plus acres in Majuro Atoll. Kwajalein Atoll, even with over 120 hearings, would be even more difficult to resolve. Kwajalein landowners needed some way of support. They would "never understand our need for the overcrowding of Ebeye," wrote one official, "unless some attempt [is made] to pay them for their loss of land."[19]

Army

Well aware of the ideal mid-ocean location and loath to yield its place, the U.S. Navy continued a limited deployment in the Marshalls. But without a strong mission for the base, officials even considered closing out its presence entirely. It would be not the Navy, but the U.S. Army, already present as well, that would name the potential significance of Kwajalein Atoll.

The close of World War II and onset of the Cold War had turned American military planning toward the weaponry of the intercontinental ballistic missile (ICBM). Because of its role in air defense during the war, it was the Army that took the lead in ballistic-missile research and testing, even while some spirit of competition for the assignment continued with the U.S. Navy. After the Pentagon spirited Wernher von Braun and other German scientists out of Europe, Operation Paperclip, the ballistic-missile team in Texas joined those in Alabama to concentrate the American effort in rocketry.[20] Based on the work of the U.S. Army Corps of Engineers, the U.S. Air Force saw that merging "two war-developed technologies," the atomic bomb with Germany's V-2 guided missile technology, "could completely revolutionize weaponry and strategic warfare." In July 1954, the Air Force established its program office for the first ICBM system, the Atlas.[21]

The following year, in March 1955, the Army asked Bell Laboratories and Western Electric for an eighteen-month study on the potential for air defense. The result followed in October 1957, when the Army established the first program office for a defensive anti-missile missile under the Army Ballistic Missile Agency in Huntsville, Alabama, naming its first product the NIKE-ZEUS.[22] These competing programs would require some clarification from the Pentagon, which came in 1958. Secretary of Defense Neil McElroy ruled that while the Army "would have primary responsibility" for ballistic missile defense, the Air Force would "continue working" on complimentary radar systems, with coordinated testing.[23]

As the Army planners, with help from Bell and Western Electric, began to search for a suitable test site for their new system, "Kwajalein Atoll in the Marshalls began to look more and more attractive." Clearly, developing and testing against a long-range missile would require exact distances and appropriate facilities. Not only was the 4800-mile distance to the Marshalls exact for a potential target-missile launch from Vandenberg Air Force Base in California, the deep lagoon of Kwajalein Atoll was a desirable landing place for ICBMs not intercepted. Kwaj facilities already included an airstrip, a harbor, housing areas, and other necessities for an interceptor defense-missile test site.[24] Thus, it was the U.S. Army that again recognized the strategic importance of Kwajalein Atoll and the Marshall Islands.

By 1959, "site preparation" began; in 1960 "facilities for an operational NIKE-ZEUS battery began to appear." By 1961, the Army's contractual personnel had assembled on the island, the Navy's having handed over merchandising, transportation, maintenance, and community support.[25] Even as jurisdiction shifted, however, the Army still needed to travel the circuitous route to request land and testing space. Typically, the Army's Engineering District, Honolulu, would request through the Navy's Pacific Division, Bureau of Yards and Docks; then, the Navy bureau would formally request that the TTPI "negotiate with Marshallese land owners for the desired property rights." The Trust Territory Attorney General would actually do the negotiating. The Trust Territory received any property for the U.S. and assigned it to the "appropriate" agency "for defense purposes."[26] While the process proved cumbersome, the Army would soon view with gratitude the role of the TTPI officials, if not that of the Navy.

At the outset, the island of Gugeegue in Kwajalein Atoll became the site for the range communications transmitter. The Army's Advance Research Projects Agency selected Roi-Namur as the site for the Pacific Range Electromagnetic Signature Studies Program (PRESS), the forerunner of many extensive and increasingly sophisticated tracking structures on Roi.[27] On these islands, work went forward with little reaction from the Marshallese. The same would not be true for the island of Lib, southwest of Kwajalein Atoll. In November-December 1961, as a precaution against unforeseen mishaps, the Navy evacuated 234 native Lib residents, moving them to Ebeye and thereby created a "Zeus Corridor," south of the atoll, and protective of Kwajalein.[28]

Thus occurred the first milestone in what would be another long controversy over property rights with indigenous landowners. While Lib did not lie in what would come to be known as the mid-atoll corridor for later missions, the case, nevertheless, set a significant precedent. On 15 September 1961, Lib officials signed a Memo-of-Understanding (MOU) with Trust Territory and Pacific Missile Range, Kwajalein officials after the promises of: (1) a village to be built on Ebeye; (2) subsistence payments for Lib residents; (3) job opportunities at Kwajalein; and (4) a new village on Lib when the people returned after what was billed as a "temporary dislocation," which lasted five years. According to a later Army assessment, "the repatriation of the Libese to Lib was a highly successful and popular operation." The Lib people "assisted" in designing their new facilities, and the Army followed "every recommendation." But not until 1966.[29]

Kwajalein Land Use Agreement

The initial major success for the Army's mission altered the entire landscape—and presaged the first significant Land Use Agreement. On 19 July 1962, the seventh test "turned out to be the magic number," when the NIKE-ZEUS launched from Kwajalein successfully intercepted an ICBM, an ATLAS D, fired from Vandenberg Air Force Base, California, "hitting a bullet with a bullet." The feat would be repeated on 12 December of 1962, and in eleven subsequent attempts. It is pertinent to recall that "successful intercept" at the time meant within the lethal range of the nuclear warhead the ZEUS was designed to carry.[30]

Political impact from the extraordinary news made its way to the U.S. Congress. The significance of the dilemma facing the military occupying the former Japanese mandates in the Pacific was beginning to be apparent. Despite the perceived need for defensive use, the Marshallese people had no intention of simply allowing the Americans to take their land. Members in the House of Representative expressed the same bewilderment German colonizers had in the nineteenth century and Trust Territory officials exhibited in the twentieth century. Looking for agreement to define "just compensation" for leased land in the islands, one complained:

> there is no analogy between the common American idea of an absolute owner and the Marshallese idea of a holder of any one of the levels of rights in common kinds of landownership in the Marshalls. The present Marshallese system of landownership is basically feudalistic.[31]

The members could see no similarity in the Western world to the Marshallese claims. Since such ties to the land were beyond their comprehension, the American lawmakers were reduced to justifying their own judgment: Kwajalein was in pitiful shape after the war, "a desolate spot with hardly a coconut tree in sight," they decried without mention of the cause of this desolation. That in itself, they believed, allowed U.S. control and use of the land.

This exercise in rationality did not change the problem. The Marshallese claimed that they owned the land the U.S. wanted. Furthermore, the House of Representatives report reluctantly admitted that the atoll was more than a "denuded coral rock formation"; in fact, it held high value for the U.S. Having been through the justification process, the report called for a settlement of "remaining land claims," extending the Court of Claims for one year from enactment of the bill under consideration. The bill would apply to all islands the U.S. occupied in the Marshalls and put in motion years of continued attempts at "final settlement."[32]

The success of the ZEUS intercept immediately bolstered the bargaining position of the landowners. With the U.S. Congress (read Interior) now pushing settlement, in October, Marshallese leader *Iroij* Amata Kabua traveled to Saipan to deal personally with the High Commissioner of the Trust Territory, making the case for just compensation for "public lands" used by the military at Kwajalein. The Americans were hopeful that this gesture on his part indicated a willingness to come to some resolution. They were already aware of his formidable leadership, since at the time, Kabua also was part of the effort to bring legislative representation to all of the Trust Territory, as will be recounted below.[33] *Iroij* Kabua would continue to be a central figure in the history of the Marshalls.

What followed in December 1962 was an agreement between the Trust Territory Attorney General and Marshallese officials for initial settlement of the largest claim for land use in the Kwajalein Atoll. The U.S. essentially rejected the Marshallese claim of "indefinite use rights," but agreed instead to a fixed period of twenty-five years for U.S. use with the option for renegotiation in seven years. Deciding to "forget past offers and differences," a new formula of $500 per acre would grant $375,000 for eighteen years past use, plus seven years future use, for 750 acres in the Kwajalein Atoll and Dalap Island in Majuro Atoll. The U.S. agreed that excluding from this agreement other complex claims surrounding Majuro would speed the process and allow military use of Kwajalein to proceed, as Kabua indicated.

This meeting between nine Marshallese leaders, including Amata Kabua, District Administrator Jalle Bolkeim, and the Trust Territory Attorney General, R.K. Shoecraft, represented a real breakthrough. With some optimism, Shoecraft recommended forwarding the deal to the Department of the Interior, predicting this "a firm offer" the Marshallese had accepted; upon approval, the amount would be placed in trust with the Trust Territory government.[34] In March 1963, the agreement between the Trust Territory and the United States showed Interior with administrative responsibility.

In Washington, any momentum would be welcome news. President Kennedy grew impatient with the realization that Executive action would be necessary for appropriate handling of the Trust Territory challenge. In May 1963, another successful and startling test, this time a NIKE-ZEUS satellite intercept, underlined the importance for America of the missile program—and Kwajalein.[35] The president's effort and the complex politics of the 1960s will be covered fully in the next chapter.

On the ground, the Army was in a hurry and saw it as a simple matter: a new mission, a new need for land, clearly the "most practical and economic approach." After the successful NIKE-ZEUS intercept, the follow-on was the NIKE-X system. In light of the perceived continuing ICBM threat, the Army's task would include sophisticated radar systems, as well as additional two-stage missiles such as the SPRINT as part of the NIKE-X project. Kwajalein would support these tests as well as those conducted by the U.S. Navy and U.S. Air Force.[36] The Air Force maintained bases on other islands in the Marshalls.

Secretary of Defense Robert McNamara clarified the obvious: "Since the operations are dominantly Army," current support seemed an "unnecessary expense to the Navy...." On 1 July 1964, the Navy's Pacific Missile Range Facility, Kwajalein, became the Kwajalein Test Site, with Colonel Glenn Crane the Army's first Commanding Officer and Project Manager for NIKE-X. Firings under the new program were set to begin 1 August 1964. Anticipating new personnel and facilities, engineers added dirt fill dredged from the lagoon to add some fifty-five acres of land to the western part of Kwaj. Another thirty-eight acres added to the northern end brought the size of the island to 741 acres.[37]

The changeover also brought an effort at community building, the Americans seeking "closer ties with their Marshallese neighbors" on Ebeye.[38] Friendly excursions would not hide the fact, however, that for Army personnel and the increasing number of contractors on Kwajalein, other "building" included a golf course, community structures, and a theater. The startling difference between the space and green enjoyed by Americans compared badly to the crowded conditions on Ebeye. The contrast would continue to bring criticism for the occupiers.

Further, with the decision to target the perfect, deep lagoon in Kwajalein Atoll, the next inevitable need was for a landing zone that did not endanger the people. For this necessity, the Army added to the Zeus Corridor south of Kwajalein the "Mid-Atoll Corridor," the central two-thirds of the lagoon. This safe area included the islands in the western (Ralik) chain "north of Ennylabegan and south of and including Yabbenohr," and islands in the eastern (Ratak) chain "north of Bigej and south of Ennubirr."[39]

From the Marshallese perspective, of course, the proposed "safe" area against accidental mishaps meant the evacuation of more islands and distress for more of the local population. The Army's attempted use of the example of Lib to demonstrate "good faith on the part of the Department of Defense to fulfill its commitments in a spirit of understanding and cooperation" seemed lame.[40] With that repatriation not until 1966, the logic was not particularly persuasive at the outset. For the Army, the painstaking community meetings seemed interminable.

Meck Island, 1963

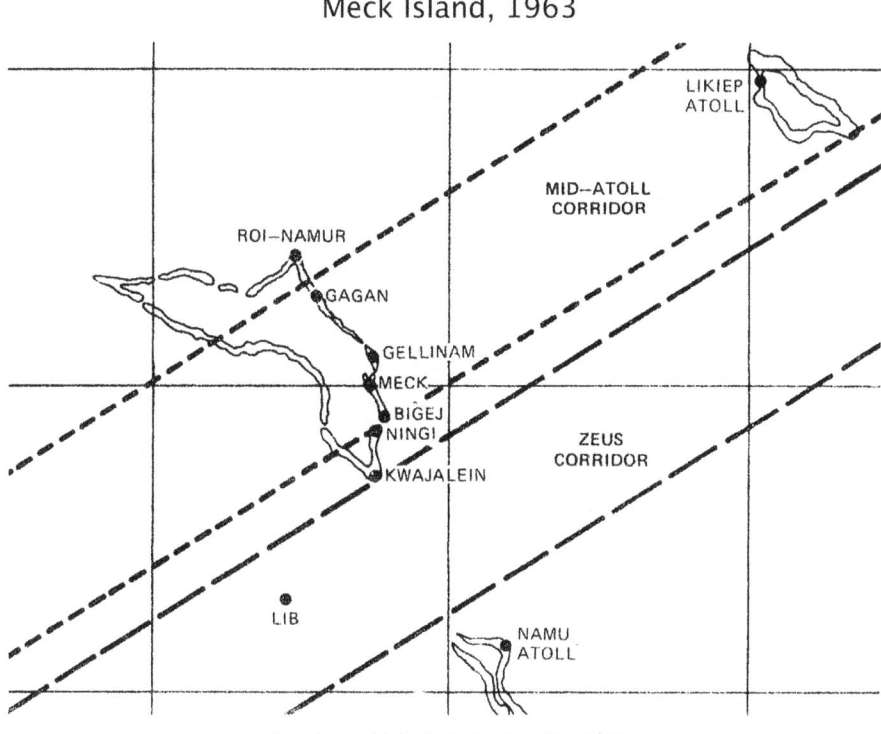

Reentry Vehicle Trajectories, Kwajalein

Mid-Atoll Corridor, Kwajalein Atoll (U.S. Army drawing).

In 1964, with authority in transition, Army land requests took the usual circuitous route beginning with the Navy. The plan to create a "safe area" would require moving even more occupants to Ebeye, and the Trust Territory government exercised caution not to exacerbate the problem of overcrowding there. Admitting the fear of more "international criticism," even Secretary of the Interior Stewart Udall expressed concern. "I do not feel," he wrote, "that any new leases can be seriously considered for the Pacific Missile Range [Kwajalein], or any more Marshallese relocated at Ebeye, until a healthful community is available to receive them."[41]

For the Army, then, the next task would be selling the Marshallese people on the benefits of relinquishing more of their home islands to another military necessity, spelled out in a seven-million-dollar "Ebeye Improvement Program." A series of meetings in January and February 1963 had already outlined new school facilities on Ebeye as well as shelters for Navy use.[42]

On 11 December 1964, the NIKE-X Project Office signed a MOU with Trust Territory officials to provide subsistence to inhabitants "actually moved who were deriving a livelihood from the land." It also expected that the Trust Territory would assist in "determination of eligibility of inhabitants for subsistence payments...." At the time of the MOU, both recognized 158 people eligible for amounts of $25 per month. Not surprisingly, the "Marshallese started complaining that this was inequitable immediately after the move was completed."[43]

The next day, on 12 Dec 1964, Trust Territory Attorney General Shoecraft took another turn at convincing islanders to accept being relocated from the Mid-Atoll Corridor. Minutes of the meeting revealed Shoecraft's effort to assure the people they would be well cared for, that the move was temporary, that the Lib experience showed the military's good faith, even though repatriation had not yet been realized. The new Ebeye project, he said, would provide even better housing, "better that anywhere else in the Trust Territory."[44]

In addition to housing, Shoecraft took credit for obtaining from the Army on their behalf promises of "fresh water facilities, adequate power for each house ... food ... the opportunity to have jobs at Kwajalein just as was provided the people of Lib, opportunity for education, and medical care." Patiently he explained mid-atoll corridor to mean:

> nothing more than a sort of dividing line, or rather two dividing lines splitting Kwajalein Atoll in the middle, and this corridor is nothing more than the place where the Military will be landing missiles fired from other areas, and although the missiles will not be aimed at any of the islands it was considered too dangerous for people to be living anywhere in the vicinity of the corridor.

He included an appeal, similar to that the Navy first exhibited, from his patriarchal view of authority as well as to civic pride: "you gentlemen are the leaders of the community and you are the gentlemen upon whom we will be depending for assistance in making the project as successful as possible."[45]

Despite the careful tutorial, the Marshallese people, through their leader Amata Kabua, relentlessly pursued the essential questions: How will the people return to gather food? Why will the landowners not benefit? The time for returning to the islands for gathering food could be accommodated, but Shoecraft had to admit that the landowner question continued to puzzle U.S. officials. This "whole matter represents quite a problem," Shoecraft confessed, "and, for the life of me, I can't figure out yet just how we're going to work it out," though all present expressed some interest in compensation for land use.[46]

The Army's effort at census ran afoul of the same suspicion the Navy had experienced in 1953 with Ebeye payments. Mr. Jalle Bolkeim, Magistrate of the Atoll, had been incensed that he had not been informed about a census. "Why was my office not consulted at the time the census was taken?" he stormed. "The census is not correct." Part of the reason for the "low population figure" is that the date of tally "was near Christmas time when a lot of the people had left the islands and came to Ebeye."[47] Based on their numbers of 216 inhabitants, planners had counted only 115 natives to receive payment. Shoecraft's despair was well founded—the Marshallese would not be taken lightly.

The Army was confident, nevertheless, that the minor issue of resettlement should not impede the onset of the missile testing. Relying on the MOU of December 1964, the Army attempted to move ahead in systems design and with expanded need for land. Working through the Trust Territory officials, two revisions of the agreement signed in December 1964 would be necessary. The first came in May 1966, with Addendum Number One granting $2,000 per month for indigenes; the number changed to 148 "family heads for distribution to all who have land rights in the Corridor in accordance with Marshallese custom." The military continued to defend its solution that the people would be allowed to enter the area "for harvesting and other activities on the average of four times a year...." This in addition to "compensation for loss of their copra crop, harvested or not."[48]

The second revision came soon thereafter, required by the islanders' "refusal to accept the $2,000 per month lump sum payment." The Army saw itself as cooperative and long suffering. By 30 August 1967, with a total of $30,000 unclaimed cash, officers agreed to renegotiation, but "expressed surprise over the Marshallese dissatisfaction." Ever ready to "'effect a final resolution to this matter'" project office officers met with Trust Territory officials in March 1968, requesting their aid to determine qualified recipients and please to be specific about the dissatisfaction. Their effort through conference with three *Iroij* leaders on 15–17 April 1968 produced a new Memorandum of Concurrence agreed to by "K. Kabua, L. Kabua, and A. Loeak."[49]

Thus, on 25 April 1968, Addendum Number Three to the 1964 MOU sought to meet the demands. The Marshallese had insisted on an agreement that came closer to just compensation for their anticipated loss. The April Concurrence stipulated that the Army would: (1) provide a boat to transport Marshallese from Ebeye to Kwajalein for work; (2) pay annually $120,940 as compensation to mid-corridor people; (3) pay for loss of copra crop– "sum to be determined on the basis of one hundred (100) tons per annum average crop" as set by the Trust Territory Copra Stability Board; and (4) pay $28,780 to fifty people who should have been included the first time. The Trust Territory would assume responsibility for proper distribution of these funds.[50]

The Army tried to make this the last round by rescinding the original paragraph allowing for renegotiations. Further, the number of 198 persons now deemed eligible for payments was to be "final, binding and a conclusive number, not subject to future negotiations toward possible increase...." Meantime, in Washington, Secretary of Defense McNamara pondered the dilemma of the Soviet threat in increasing arsenals of ICBMs, now designed with multiple warheads.[51]

By November 1967, the SENTINEL System Command (SENSCOM) had replaced NIKE-X, engendering new testing with new requirements. In the following year, April 1968, concurrent with the signing of Addendum Number Two, the Kwajalein Test Site became the Kwajalein Missile Range (KMR). In Huntsville and Washington, D.C., General Alfred Starbird became the first official Ballistic Missile Defense Program Manager. As part of the ever-developing hierarchy for the U.S. Army's advanced technology, the entire NIKE-X development program from SENSCOM and a major portion of the DEFENDER research project from the Advanced Research Agency, together formed the Advanced Ballistic Missile Defense Agency (ABMDA), reporting directly to the Secretary of Defense. Projected locations for the deployed defensive missiles included seventeen sites across the fifty states.[52]

Relative stability would be relatively brief, however, as the 1968 U.S. presidential election would bring Richard Nixon to the Executive Office, with a new group of decision makers to define "missile defense." Also, with the signing of the 1968 Memo of Concurrence and a collective sigh of relief, those aware should have noted a statement to the High Commissioner of the Trust Territory signed by the three *Iroij* who had agreed to the MOU. The Marshallese had in no way forgotten their primary concern for the land. The content of the MOU again reflected the insistence that any "policy determination" should include for landowners "payment" of:

> a proper rental and damages for any destruction or change of the nature of the land effected since the land has been held by the United States of America in its trusteeship and possession on behalf of the Marshallese owners. We are adamant that we will never agree to or accept less than the foregoing which represents our law and custom. We believe that which we seek is in accordance with principles generally accepted by all civilized nations. We will continue to press for justice with the United Nations and with the President and Congress of the United States of America.[53]

Six—The Trust Territory of the Pacific Islands

The effort of the U.S. military to meet the requirements of a robust missile program had brought major changes for the Marshallese, especially the former landowners, and the entire Kwajalein Atoll. Trust Territory officials had provided a negotiating presence for settlement in the 1950s and 1960s, working within the framework of the strategic trust the United Nations had granted the United States. That framework, however, had further revealed the underlying contradiction of the military's "strategic" control versus the mission of "trust" to bring the people of Micronesia to self-determination. That contradiction was still to be reconciled.

Seven

The Congress of Micronesia

John F. Kennedy's Administration began the decade of the 1960s with optimism and appetite for a new frontier to conquer. The stirring words of the president's inaugural address vowing to "pay any price," or "bear any burden" reflected an idealism yet to meet the reality of Cold War politics.

For the future of the Marshall Islands, a former frontier and the idealism of a previous generation would be pivotal. The United Nations (UN), now come of age and nearly doubled in size by new-nation members, was ready to confront remaining remnants of colonialism in the trusteeships created after the Second World War, only three of which remained by the 1960s. Prior to Kennedy's election, the UN issued Resolution 742 on 26 November 1953, outlining "factors indicative of the attainment of independence or of other systems of self-government." These included "opinion of the population ... freely expressed," and "freedom of choosing on the basis of the right of self-determination...."

Then, in December 1960, months after Soviet Premier Nikita Khrushchev had allegedly banged his shoe on the lectern in New York, claiming (loosely translated) "we will bury you," a vote came. With the U.S. abstaining, the UN General Assembly adopted Resolution 1514, "Declaration on Colonialism," in part stating:

> Immediate steps shall be taken in Trust and Non-Self-Governing territories or all other territories which have not yet attained independence, to transfer all powers to the peoples of those territories, without any conditions or reservations, in accordance with their freely expressed will and desire, without any distinction as to race, creed or colour, in order to enable them to enjoy complete freedom and independence [UNResolution1514,14Dec60].

The following day, the Assembly adopted UN Resolution 1541, issuing "principles which should guide Members" in shepherding transition to " a full measure of self-government." These included acceptable choices of: (1) becoming a sovereign independent State; (2) free association with an independent State; or (3) integration with an independent State.[1]

The second, perhaps least understood at the time, would prove to be the preferred option, but also the most elusive. It called for "respect" for the "individuality of cultural characteristics" of the territory, as well as for allowance of the "freedom to modify" status through "constitutional process," without "outside interference." A tall order, in brief: "Associated Statehood describes a system of relationship between a metropolitan country and its dependency, as determined by the will of the peoples concerned."[2]

This language, with its deliberate resolution aimed at existing remnants of empire, brought an onslaught against the United States. The Trusteeship Council of the UN, which up until that time had exercised little oversight in the case of the Trust Territory of the Pacific Islands (TTPI), now turned a skeptical eye on the impossible "fragmentation" of joint authority exercised by competing American departments of the military, both Navy and Army, Departments of State and Interior, not to mention overlapping assignments of Trust Territory officials, dealing with the diversity of cultures among islanders. In 1961, the council's Visiting Mission, having toured Micronesia, was "sharply critical" of American stewardship in every area: education, economic concerns, war claims, non-existent health care in the Marshalls, and poor living conditions in Kwajalein Atoll. The mission even underlined the need for a legislative body of Micronesians, the crucial topic followed below.[3]

The new administration seemed "stunned" that the arrows were not only from traditional anti–American detractors, but allies such as the New Zealand member, Ambassador Frank Corner.[4] President Kennedy quickly responded by confirming that America's commitment to "self-determination," promised in the very structure of the trusteeship, would be honored. The U.S. would be on the right side of history.

On 25 September 1961, just three days after Congress had authorized his cherished plan for a Peace Corps, Kennedy made his maiden speech before the UN General Assembly. In the context of a full endorsement of the UN mission, he described the American position, supporting the "expeditious movement of nations from the status of colonies to the partnership of equals." Then, observing that "the tide of self-determination has not reached the Communist empire," he deftly noted:

> My nation was once a colony, and we know what colonialism means: the exploitation and subjugation of the weak by the powerful.... Let us debate colonialism in full—and

apply the principle of free choice and the practice of free plebiscites in every corner of the globe.[5]

The president's speech, "sealed the U.S. position" on colonialism and sent his staffers scrambling to deal with the embarrassing contradiction in America's very-visible cupboard. Their quest was how to accomplish the conflicting goals of allowing self-determination while maintaining strategic control—the challenge of American policy in the Pacific from the beginning, and "no less cynical than the concept of strategic trusteeship" itself.[6] Kwajalein Atoll and the new technology in missile defense would provide one significant part of the controlling drama.

Despite the expertise of "the best and the brightest" in the administration, admittedly the first string had little to no knowledge of the Pacific arena. The president himself, with naval experience during the war, perhaps was most knowledgeable, and because of that experience, held a personal desire to see justice done in the Trust Territory. At least one Washington official reported Kennedy "obsessed" with the Pacific and his desire to bring modernization to the islanders.[7] Without doubt, the president felt an affinity for the water. On one occasion, he held that "all of us are so committed to the sea … because we all came from the sea … and when we go back to the sea … we are going back from whence we came." Underlining the U.S.– Australian friendship in those comments, he further reminded his listeners of policy: "we value very much the fact that on the other side of the Pacific, the Australians inhabit a very key and crucial area, and that the United States is most intimately associated with them."[8] As a U.S. Senator, Kennedy had supported statehood for Hawaii in 1959 and "assumed" the Pacific islanders were "victims of colonial-inspired racism…." Now he wanted the Trust Territory to be part of his larger vision.[9]

Those charged with finding a new, creative approach for Micronesia would be the Under Secretaries, who would find and continue to make the encrusted positions of the conflicted departments hard to overcome. Acknowledging the matter of "presidential significance," National Security Advisor McGeorge Bundy, tapped his Assistant Carl Kaysen to ride herd over a reluctant committee of Under Secretary of the Interior John Carver and Under Secretary of State Harland Cleveland, sometimes joined by representatives from the Department of Defense (DOD).

In April 1962, with his National Security Action Memo 145, the president did not mince words. Since the origin of the trusteeship, he said, the U.S. had carried out its "obligation" in a manner to "change as little as possible" the "customary way of life" of the indigenes. His administration, however, now recognized "fundamental changes" in the "outlook of the peoples of the remaining dependent areas" and as well "in the attitude of the rest of the world toward these areas...." In the best interest of the United States, we need a "greatly accelerated program" for political, economic and social development." Further, he intended to allow "a real option" for the islanders, "freely expressed," to move into "a new and lasting relationship" with the United States "within our political framework." Thus was the president's clear direction for the Task Force of Under Secretaries.[10]

Kennedy followed his memo with his own action, requesting an increase in appropriations for the Trust Territory. On 19 July 1962, the president asked Congress for "authorization for an increase in funds" from a former ceiling of $7.5 million to a ceiling of $17.5 million for "administration" of the Trust by the United States. In his 1963 Annual Report to the Secretary of the Interior Stewart Udall, High Commissioner M. W. Goding would relay the news of the funding as a "new era," claiming it "unmistakable" that this was a "blueprint of acceleration and change" for the area. The dollar amount in appropriations would continue to increase, but with that commitment would come an ongoing dilemma facing the U.S. Should America "fail to maintain and increase funding, it can be charged with retarding, or at least with not adequately promoting development."[11] On the other hand, with more American financial backing, the U.S. would be "charged that this made Micronesia more and more dependent," thus preventing the option of self-government desired by the islanders. For the Department of Defense, that would not be its concern. Representative Wayne Aspinall (D–CO), Chair of the Interior & Insular Affairs Committee, supported the appropriation bill for the "economic and social development" in the TTPI, but Aspinall was quoted as saying, "we've got to have these islands—for military purposes."[12]

The president would see the full dimensions of the contradiction. Added to his personal interest in Micronesia, Kennedy was learning more about the government's ongoing efforts since World War II to field an antimissile system against a new generation of strategic threats, including the intercontinental ballistic missile (ICBM). Because of its air-defense role during the war, the U.S. Army had taken the lead in the nation's ballistic-missile defense—and Kwajalein in the Marshall Islands had become the ideal location for testing—valuable real estate for the Defense Department. As already noted, in 1959, "site preparation" had begun; in 1960 "facilities for an operational NIKE-ZEUS battery began to appear"; and by 1961, the Army's contractual personnel had assembled on the island.[13] A clear mandate to complete testing, however, would not be simple to accomplish. There was the question of land ownership in Kwajalein

Atoll, not to mention the inter-service rivalry and intersecting missions. It was not until 1963 that the seminal agreement with Kwajalein landowners would be sent to Interior, and in 1964 that the Army actually would have its command structure in place. As already noted, in 1986 the Army would rename the Kwajalein Test Site the Kwajalein Missile Range.[14]

Meanwhile, in 1962, President Kennedy, having just focused on the increase in funding for the Trust Territory for social, political, and economic development, found himself in the midst of sobering Cold War realities. Since April, the Soviets had taunted the U.S. saying publically that the United Nations should be involved in a changed status for the Marshalls because of the military build up. Soon to be embroiled in the terrible confrontation with Khrushchev in the fall, the best news of the summer may have been the word from Kwajalein. On 19 July 1962, the seventh test "turned out to be the magic number," when a NIKE-ZEUS missile successfully intercepted an ICBM fired from Vandenberg Air Force Base, California.[15]

Skeptics noted that one intercept would not guarantee success against a rain of missiles. Still, the Army claimed America's first defensive-missile intercept against an ICBM equaled the extraordinary result of "hitting a bullet with a bullet." Other successful tests would follow. The impact of this accomplishment would be lost neither on international competition nor the administration. In October 1962, the very month of the Cuban crisis, the president made the "Assignment of Highest National Priority to Project DEFENDER," a part of the Advanced Research effort in missile defense.[16]

Encouraged by seeing the crucial role played for the missile-defense program in the Marshall Islands and Kwajalein, President Kennedy nurtured the idea of transforming all of Micronesia—but even while maintaining it "within our political framework." The president was primed for an update. But Bundy's assistant Kaysen had handed off the Task Force assignment to his assistant Michael Forrestal, who had not been impressed with any desire of the Under Secretaries (State/Defense/Interior) to move ahead. Despite his effort at encouragement, there was "no sense of urgency." Forrestal had made his own on-site appraisal of Micronesia and found that the situation in the Trust Territory was "truly appalling."[17]

In March 1963, therefore, after receiving Bundy's progress report consisting of "no progress" from the Task Force of Under Secretaries, Kennedy issued his National Security Action Memo 229, directing members to come up with an agreed plan. "Since more than a year has passed since the Task Force ... was established," the memo began with plaintiff tone, "I would very much appreciate having a report on the progress we have made toward our objective for the TTPI."

With the president's signature on this Action Memo, Bundy himself got busy with a plan. His design spelled out all the areas the UN mission had noted of need: health care, education, economic concerns, and war claims. Significant was Number Seven, the last: "Additional steps we should take to prepare the Trust Territories for an eventual plebiscite."[18] While an essential part of Kennedy's original task, this goal of free choice for the islanders would provide the core divisive issue with which American policy makers would struggle over the next twenty years, each department having its own reason for not trusting the outcome in such an open process.

Overstepping the Secretaries, Kennedy realized that the Executive must act. With the successful ZEUS satellite intercept demonstration reinforcing the strategic importance of the Trust Territory, on 9 May 1963, the president issued National Security NSAM 243, with instructions:

> to survey the political, economic and social problems of the people of the Trust Territory and to make recommendations leading to the formulation of programs and policies for an accelerated rate of development so that the people may make an informed and free choice as to their future in accordance the U.S. responsibilities under the trusteeship agreement.[19]

Kennedy then appointed the intelligent, resourceful, and "acerbic" Anthony N. Solomon to head what became the Solomon Task Force. Solomon, Harvard Professor of Economics and later Assistant Secretary of State for Economic Affairs, assembled a first-rate team of nine advisors from both "Government and non–Government," who served for "different periods of time up to six weeks" between July and August 1963.[20] The Mission visited the six district centers of the Trust Territory and held discussions with "seven assemblies of local people, eight legislative committees, seven municipal councils and three women's associations." Importantly, they took care to interview indigenous persons in every strata of island society, including a "representative sample" of outlying islands. Even more admirable was the group-discussion process by which they agreed on their recommendations for an overhaul of American oversight.[21]

Upon their return, in several additional weeks, the group compiled a voluminous review of their "Mission" that became known as the "Solomon Report" and submitted their findings. Initially, they marked as unclassified the second and third volumes, covering social, educational, and economic development, but the State Department quickly changed that ruling. State insisted that the entire report be classified because of the "secret political policy objectives" revealed in those pages. Only through the surreptitious action of a staffer would the content bear wider scrutiny by the House of Representatives Interior Committee.[22]

The nefarious "political objectives" started with consideration of "preparation for organization, timing and favorable outcome of a plebiscite," the "informed and clear choice" the president had requested. And after achieving the desired positive result, the report asked, what problems would remain for the U.S. with a continuing affiliation with Micronesia. Simple enough, though it would bring a rush of charges that any preplanned coordinated plebiscite to ensure a favorable outcome for the United States would hardly be a free choice.

Nevertheless, the Solomon Report went on with an "integrated master plan for action" to be achieved by 1968. This included impossible objectives. Even the opening sounded rather sweeping: win the plebiscite under circumstances that would "satisfy somewhat conflicting interests" of Micronesians, the UN, the U.S., and oh yes, "along lines satisfactory to the Congress"; be "appropriate" to "present political and other capabilities" of the people themselves; and then, provide "flexibility" to accommodate the "measure of local self-government" the U.S. Congress would be willing to grant.

That was only the impossible first. Second would be "achieving rapidly minimum but satisfactory social standards in education, public health, etc." The third would seek to raise "cash incomes" through "development of the current, largely crop-gathering subsistence economy."[23] One can easily predict the forthcoming decades of conflict.

In October 1963, even before the scheduled meeting, the president had read the summary and was ready with "sharp questions." After hearing Solomon, he turned to Udall and proclaimed: "I want this implemented A to Z."[24] The National Security Action Memo he signed 25 October put that sentiment into print:

> The report contains recommendations concerning programs and policies to implement the policy established in NSAM 145, dated April 1962. The Departments of State and Interior in cooperation with other departments and agencies of the Government as appropriate, are requested to develop and carry out necessary plans and programs to carry out recommendations of the report that are feasible and acceptable for implementation.
>
> Please report to me by November 31 on the actions taken or contemplated with respect to the report.[25]

Adding to Kennedy's determination was additional information in early November. He "exploded" with anger after learning of a polio epidemic in the Marshall Islands through the past summer, which he thought "inexcusable." Though the polio vaccine had been used in the U.S. for years, Interior had failed to administer it to the islanders.[26] Two American children contracted the disease on Kwajalein, compared to 192 Marshallese on various atolls, mostly children but ranging in age to adults, with eleven deaths. Retroactively, those charged with health in the islands were forced to call on the Centers for Disease Control (CDC) to secure the Sabin oral vaccine. A rescue team of doctors made haste to redress the problem before the entire Trust Territory knew the ravage of this crippling disease.[27]

But indignation regarding conditions in the Trust Territory, as well as the president's determination to bring change, would be overwhelmed by the tragedy of 22 November 1963. With the death of John F. Kennedy, the Solomon grand blueprint was "deep-sixed," all to the relief of the contingent among Pacific policy makers who were fearful of change.[28]

Just as President Harry Truman had insisted on unanimity among advisors after World War II, the new chief executive, Lyndon Johnson, refused to enter the fray between departments. Perhaps knowing that Interior would be "irrevocably opposed," Johnson declined to hear personally the State Department's recommendation that a Special Assistant for Micronesia reporting directly to the Executive would be needed for progress.[29] Instead, Johnson relied on the coalition of Interior and the House Interior Committee, chaired by strong-willed Wayne Aspinall, with whom he had worked in the Congress. Aspinall, who had earlier agreed to increased appropriation for the Trust Territory, now allowed Under Secretary of the Interior Carver to bury the Solomon Report.

In 1964, Carver denied the UN Visiting Mission access to the report, dubbing it an "internal working document." Further, Carver denied all indicators from the UN Trusteeship Council that the people of the islands were eager and ready to move forward toward some plan for future status. He had not believed the Visiting Mission report in 1961 that there was "considerable dissatisfaction and discontent," and now denied as "untrue" that the people of the territories even wanted "clarification of their relationship with the United States."[30] He rejected any need for plebiscites in the separate districts of the Trust Territory, which Solomon had recommended, "at least for the near term." Later assessment blamed the Interior Department's "Indian reservation" mentality, never making the effort to "understand the cultures" of the Pacific, but seeking to maintain the status quo. The overall plan was to keep Micronesia as one unit, permanently held by the U.S. through some future prescribed vote—only when certain to yield the "correct results."[31]

Seeing it differently, the State Department's "principal and continuing responsibility" was to report to the UN on the territories and to avoid international condemnation of America. Reflecting that difference, Under Secretary of State Cleveland's direction, officials attempted a definitive "State Department Planning Memo." The plan outlined a course of action needed to reach the conclusions the Solomon Report had defined. Also, it tracked the way to "free association" recommended by the Visiting Team member Ambassador Frank Corner of New Zealand, the path the Marshall Islands ultimately would choose.[32]

Consensus, however, could not exist without Interior, and Carver would have none of it. From his viewpoint, State was interfering in his department's own jurisdiction, thinking it could do "Interior's job better than Interior." Carver grew "testier and testier" with each new effort of "incursion" into what he saw as his area of responsibility.[33] Discouraged State Department official Donald McHenry was "so pessimistic" that he considered an appeal through Secretary of State Dean Rusk and Secretary of Defense Robert McNamara to the president. He and colleague Elizabeth Brown resorted to working behind the scenes with Arthur Goldberg, American Ambassador to the UN, to keep the Trust Territory issues alive. McHenry would prove a significant person for continuity of policy when he himself became America's UN Ambassador in the 1970s.[34]

The Congress of Micronesia

With this morass of conflicting views and delayed decisions in Washington, it would be the people of Micronesia themselves who would engender the necessary force for a breakthrough. As noted on Kwajalein, the Marshallese had only just begun to realize the power of the claim to have a part in deciding their own future. In the whole of the Trust Territory, legislative representation would provide the wedge.

After creation of the TTPI, the attempt to leave the life of the indigenous people as it had been only led to condemnation that the United States had not a trust but a "rust territory." In the intervening years between victory in the war and the politics of the 1960s, attitudes had not remained static. For the islanders, the wish to be left alone had morphed into fear of neglect, even if "benign neglect," and then an emerging "mood of expectancy," anticipating change.[35] While knowledge of their developing political consciousness may have escaped some in American legislative circles, among the people it had matured over decades.

In addition to the effort to encourage a work ethic and economic development to some extent, the U.S. Navy may be credited with planting the seed for political awareness among the islanders. While bearing the print of Western concepts of "self-government," the encouragement of representative atoll and island councils after the war was a forerunner of the legislative push to come. Not surprisingly, that attempt sometimes ran afoul of the *iroij laplap* (paramount chiefs), raising their suspicions even when they were offered respectful "ex-officio" positions on the councils. The idea of "secret ballots and public debate" could alter forever their cultural power.[36]

Even while acknowledging the Navy's first effort, with the creation of the trusteeship in July 1947, President Truman's Secretarial Task Force had recommended transfer of the TTPI to a civilian agency. What followed was the Executive Order 9875, granting short-term control to the Navy, but with the expectation that this would change, as it did in 1951, when the president transferred jurisdiction to the Department of the Interior.

In the four-year interim, the Naval Administration took several first, positive steps. Interim Regulation 4–48 created a Legislative Advisory Committee, which would "draft regulations, process laws, consider legislation" felt to be "desirable" for the territory, and advise on "policy issues." It was comprised of five members appointed by the high commissioner "from among the heads of Territorial departments." The overall ambitious plan was next to expand that committee's membership to include indigenous representatives from each administrative district, eventually evolving from "advisory" to be a "true legislature representing the inhabitants of the Trust Territory...." But alas, it was not to so evolve. With the transfer to Interior, the "demise" of this version of a Legislative Advisory Committee followed in December 1952.[37]

Also within the interim period, the Navy experimented with what became the "successful vehicle" for a representative Advisory Council, the "institution of a Territory-wide legislature." In 1949, the first "direct representation of Micronesians in a Territory-wide meeting" occurred in Guam. Administrative personnel plus "two inhabitants for each district" met to discuss economic issues. Members of the Trust Territory Headquarters Staff attended, including the Deputy High Commissioner. Also on hand were civilians from the office of the Chief of Naval Operations, administrative personnel from each district, and indigenes from each district the administration had appointed as representatives.[38]

Not impressed with this awesome group, the islanders immediately brought to the table the same matters they had raised from the beginning of the American occupation. Always the first, "perennial issue of contention" would be: what about the settlement of land claims and the return of their property? Of course, matters such as fishing rights, boats, and possible industry beyond agriculture were all of interest, but what about the settlement of land claims?[39] To the U.S. military, this was a familiar pattern.

For the Marshallese, the entire move toward self-government was a welcome step. That very year, they were moving toward their own local constitution with the leadership of *Iroij* Amata Kauba, who would be key in negotiating the initial Kwajalein Land Use Agreement with the U.S. Army, as already recounted.

Both Kauba and Dwight Heine had studied in Hawaii with constitutional scholar Norman Meller. The two of them would make significant contributions in the growth process toward political maturity of all of Micronesia. In remembering the various island cultures and languages in so vast a region as the Trust Territory, it would become clear that America's preferred agenda of a single form for permanent solution would be difficult if not impossible to achieve. The various divisions would become apparent in the long process now before the indigenous peoples.

While this first attempt of the Navy would not be considered exactly "a Territory-wide legislative body," it certainly was a prototype. With the shift of jurisdiction to the Interior Department in 1951, however, no "comparable gathering" convened until 1953. When it finally did occur, under the Eisenhower Administration and a new Secretary of the Interior, Douglas McKay, the effort was labeled the "First Trust Territory Conference on Self Government" and was held on Truk (Chuuk).

For this conference, two representatives from each of the five administrative districts at the time attended, invited to discuss "any topic pertinent" to local "social, economic, or political problems." With such a broad agenda for a general meeting, the delegates began with basics, first the "arduous chore" of translation for their various languages. Second was the effort to understand each other's situation, the representatives gaining new insight into the plight of each region. Some would say, "they knew there was no Micronesia." Still, overall, they expressed their mutual desire for "playing a greater role in their own governance." There would be among the people at least unity of purpose to move forward.[40]

Progress was slow in the remainder of the 1950s. While delegates and advisors had expected that regular, comparable conferences would follow this first effort, it would be three years before another. Perhaps expecting a miracle with the first try, the Trust Territory High Commissioner erroneously reported to the UN Trusteeship Council that "no significant results" had come from the Truk (Chuuk) meeting. It had been held "prematurely." It was not until 1956, therefore, that the Trust administrators even called an inter-district conference for Micronesian leaders at the Trust Territory Headquarters on Guam (later moved to Saipan). There these seminal players discovered the value of speaking with each other informally in small social gatherings away from the conference table. This would be the way in which they learned a cohesion that would prove to them the combined power of representative governance. Next, they requested another conference to involve the entire Territory in at least exploring some unity of their cultures.[41]

In 1957, the second inter-district conference convened with a great sense of purpose. This time the report to the Trusteeship Council would claim it was "the outstanding event of the year," with request for such meetings annually. Energized by the exchange of views on common problems, the people were beginning to understand "broader aspects of the Territory's needs" rather than just "interests of their respective localities." At their third meeting the next year, the delegates decided to call themselves the "Inter-District Advisory Committee to the High Commissioner," thereby "signifying" the desire for "their consultative function." The committee sought continuity by creating two-year, staggered terms for each district's two delegates, which they achieved in 1959. Then, in 1961, they "reconstituted themselves" as the Council of Micronesia. Dwight Heine of the Marshalls served as Council Chairman.[42] Only a short step remained to claim their legislative role as the "Congress of Micronesia," with representatives for the entire Trust Territory.

While American advisers in the Territory played a part, "power was shifting" to the indigenes, but a little too fast for some in Washington. The Congress of the United States had made clear its own power to "annul any enactment" of the body. Interior continued to emphasize its jurisdiction for "territory" according to the U.S. Constitution. Nevertheless, the "consensus of opinion" among islanders, was monumental: they could agree on the goal of self-government "without need to work toward a common Micronesian culture."[43]

In September 1964, in its Order No. 2882, the crucial step taken was by the Secretary of the Interior, who authorized creation of the Congress of Micronesia, which was executed with President Johnson's Executive Order. In his annual report, High Commissioner M. Wilfred Goding called it "by far the most important event of the year," after "long years of preparation." The Council of Micronesia, had "devoted almost two years to its study and by resolution recommended the final form" of the congress. That form would be a two-house body, a House of Delegates (Senate) and the General Assembly (House). General elections for the congress followed in

January 1965, with Amata Kabua elected to the House of Delegates and Dwight Heine to the General Assembly from the Marshalls. There would be two senators from each of the six districts elected for four-year terms. Representatives in the House would be based on population and elected for two-year terms. It would be understood that legislative power of the congress extended only to its "rightful subjects," and "no legislation may be inconsistent with treaties or international agreements of the United States...."[44]

The visiting mission of the UN Trusteeship Council could then note "with satisfaction" that the policies of the trust "Administering Authority," that is the United States, rested on a "firm commitment" for the "unity and territorial integrity of Micronesia." This congress of the islanders would provide a "forum for discussion" through which "the thinking and desires of the Micronesians can be made known...."[45]

Accepting the very existence and defining the role of the Congress of Micronesia became part of the continuing struggle between the various Departments of the Interior, State, and Defense. While unity of the Trust Territory may have appeared beneficial from the broad view, the reasons for that conviction among the Americans were not necessarily based on regard for the islanders. Through the interdepartmental debate, demands from the Department of Defense remained constant. Theirs was a growing concern for strategic advantage in Oceania. By 1965, with the escalating crisis in Vietnam before them, the Pentagon asserted that "control" of the TTPI was "essential to U.S. national security interests in the Pacific."[46] The DOD urged bringing the Trust Territory within some "permanent political framework" with the U.S. Nevertheless, though he had authorized the Congress of Micronesia in the previous year, in February of 1965, through a budget memo, Johnson quietly terminated the Solomon Task Force.[47]

Basic differences between the Departments of State and the Interior continued unabated. For the reasons JFK had realized, State officials favored placing the Trust Territory jurisdiction under a "presidential special assistant." For Elizabeth Brown, now UN Political Affairs Adviser in the State Department, the U.S. goal should be "to remove all our territories including the TTPI from international scrutiny." Interior Under Secretary Carver, with agreement from Representative Aspinall in the House Committee on Interior and Insular Affairs, still feared loss of military control if any real self-government were granted. In January 1966, a meeting to resolve differences resolved nothing. Carver claimed "to have listened" to the arguments of State and "discounted all of them." Interior had matters "well in hand," as problems currently "do not now exist."[48]

Secretary of the Interior Steward Udall disliked controversy between the departments. While he saw that Under Secretary Carver was "too personally involved," he also resented what some saw as the "sensational effort" to transfer the entire Trust Territory to the State Department's oversight. In what some saw as a "delaying tactic," Udall suggested exploring the possibility of "expanding Hawaii to include the Trust Territory." Greeted by a gasp, after this, everyone took a breath. In the next months of summer, Carver would accept an appointment to the Federal Power Commission and leave Interior, though his successor would follow the same basic views for the department.[49]

By coincidence or design, President Johnson finally responded to Trust Territory concerns by a means acceptable to him. Deciding that Interior and the Peace Corps could "handle the Trust Territory," he agreed to "unleashing" the Peace Corps in Micronesia, a "juggernaut ... in motion." Publically endorsing their mission for the territories, but unwilling to hold a press conference, in May 1966, the president allowed UN Ambassador Goldberg, Peace Corps Director Jack H. Vaughn, and Secretary Udall to make the joint announcement.[50]

Peace Corps volunteers, inspired by such an "extraordinary and unparalleled opportunity," would bring the islands to public consciousness in a way not seen since JFK's effort—and perhaps the corps' link to Kennedy provided a justification for the president. With an overwhelming ratio of 195/1, the volunteers would make a huge impact on the thinking of the Micronesian indigenes, in subtle and sometimes overt ways as lawyers, advisers, and teachers, influencing their demands for change even in the short term, while causing some consternation among governmental staff. Later, President Nixon, suspicious of that influence, would ask his assistant John Erlichman to investigate the "meddling" of the corps in Micronesia, perhaps "illegal political activity."[51]

Meanwhile, impatient with inaction from the United States, in August 1966, the Congress of Micronesia, through the Trust Territory High Commissioner, had petitioned the president to establish a commission to move forward on their "future political status," to "ascertain their wishes ... and to study and critically assess the political alternatives open" to them. The congress expected this would occur with consultation between American officials and the islanders themselves, and optimistically hoped for a report in two years.[52]

While that was unlikely, in Washington, Interior officials now proposed a presidential commission composed of U.S. executive branch officials, U.S. Congress members, Congress of Micronesia members, and even two "members of the public." This commission would consider options for future status, but even with Carver no longer in the picture, Interior felt that "territorial, non-self-governing relationship" would be the right option, and was still unwilling to consider State's proposal for possible "free association." Each department needed the support of DOD, which tended to side with State. And so it continued until April 1967, when officials from the three finally agreed on a tentative schedule for a plebiscite and possible alternatives for ending UN oversight of the U.S. occupation. Interior relied on future congressional action blocking any "free association" option. But more visibility had come in October 1966, when Senator Eugene McCarthy (D–MN) offered a ringing speech to the Senate with its focus on Micronesia. McCarthy included well-deserved criticism for Interior and the U.S. for neglect and "the kinds of policies for which we have faulted the European colonial powers."[53]

When the Congress of Micronesia convened its third regular session in July 1967, the Senate elected John Ngiraked of Palau as president. Senator Amata Kabua continued to serve as Senate floor leader. Having no meaningful reply to its request for action from the U.S. on political status, and discouraged with the pace of response to its request of the previous year, the congress attempted to generate momentum by creating its own "Commission on Future Political Status," with one member from each of the six districts. The commission was chaired by Senator Lazarus Salii from Palau, while Senator Amata Kabua represented the Marshalls.[54]

The timing was right. President Johnson's NSC Advisor Walt Rostow and Domestic Advisor Joseph Califano urged the president to make the Executive part of the strategy, reminding him that JFK's Memo No. 145 in 1962 had not yet been acted upon. Again choosing not to make a public announcement, on 21 August 1967, Johnson sent to the Speaker of the House and President of the Senate a resolution to establish a presidentially appointed "status commission." It was the first legislative proposal by the executive branch regarding this issue for the Trust Territory since Kennedy's effort. And with Aspinall's leadership, the Congress failed to enact it. Some would later judge the failure to enact Johnson's commission proposal as a "major mistake" for the U.S.[55]

In 1968, the momentous year for the Vietnam War, a beleaguered President Johnson would be hard pressed to concentrate on solutions for Micronesia. Yet, in January, the month of the Tet Offensive, a congressional delegation of three senators and seven representatives toured the various districts of the Trust Territory and met with various members of the Micronesian commission. Without a presidential commission and one overall message, however, the conflicting comments from the congressional visitors "left some confusion" with the Congress of Micronesia representatives. The how and when regarding plebiscites was unclear. What did defining their "choice" mean when the various districts had different answers for their future? The trip only underlined the impossibility of the single solution Americans sought. And, once again, the report from an actual on-site visit brought back the familiar condemnation: "staggering" problems left unresolved; "blistering attack" on Interior for its neglect. And even with this new focus, questions remained of how to begin preparing the islanders for a meaningful choice, since free association remained anathema to Interior.[56]

Equally troublesome, whatever choice must guarantee continuing control for the needs of the military, which faced growing protests from Marshallese in the mid-corridor of the Atoll, whom the Army had relocated from their home islands because of missile tests. In August 1968, they petitioned the Congress of Micronesia for more and fairer compensation for eviction from their property. Their congress responded by offering to the Trust Territory High Commissioner a resolution requesting that settlement negotiations be reopened. In October, on the very eve of the presidential election, a memo from the Joint Chiefs of Staff underlined again the strategic importance of the TTPI and Kwajalein Island.[57]

In the following year, the final report of the Future Political Status Commission authorized by the Congress of Micronesia began with this introduction: "As the United Nations becomes increasingly unwilling to accept the continuance of political dependency, as the United States defines and clarifies its interests in Micronesia, Micronesians themselves must decide what their own purpose and destiny should be."[58]

And so they must. But any hope for progress on resolving "future status" of the Trust Territory awaited more hearings, new perspective, and new presidential leadership.

Eight

Micronesian Status Politics

The presidential election of 1968 brought to the White House the administration of Richard Nixon, whose turbulent years in office would mark a watershed in the politics of the United States in many ways. Certainly, the Nixon years brought a renewed attention to the Micronesian question, as the executive branch would be more directly involved in defining the future status of the Trust Territory.

With the people of the islands now fully engaged through the Congress of Micronesia, their Future Political Status Commission made its final report in July 1969, ending two years of work. The commission wrote that its original mandate has been "joined by a larger mandate...." What may have seemed a "long-term investigative exercise" had become "an imperative primary issue."

The four areas of the commission's inquiry closely matched those outlined in the Solomon Report: (1) political education and action; (2) alternatives for future political status; (3) procedure for determining the will of the people; and (4) comparative analysis of "other territories and developing countries." The commission had done its work by consultation with the new Secretary of the Interior Walter J. Hickel, various military agencies, U.S. congressional groups, and with public hearings in the six districts. The summary of inquiry was followed by the statement of their conclusion. The first choice for future status would be: "A Self-Governing state in Free Association With the United States." The "recommended second choice" would be independence.

The argument for the first choice spelled out an amazing logic in "two inescapable realities: the need for Micronesian self-government and the fact of long-standing American interest in this area." True, a "re-definition, renewal and improvement of the partnership" was needed, but the members credited the U.S. with a choice for "democratic, representative, constitutional government." With no anger but incredulous appeal, the commission asked the unbelievable: "How, then, will America benefit by entering into association with Micronesia? How can Micronesia hope to reward continued American contributions to its development?" The U.S. military would have a ready answer for this self-imposed question. But no need, the commission gave the perfect response: they had "one item of material value" to offer, "an item which is most precious in Micronesia and to Micronesians: the use of their land." The people "recognize that their islands are of strategic value...." They "would accept the necessity of ... military needs." With the realization of potential risk of danger or attack, the necessary "conditions would not be lightly undertaken...." Nevertheless, "as a self-governing state we would be far more prepared to face these prospects than as a Trust Territory."

The use of their land! It was the perfect answer for the U.S. Army. And in the wording, one can see the unmistakable hand of Amata Kabua, a member of the commission and also active at the time in negotiations with the Army for lease of Kwajalein Atoll. But so as not to sound too sanguine, the commission warned: "talk of land acquisition by any outside interest—let alone the military—aggravates long-standing land problems and appears to create new ones." No, the elusive Kwajalein Land Use Agreement yet lay long years in the future.

At the time, in 1969, the commission did not request any legislation from the Congress of Micronesia, but deemed that "premature." It did, however, hope that members would read the position papers offered, reach the same conclusion of the commission, and proceed with negotiations with the United States to accomplish resolution.[1]

With the Micronesians pressuring change, the Nixon Administration reassessed the situation. The possibility of agreement between the Departments of the Interior, State, and Defense had increased, but the Defense Department increasingly saw its role as primary. Having received intelligence that the Vietnam War "could not be won militarily," ending the war became a number-one priority. In that context, Nixon was reminded by more than one advisor of the significance of Micronesia should the U.S. succeed in withdrawing from South Asia. All agreed that because of Guam, the Northern Marianas were crucial, while the central-Pacific location of Kwajalein Atoll in the Marshalls looked equally vital.[2]

The administration had inherited the robust U.S. Army missile-defense program, and now some stability with the Marshallese landowners. After a review in 1969, officials adopted the essentials, but chose the new name of SAFEGUARD (SAFSCOM). The four components of the system included perimeter-acquisition and missile-site radar, as well as the SPRINT and SPARTAN missiles. SPRINT was "the two-stage, extremely high acceleration missile of the NIKE-X project," while the SPARTAN was a "three-stage, long-range missile...." Both were designed to carry a nuclear warhead. Gone was the urban-defense concept, with the decision to concentrate on the defense of land-based ICBMs.[3] Kwajalein Missile Range remained at the core of the program, essential for the testing of missiles.

In the summer of 1969, Micronesia came to center stage through the president's well-publicized, fact-finding trip to Asia. A stopover on Guam provided the opportunity as Nixon struggled to articulate the basic national security dilemma—how would the U.S. withdraw from Vietnam while not seeming to abandon its allies. In his memoirs, National Security Advisor Henry Kissinger remembered the event at "the end of a long day," in an "officers' club...." In this "informal background chat" with reporters, the president framed the words that would take on a life of their own. Reporters first labeled the off-the-cuff effort the "Guam Doctrine," but later, Kissinger claimed that after being asked repeatedly about his remarks, Nixon "soon elevated them to a doctrine," christened with his name as, the "Nixon Doctrine."[4]

In his Vietnam speech of 3 November 1969 and in his Foreign Policy Report of 18 February 1970, the doctrine would become: (1) honor present treaty commitments; (2) provide nuclear shield for an ally or in our security interest; and (3) with other, conventional aggression, provide aid, but the nation directly threatened would assume primary responsibility for providing its own defense. America would help "the defense and development of allies and friends" but "cannot—and will not—conceive all the plans, design all the programs, execute all the decisions and undertake all the defense of the free nations of the world."[5]

In that initial Guam encounter, in wide-reaching answers to various questions, the president underlined the significance for U.S policy, as "potentially the greatest threat to [future] peace will be in the Pacific." According to a reporter's account, Nixon began his remarks with familiar historical perspective: "Whether we like it or not," he said, "geography makes us a Pacific power ... Indonesia [at] its closest point is only 14 miles from the Philippines, when we consider that Guam ... of course, is in the heart of Asia...." And, "when we consider the interests of the whole Pacific as they relate to Alaska and Hawaii, we can all realize this." For the U.S. "involvement in war so often has been tied to Pacific policy or lack of Pacific policy as the case might be."[6]

Nixon might well have included the Trust Territory in his list, surely on his mind and reflected in the poignancy of his remarks. For earlier in that long July day, the president also had talked with a five-person delegation from the Congress of Micronesia, a meeting arranged by Secretary of the Interior Walter Hinkle as the chance for Nixon to express interest in the ongoing dilemma. In anticipation of this opportunity to meet with the president himself, the Congress of Micronesia had rushed through Joint Resolution No. 31, which stated in part "that the president and the Congress of the United States are urgently requested to give serious consideration to the future political status of Micronesia and the ways in which this status should be finally resolved."[7]

Thus arranged in a fifteen-minute encounter, those who met privately with Nixon and Kissinger included Senator Lazarus Salii from Palau, who served as Chairman of the Future Political Status Commission and headed the group. Also along were two now familiar Marshallese. First, Amata Kabua, President of the Congress of Micronesia Senate, said to be "smooth, elegant, [and] incredibly cool," participated in the proceedings "from behind dark glasses." Known for his "confident, in control, unintimidated" manner, in another setting, some had dubbed him Amata KaBuddha. Then, Dwight Heine, future Speaker of the General Assembly(House), was also in the group. In the Congress of Micronesia, delegates would come to appreciate Heine's leadership with the "ability to work behind the scenes in reconciling disagreements."[8]

President Nixon asked several questions, and while the record does not reveal his personal impression, what followed the encounter would be a pivotal change in momentum. Back in D.C., Secretary of the Interior Hinkel confirmed the invitation to begin actual status negotiations and began what became eight rounds of dialogue between October 1969 and June 1976. Negotiations would come to be titled the "Micronesian Future Political Status Talks."[9]

In the First Round, held in Washington, eleven points of contention regarding independence were the basis for discussion. Paramount among these was "unqualified control over their land," always of crucial significance, and any use by the U.S. "for military or other purposes" must depend on negotiations "between the two governments." The Marshallese insisted on more self-government as a sovereign country, far beyond what Americans expected or were ready to consider—way "out of the ball park," as one supposedly muttered. On the other hand, there was some agreement that governance could be based on their local constitutions, good to hear since the Marshallese already claimed their own.[10]

Initially unimpressed, Kissinger was hampered by none of the restrictions of concern for Marshallese or any other Micronesian sensibilities. His famous dictum was: "There are only 90,000 people out there. Who gives a damn?"[11] Kissinger's solution was eminent domain—take whatever land the U.S. needed for its own purposes, essentially the position of DOD over the long years of negotiations, but a concept completely unacceptable to islanders. That same brand of imperialism had been well burned into their collective memory by their former Japanese occupiers.

Having already been a prime representative of the people in negotiations with the U.S. Army, Amata Kabua seized on the concept and "sponsored an eminent domain bill that would have given islanders control of their own land," an argument the Congress of Micronesia viewed unhelpful and vetoed.[12] Kabua, said by Senator Lazarus Salii to be the one person who could have "kept the old Trust Territory together," in fact, often worked against Micronesian unity and seemed to struggle with his decision regarding the best outcome. Later, local political competitor Carl Heine would claim that the primary motive for *Iroij* Kabua in considering a separate identity for the Marshall Islands was his own personal gain, as he was a landowner, while American revenue from military lease at Kwajalein Atoll was then shared with the entire Congress of Micronesia. More of this unity debate will be followed below.[13]

The impasse over the issue of land, considered "key to an agreement" by Secretary Hinkel, rendered the First Round of discussion a failure, but nonetheless proved instructive for both sides. Clearly, with such large stakes in the outcome, Interior could not negotiate alone. Defense must be at the table, along with the State Department, still maintaining a "principal and continuing responsibility" to report on U.S. territorial affairs to the UN. For their part, the Micronesians wondered if their "varying interpretations" of independence and forms of free association "might well have confused the Americans," with some leaning toward requesting the United Nations to assist their cause.[14]

Whether or not the Americans were baffled by the concept, certainly some, including Kissinger, were opposed to it. The U.S. stance was unrealistic but tenaciously held: (1) the entire Trust Territory must remain as one entity under U.S. jurisdiction; and (2) a controlled plebiscite must be conducted to guarantee results. With "profound differences" between the Americans and the Micronesians, by the Second Round in July 1970, the islanders stood firm on their "essentials," so-called Four Principles:

(1) Sovereignty in Micronesia resides in the people of Micronesia and their duly constituted government.

(2) The people ... possess the right of self-determination and may therefore chose independence or self-government in free association with any nation or organization of nations.
(3) The people ... have the right to adopt their own constitution and to amend, change, or revoke ... at any time.
(4) Free association should be in the form of a revocable compact, terminable unilaterally by either party.[15]

With these, the best the U.S. could offer was support "in principle" for the Micronesian "desire for a constitution." But this reluctant acceptance of even the concept of an independent means for governance provided a significant win. In response, by House Joint Resolution 102, the Congress of Micronesia then established a Joint Committee on Future Status, with Senator Salii again as Chairman. The congress enlarged the committee by two members from each of the six districts and authorized its representatives to continue the negotiations with America, as long as necessary to win these terms. Further, programs for political education and the study of the economic aspects of free association would be needed.[16]

National Security Advisor Kissinger now began to feel "some urgency." With the departure of Secretary of the Interior Hinkle from the administration (for the sin of privately criticizing handling of the Vietnam War), Kissinger could now apprise the president of the lesson JFK learned back in the 1960s: the Executive needed some direct link to policy for the settlement of the complex Micronesian legacy.[17] In 1971, the appointment of Franklin Haydn Williams, well qualified with experience in the Trust Territory through DOD, engendered hope. Personnel in the Departments of State and Defense breathed a sigh of relief, while even staff in Interior entertained mixed reactions.

Equally significant in 1971 was creation of the Office of Micronesian Status Negotiations. Though an Office of Territorial Affairs had existed under Interior, this office would operate instead under direct control of the President's Personal Representative Williams, who would hold Ambassador status. While administratively housed with the department, which would allow easy consultation, the new office was independent of Interior's jurisdiction and headed by strong directors: first, Arthur W. Hummel; then Admiral William J. Crowe, who would rise one day to the post of Chairman of the Joint Chiefs of Staff. Crowe's appointment reassured the Pentagon that its interests would be protected in the negotiations. The new Secretary of the Interior, Rogers Morton, now named a new Deputy Assistant Secretary for Territories, with linkage to the Micronesian issue.[18]

Prying total control from the Department of the Interior would have multiple benefits. The overlapping interests of State, Defense, and Interior had kept hostage any resolution of the Micronesian question for decades. As even Kissinger now recognized, the Congress of Micronesia's growing preeminence, along with increased dissatisfaction in American leadership, might well jeopardize the desire of islanders to be a part of America's empire in the Pacific at all. The situation held shades of the German Commander Ahlert, fearful of challenging the power of a former *Iroij* Kabua, Amata's ancestor, back in the nineteenth century.

Already the former U.S. demand for unity of the Trust Territory seemed an anachronism. The Marianas were moving decisively toward commonwealth status, while the Marshalls continued to insist on self-governance. Ominously, young Micronesians pushing for independence from America obtained a "still-classified portion" of the Kennedy Administration's Solomon Report. They wasted no time using the discovery to claim a U.S. secret plan to "take over" Micronesia. Ambassador Williams, with visibility and clout of the Executive behind him, moved quickly to work toward a draft compact of free association.[19]

Even with all hands on deck and all players in decision making now fully engaged, the obstacles to successful negotiations still seemed overwhelming. In October 1971, in Hawaii, Round Three brought some progress, as the Americans shifted their stance and accepted three of the four basic principles the Micronesians had demanded. They accepted three: sovereignty, self-governance, and local constitution; but not the fourth, the "right of unilateral termination." Williams explained that the U.S. saw any agreement not as a treaty, but as a "binding Compact" with legal implications, requiring legislative approval on both sides.[20] Still not convinced, the Micronesians justifiably feared unilateral control by the U.S. if they were unable to cancel the compact at their will.

A momentous year awaited in 1972. In April, the Fourth Round, was held in Palau, Chairman Salii's home. On Easter morning, talks began with a religious tone and statement of good will from Ambassador Williams, who expressed the desire for "a mutually beneficial relationship" between the U.S. and Micronesia.[21] As before, the matter of sovereignty and the future autocracy by the United States were dominant. Could the Micronesians withdraw from a compact of free association if or when they might wish to in the future? Would they hold out for the option for independence? And how would future rounds go forward? Already impatient, the Northern Mariana Islands balked at continuing the same format and requested separate negotiations with the United States, which the Americans granted.[22]

In July-August 1972, the Fifth Round of talks returned to Washington, hosted by the Office of Micronesian Status Negotiations. In opening statements, Ambassador Williams and Chairman Salii agreed on a purpose to move forward with a draft of a compact of free association. Williams began with the definition of free association as "shared responsibilities and obligations," one party with "internal affairs" and the other "authority of foreign affairs and defense." He added: the "first order of business" would be to "determine whether we are or whether we are not both seeking the same kind of future relationship." Goals of the U.S. would include "your full self-government" according to the "freely expressed wishes of the people of Micronesia," while America has "continuing responsibilities" for maintaining "peace and stability in the Pacific" that would extend "beyond the termination of the Trusteeship Agreement."[23]

With genial agreement of purpose, the delegation agreed to a small committee that worked diligently to prepare a draft compact in three weeks' time, allowing them to limit the "plenary meetings" to only two sessions. In closing, Williams issued something of an apology for the "hottest and most uncomfortable" summer weather in D.C., that lacked the "cooling summer trade winds" of the islands. Having thanked the Micronesians for their hospitality in his previous visits through the Trust Territory, he now anticipated the next round of negotiations would be in only a few months in Oahu, Hawaii. He quoted from the report of the Congress of Micronesia's Future Political Status Commission in July 1969 and claimed that the "patient" talks over the past three years "have brought you closer to the goals you set for yourselves...." All seemed to agree that the ground was laid for the next level of detail to spell out the general goals. All the affable and cordial language could not paper over, however, the considerable hurdles that yet lay ahead, such as "agreed land arrangements for U.S. military purposes" and "future financial arrangements."[24]

These hurdles were not long in arising, quickly jeopardizing the next round of talks and seeming to bring inevitable divisions for resolution of TTPI. After the good will of the summer talks, the Congress of Micronesia levied a blow that the U.S. would view as raising "inconsistencies and contradictions and repudiations" of agreement just reached.[25] In "Second Special Session" in Palau, the congress passed a Senate Joint Resolution No. 117, which authorized and directed the Joint Committee on Future Status "to conduct negotiations ... regarding the establishment of Micronesia as an independent nation, while continuing negotiations toward Free Association." Dealing with "present dissatisfaction" of its various members, the congress felt "there will have to be some political alternative available" in order that "resolution ... might not be delayed." Ominously, the report added "there is an important and growing sentiment in Micronesia for independence, on its own merits." The "only acceptable type of plebiscite ... must include a choice of more than one political alternative."[26]

Caught off guard, the Americans refused to continue with the Sixth Round, which became a short, one week version, with mutual attempts at clarification and little agreement. "Both sides agreed that the talks should be temporarily recessed" to allow for consultation on "substantive decisions necessary" to continue. Each side warned the other. Americans advised: "if your original goal of free association does not continue to be an objective which you can support, we will have to reconsider our own position."

In turn, the Micronesians stressed "the urgency of completing the negotiation of a draft" of free association. And "you should recognize the inevitability of developments of this sort" realizing the talks were "now into their fourth year." Exact specifications in matters of finance and "land requirements" could not be agreed upon until the final document. And, with a final slap, the committee reminded that their "mandate" does "encompass the entire present Trust Territory and not only five out of the six districts." The "unilateral action" of the U.S. in holding "separate negotiations with the Marianas" does not "relieve this Committee" from its "obligations with which the Congress has entrusted us."[27] The warm tone of the summer was only a memory.

In the Congress of Micronesia, however, there was growing friction in the question of how to proceed. The "Independence Coalition" that had pushed for the reversal of the summer's intent, was weakened in the November elections by significant losses. The next step for the congress, therefore, was to seek direction from the people themselves. The congress instructed the Joint Committee on Future Status to fan out to the six districts for feedback from the constituents of the Trust Territory, which they did in the following year.

In July 1973, the Eastern District Hearings only would enhance Senator Amata Kabua's standing, as he sat on The Joint Committee on Future Status Subcommittee for the Eastern District that included the Marshalls. Further, Kabua's leadership continued to display a certain political verve. In his reflections before the Congress of Micronesia the year before, Kabua, had disparaged Western efforts at developmental help for the Trust Territory, saying that the "number of studies" was "exceeded only by the number of speeches on economic development." In even earlier speeches he had disparaged any association with the United States, warning that Native Americans had been forced from their land and confined to reservations.

Reversing that, in June 1973, he pushed the envelope by claiming: "We don't believe in a middle road. We would seek either independence or statehood." But it will be remembered that in his report for the Future Political Status Commission, he had asked how Micronesians could repay America for its protection; then, shrewdly recognized the "strategic" importance of Kwajalein land for the U.S. military. Now, the savvy "KaBuddha" decried unity, making instead his "bold decision" to seek future separation for the Marshalls from "association with other districts of Micronesia."[28]

The Hearings of 1973 would offer more visibility. The members traveled to several locations for numerous meetings to inform the people about choices and entertain questions from the locals. There were: all-day sessions on Ebeye, 19–20 July; one session on Jaluit, 22 July; and multiple sessions on Majuro, 24–25 July. The Majuro sessions included one held before the Nitijela (parliament), and one before a group of "Administration Employees" that included at least one Trust Territory employee, who was persistent in her questioning. On 24 July, there was also one short public meeting at Laura Village, on the small island of Laura, just west of Majuro, still bearing the name bestowed by American servicemen during the war.

With every group, the comments were amazingly similar: Who is pushing for change—the Americans or Micronesians? It's too fast; why the rush? We're not ready to make a decision—we need more information. Explain the difference between Free Association and Independence. (Answer: patiently repeated listing of advantages, disadvantages.) Why two and not four choices—how about Status Quo or Commonwealth? (Answer: The Trust is temporary; in commonwealth, we fear loss of identity.) What does the commission think is the best choice? (Answer: We are here to listen). Where is the political education needed to make an informed choice? (Answer: A new Political Information Committee will be making an effort). Make a strong effort—to outer islands also. We need booklets to read—not just radio. Many on outer islands do not have radio. Many do not read. Need translation into Marshallese. Do we have the resources to maintain Independence? (Answer: probably not.) Would we be vulnerable to attack or takeover if not associated with a power like the U.S.—memories of Germany and Japan. Which choice would be better to retain our own culture and traditions? (Answer: probably Free Association.) What about Unity of Micronesia versus separate negotiations for the districts? Why did the Marianas get separate talks? And always: What about the leased or occupied land? What is the meaning of "public land," eminent domain, and to whom should land be returned: a central government, districts, or individual original landowners? (Answer: that will be up to local constitution.)[29]

The attitude displayed by the Marshallese proved instructive. And after decades of haggling in Washington, all this sounded familiar. The weeks of discussion and comments perhaps would have been gratifying for former Secretary of the Interior Carver, who had resisted any rush to change the status quo. But while the reputation of the United States seemed solid for the most part and the Trust beneficial, the High Commissioner's holding ultimate power riled some of the islanders. One recent example of cause was the HC's veto of a resolution passed by the Congress of Micronesia for a Maritime, Law of the Sea claim for autonomy. Kabua also sat on the Law of the Sea Committee.

In a striking memo to the president, Henry Kissinger, now Secretary of State as well as National Security Advisor, reported with some concern that the Fifth Round of talks had been suspended when the islanders "insisted" that the U.S. negotiate "an independence option" simultaneously with "the free association option." He sought to clarify his own game plan against the independence move. Now he agreed with the majority of the American players, State, Interior, Justice, as well as Ambassador Williams, that the U.S. should agree to an offer of independence—if only, as only Kissinger could word it, to "spike" the effort of Micronesian radicals to sabotage the free-association option. He admitted, however, that "Defense dissents," of course, fearing the islanders would actually accept such an offer. Insisting on the exception of making sure the U.S. "would retain basing rights in Kwajalein Atoll (our missile testing facility)," Kissinger explained to Nixon that he was willing to consider the "small risk" the Micronesians would select the option of independence. The president's instructions to Williams, he expected, would ensure a "reaffirmation that our preferred alternative is Free Association, and a definition of the essentials of that relationship."[30] Kissinger now saw the beauty of free association.

Thus instructed by Kissinger's plan, in November 1973, in the Seventh Round of negotiations, America's new position was on the table with discussion of the implications for every option from commonwealth to independence. Also, there were major concessions regarding land and the previously assumed power of eminent domain, so reminiscent of the Japanese declarations. Now the U.S. would cede to local control the so-called "public land" held—sixty percent in Micronesia overall; thirteen percent in the Marshalls. Eminent domain "would cease at the conclusion of the Trusteeship." One remaining dispute was the amount of U.S. financial aid to each district; the Micronesians had asked for $100 million annually. Even after the expected U.S. programming, now mentioned were amounts wildly divergent, between a $43 million and $80 million annual grant.[31]

As talks continued between the U.S. and the Marianas, the measure of support for unity of the Trust Territory waned. With the financial matter still unsettled, in March of 1974, the Marshallese Nitijela (parliament) requested direct status talks for the Marshall Islands. On the other hand, at the same time, some progress toward unity continued. The Congress of Micronesia agreed to complete negotiations on the draft compact, and in June, the congress elected delegates to a constitutional convention. By July 1974, with informal talks between the U.S. and the Future Political Status Committee, when the Americans offered to discuss the independence option, there was little response. Both sides now agreed on 1981 as the target date for a draft compact.[32]

In the Marshalls, the debate continued, even in the wake of the request for separate talks with the United States. In one clear voice, Carl Heine published a powerful analysis of the issue as he viewed it "at the crossroads." Heine, a Marshallese by birth, had been educated in the United States and served in Yap as deputy district administrator for the Trust Territory government. Also, he was staff director for the Congress of Micronesia Joint Committee on Future Status. In his "reappraisal of the Micronesian political dilemma," he made an impassioned call for support of free association. Claiming that he, as a Micronesian, could speak to and for his fellow islanders, he delivered a scathing review of those showing a "provincialism" in attitudes that worked against free association, a "complete obsession with an archaic past." Mostly, it was the "traditionalists, the landed paramount chiefs" who were opposed. "Micronesia should be looking forward, not backward." Complete independence from the United States was nothing more than "a nice dream, a tale, a myth...." Further, the U.S. trusteeship primarily had been "advantageous." The "finest fruit of American colonialism in Micronesia" had been to grant the "right of self-assertion," so different from the colonialism of Germany or Japan. It was, after all, "the United States who informed Micronesians of their right to self-determination...."

Heine did not shirk the central issue of land ownership, recognizing that "who governs" was clearly related to "who owns the land." But he argued that free association strikes the correct balance—a just compromise offering "both a challenge and an opportunity." Equally strong was his criticism of the "young Micronesians," radicals, "their bitterness inflated and influenced" by "these self-appointed outside advisors."[33] Perhaps this was a reference to Peace Corps volunteers?

Local Marshallese politics may have influenced published versions of the debate. In 1974, at the time his book appeared, Heine, known locally as "Lon," planned a run for Kabua's seat.[34] Heine, critical of *Iroij* Amata's entrenched political power and family, was frequently the "opposition" candidate against him. Heine claimed Kabua's position on separation for the Marshalls was based on the financial benefit Kwajalein brought the islands and specifically the landowners, and more specifically, to Kabua himself. Kabua wanted the entire revenue to remain locally and not shared with the congress.[35] But in November, in the Congress of Micronesia election for the fifth Senatorial District, the tallied vote would read Kabua (incumbent), 2902; Carl Heine (challenger), 1671. Heine's effort would be denied.[36]

Whatever the debate, potential or possible progress again would be stymied by American politics. Even mentioned by one alert Marshallese person the year before in the Eastern District Hearings, the full import of the ongoing Watergate scandal fell in August 1974. With the resignation of Richard Nixon, Micronesian polity once again would be caught in the transition of executive power. President Gerald Ford, the only unelected president to serve the United States, faced a myriad of matters demanding resolution, including the long-held American illusory hope for unity for the Trust Territory.

By 1975, any progress was made behind closed doors, while the new president confronted major decisions in domestic issues following Nixon's resignation. Meanwhile, momentum for commonwealth status had continued in the Northern Marianas. But when the Congress of Micronesia attempted a referendum to consider options, a low turn-out vote was inconclusive. More significant, from July to November 1975, a Micronesian Constitutional Convention was held in Saipan, crafting a constitution for a Federated States of Micronesia (FSM). On 8 November, representative from five districts, all except those of the Northern Mariana Islands, signed a draft constitution for the proposed FSM.[37]

With the long-held and unrealistic American hope of unity for the Trust Territory gone, Americans accepted the geographical reality of Guam, captive in the Northern Marianas, and the strong majority support for a closer relationship with the U.S. In July, the U.S. House of Representatives had already approved the new status. After full formal hearings, in February 1975, the U.S. Senate also approved. Thus, with congressional action, and relying on Nixon's previous authorization, on 24 March 1976, President Ford signed the agreement for commonwealth status for the Northern Marianas.[38]

In May, the Chair of the Under Secretaries Committee sought to further clarify for the president the remaining issues that now "complicated" resolution of the Trust Territory matter. Facing Round Eight in 28 May–2 June 1976, he outlined the history of the Micronesian negotiations. Included were the "security interests" of the area, all the familiar strategic claims plus the "continued growth of Soviet sea power in the western Pacific." The goal would be to achieve a "close, friendly and enduring relationship" between the U.S. and all districts of the old Trust Territory.[39] Options listed included: commonwealth status, such as the Marianas had chosen; treaty links to fully independent countries; and the primary recommendation, the free association route.

Even as Kissinger had suggested in 1973, offering independence to "spike," that is, manipulate the islanders into fearing the loss of American sponsorship, had been effective for some. This resulted in the need to prepare for the required plebiscite and "real" choice in a continuing relationship. Although still viewed as "more costly," free association was now thought to guarantee the U.S. "greater freedom of action" and protect "specified defense rights, which would include use of Kwajalein...."[40] DOD's position all along had insisted on land control for the Kwajalein Atoll. On 4 July 1976, with irony and deliberate cynicism, Marshallese Representative to the Congress of Micronesia, Ataji Balos, noted that "the command of Kwajalein Missile Range celebrated the American Bicentennial by closing Kwajalein Island to any Marshallese."[41]

Thus, the Under Secretaries Committee gave President Ford the desired agreement for his instruction to Ambassador Williams. Rather contradictorily, the old dream of "Micronesian unity" was to be included, but along with the sober reminder that it was probably "not feasible...." In that regard, however, it should be noted that the draft Micronesian constitution, signed in November 1975 by all districts except the Marianas, also was founded on "principles of unity."[42] Whatever.

Sensing the probability of losing control, the Congress of Micronesia failed to endorse the draft compact prepared by the negotiators, even though the disputed marine issues had been removed. The congress moved to establish a new Commission on Future Political Status and Transition.[43] Thus, the "inconsistencies" between the status of the compact and the FSM constitution presented increasing confusion. Williams warned the islanders that any efforts "to blur the distinction ... [could] only confuse the picture and prejudice if not preclude the prospects of eventual agreement." The members of the new commission could not "proceed in opposite directions simultaneously toward two incompatible goals."[44]

The United Nations Trusteeship Committee was equally concerned.

At their 1976 meeting, members weighed in, noting a possible contradictory mandate for commissioners. Also, the committee repeated its concern that any plebiscite must be free choice, reminding that no draft compact would be in effect should fifty-five percent of voters reject it. Seeing that the process inexorably spun beyond its purview, the old guard dolefully reminded the world that the Trust Territory government structure "in all legislative matters, including appropriations, shall be conducted through the Department of the Interior."[45]

Carter/Hilo Principles

Though with dubious clarity, the moves toward resolution were undeniable. As had occurred in the past, the realities of American politics took control. The election of 1976 placed Jimmy Carter in the White House—a president with both keen appreciation for human rights and a brilliant mind with insatiable hunger for detail. That combination would place the Executive once again in the decision-making process and undergird the momentum for success. Further, at the propitious moment, the president would appoint Donald McHenry his Ambassador to the United Nations. McHenry, then serving at the UN Security Council, was the State Department official who had nurtured the goal of settlement over disappointing years of "trust betrayed." He would now bring the promise of termination for the TTPI close to fruition. From the outset, Carter was "favorably impressed" with McHenry, and relied on his judgment in many matters throughout his presidency.[46] In the Carter years, the necessary negotiations for success, with UN approval, would finally come through the Hilo Principles.

In the early months of his administration, President Carter carefully reviewed the status negotiations. Through his National Security Advisor Zbigniew Brzezinski, the president made clear his objectives. The "broad U.S. objective should be the conclusion of status arrangements" which would: First, "protect essential U.S. political and security interests...." Second, allow the islanders to "freely determine the nature of their future association with the U.S...." Third, "permit termination of the trusteeship agreement by 1981."

With that general intent, "the U.S. negotiator first should seek a free association agreement with a united Micronesia." Recognizing the growing impossibility of that, "alternative arrangements" would include: (1) a "special treaty relationship with an independent Micronesia, or (2) a mixed arrangement embracing a free association agreement (or agreements) with those districts desiring it...." With other districts, "should they choose independence," and then seek "a special treaty relationship."[47]

In the problematic financial category, the president clarified amounts in various categories, the primary requirement to "obtain satisfactory and legally binding agreements" to guarantee "exclusive U.S. use of all land, waters, and airspace required by the Kwajalein Missile Range and its activities...."[48] At the time, the president was well aware of the implications for KMR in the ongoing ballistic-missile debate, covered below.

Previously contentious issues of marine resources and the 200-mile authority zone would be settled to the benefit of the Micronesians for their own economic development. The directive also made clear the power of the Executive, as negotiations would be conducted by a "Special Representative of the President." The National Security Council Policy Review Committee would coordinate "departmental recommendations concerning the negotiations..." with Brzezinski himself chairing the committee. The NSC Inter-Agency Group on Micronesia would offer assistance, chaired by the Counselor of the State Department. All negotiations would "be supported by the Office of Micronesian Status Negotiations."[49]

Perhaps notably, the president chose the State Department to chair the Inter-Agency Group. On another occasion, Carter had expressed his "complaint" that: "There were times you [Interior] don't support White House policy," if "I make final decisions contrary to what you recommend." This defiance rated a presidential reprimand: The slow response time from Interior to "White House correspondence referred to you" was "inexcusable."[50] President Carter seemed to have experienced the same frustrations followed since the Kennedy Administration.

This clear direction from the Executive was deliberate and timed to coincide with the next status negotiations held in Honolulu in May and then in Guam in July 1977. In the face of continuing "separatist tendencies," such clarity would be required. In August, even while voices of opposition remained, *Iroij* Kabua's directive came to fruition. A full sixty-three percent of Marshallese voters now chose to separate from the rest of the Trust Territory. In the Congress of Micronesia, *Iroij* Tomeing, Chair of the pro-unity group *Ainiken Dri-Majol* (Voice of the Marshalls), still labeled the separatist movement a "very dangerous step."[51]

Also in August, Carter appointed Ambassador Peter R. Rosenblatt as his Personal Representative with Ambassador status. Rosenblatt, formerly on the National Security Committee in the Johnson Administration, had served as negotiator in Vietnam talks. He later claimed his previous attempt to understand the Vietnamese position assisted him in the "Micronesian situation." According to Rosenblatt, the islanders by now had been "totally persuaded that they were incompetent and we were all competent." With Carter's instruction, he intended to change any lack of confidence and mistrust of American intentions. As talks continued in October 1977 and January 1978, by allowing for the remaining five districts to choose their individual paths, their sense of autonomy propelled the process forward.[52]

The long-anticipated breakthrough came in Hilo, Hawaii, signed on 9 April 1978. There all districts agreed with the United States on what came to be known as the Hilo Principles for free association. The eight basics that would finally bring an end to the Trust Territory included: (1) negotiations on free association would be concluded on "government-to-government basis," differentiated from independence; (2) the free association agreement would require a UN-observed plebiscite; (3) constitutional arrangements for governance, with the issue of unity or separation decided at the district level; (4) full internal self-government; (5) U.S. would have "full authority and responsibility" for security and defense for an initial fifteen years and then terms mutually agreed upon. This point included the issue of land, essential for the Marshallese. "Special land arrangements" would remain in effect under terms negotiated "prior to the end" of the trusteeship. It should be noted that the first tenet, "government to government," would prove significant in future debate over reauthorization after the initial fifteen years, as well as in final settlement with the landowners.[53]

The eight principles concluded with: (6) Micronesian peoples would have "authority and responsibility" for their foreign affairs "including marine resources," but through consultation with the U.S., which would maintain control to determine matters "incompatible" with its own security and defense authority; (7) "unilateral termination" would be possible, but "subject to" the provisions of Principle Five, i.e., the all-important land matter. And finally, (8) if "mutually terminated," the same levels of U.S. financial assistance would not be guaranteed.[54] It was all there, as Brzezinski proudly reported to the president. And the Department of Defense had insisted on and received security requirements compatible with the original "strategic trust" by securing the right to "strategic denial" and land control for Kwajalein Atoll.[55]

By 1979, however, the Interagency Group hit a snag in projecting the financial cost for termination of the trusteeship. This group, now consisting of representatives from Defense, State, Interior, Justice, Commerce, Transportation, Energy, the National Security Council, the Joint Chiefs of Staff, the Office of Management & Budget, and the Micronesia Status

Negotiations Office reported that the Micronesians were sensing their own negotiating power and were upping the ante for their cooperation. With negotiations of the Northern Marianas now complete, the other islanders "requested application of the method" of built-in inflation rates for compensation for those "employed in our Commonwealth Covenant...."[56]

True to his style, in responding, Carter "spent a great deal of time on the Micronesian memo and made a number of rather specific decisions." He added his personal quips to the discussion, and lowered the numbers for financial aid in every category—except for the ten million for control of Kwajalein Missile Range. As he had stated in his clear objectives, Kwajalein was essential.[57]

In July 1978, the next step was a vote to ratify the constitution for the Federated States of Micronesia (FSM). Following the president's directive, the State Department had insisted on a real choice for the people. Exercising that option, in July 1978, the districts of Truk (Chuuk), Ponape (Pohnpei), Kosrae, and Yap joined to ratify, while Palau and the Marshalls rejected it. Thus, on 31 October 1980, the new FSM signed a draft compact of free association, while on 17 November 1980, Palau agents signed its own version. Palau would remain a separate entity, while also agreeing to a free association with the United States.[58] In August of 1979, President Carter had appointed Donald McHenry, from the State Department, as America's Permanent Representative to the United Nations. It was McHenry who had shepherded the long Trust Territory settlement process for more than twenty years. Now, under his watch, it seemed headed for an appropriate conclusion.

Most significant for this study, in March 1979, the Marshall Islands had approved the separate constitution put forth by its own constitutional convention in the previous December. On 1 May 1979, the "first constitutionally elected government" in the Marshall Islands took office. The new Nitijela (parliament) consisted of thirty-three members, who, predictably, selected *Iroij* Amata Kabua as the first president. The last remaining hurdle for the Marshalls would be its own contract of free association with the United States. On 14 January 1980, representatives of the Marshall Islands and the U.S. initialed a draft compact.[59]

For President Carter, the conclusion of the TTPI in his term would have been welcome good news, adding to his major foreign policy successes such as the Panama Canal Treaties (1977) and Camp David Accords (1978). But the end was not yet. In the Marshalls, what lay ahead were protests by landowners, who demanded attention to long-simmering grievances regarding the islands of Ebeye, Roi-Namur, and Kwajalein in the Kwajalein

Atoll. Whatever the talk of American power, it would be the Marshallese people who would determine the outcome and future for their homeland.

To his credit, even with new challenges and crisis in Iran, the president's attention did not stray from conclusion of the Micronesian settlement. Internal bridges yet to be crossed included dealing with the congressional Interior committees, which continued to count the Trust Territory their prerogative. Congressman Phil Burton (D-CA), Chair of the Parks and Insular Affairs Subcommittee of the House, had a reputation for "manipulative skills," and according to some, believed himself the "great white father" of U.S. territories in the Caribbean and the Pacific.[60]

The administration already had confronted problems dealing with the arrogant attitude of the Interior Committee. True to form, on December 1979, as the Micronesian dilemma seemed close to resolution, Burton expressed his desire that the negotiations be postponed until after the upcoming presidential election. Further, he insisted that the future compact should insure proper health and education benefits for the Micronesian citizens, stating it as though these had not been taken into account, which was not true. Rosenblatt strongly rejected the idea of postponement, judging it a loss of momentum as well as bargaining position.[61] Ever mindful of the necessity of congressional approval for any completion of the process, Carter supported his ambassador while seeking balance in the search for House and Senate approval.

The election in November 1980, bringing Ronald Reagan to the White House, again changed the end game for Micronesian Status Negotiations. Carter's team hastened to comply with his final directive delivered through Brzezinski: "the President would like to sign the final agreement before January 20...."[62] But he could not. While resolution of the entire compact with congressional approval would not be achieved on this president's watch, the Carter effort had provided the breakthrough and essential foundation.

Nine

Free Association

While President Carter's effort to settle the Micronesian situation had included humanitarian concerns, defense requirements for the Kwajalein Missile Base represented a major factor in the decision-making equation, especially as tensions of the Cold War escalated during his term. Laying the groundwork for the presidency of Ronald Reagan, the debate over missile defense would spotlight collateral implications for Kwajalein, along with reinforced justification for a continuing American presence in the Marshall Islands.

Two factors were key to the changes in the 1970s, both inherited from previous administrations. First was the ongoing "delicate balance of nuclear terror," cultivated during the tenure of Secretary of Defense Robert McNamara through the Kennedy and Johnson years. McNamara feared the increasing arsenal of ICBMs was a two-way ticket of "assured vulnerability" and "assured destruction" with no limits on nuclear war.[1] The Nixon Administration had approached the survivability debate by engaging in a complicated series of Strategic Arms Limitation Talks (SALT). The initial success of SALT was a treaty between the U.S. and the Soviet Union agreeing to a Limitation of Anti-Ballistic Missile (ABM) Systems. Signed on 27 May 1972, this first ABM Treaty embodied the policy appropriately named in its acronym MAD: Mutual Assured Destruction; it would limit defensive weapons while allowing offensive ones to flourish.[2]

Treaty modifications that followed resulted in agreement between the two powers for a single ABM "hard site," meaning the defensive ICBMs, rather than deployment around cities, which planners had first envisioned. For America, the Pentagon chose SAFEGUARD missiles in North Dakota and rushed to comply with the goal of readying the site for "full operational capability" by the target date, which the Army achieved. At that point, however, political realities trumped military zeal.

The second factor in the 1970s was the war weariness of the nation after the Vietnam War and Watergate scandal ending the Nixon Administration. In 1974, after intense debate, the U.S. Congress required that the missile-defense program cease moving toward an actual prototype for missile production. Even after DOD's push to achieve the functional capability, Congress ruled that "operation and maintenance" of the SAFEGUARD system be terminated, with the exception of the perimeter-acquisition radar. Pentagon coordination through the years of ballistic- missile testing, with the primary location for experiments located on the Kwajalein Missile Range (KMR), may be seen again in this phase. The last flight in the Air Force System Test Target Program series to protect the Army's SAFEGUARD had occurred in August 1974. A few years later, when the U.S. Air Force began its new Missile X Program, the Pentagon transferred the Army's radar to the Air Force. In 1975, the Senate ratified the ABM Treaty; President Ford's signature finally put this treaty into effect in May 1976.[3]

Meanwhile, the debate over the basing and deployment of any missile system had a "major impact" on the Army's Ballistic Missile Defense Organization (BMDO) and its programs. As negative media coverage had followed the Ford Administration's flirtation with multiple protective shelters and mobile basing, it also plagued the Carter years.[4] The Army's previous achievement, nevertheless, would provide the undergirding technology for the next level of missile defense when required. Significant and predictive for that phase in the Reagan years, the Army's BMD research was moving toward interceptor technology and away from nuclear weapons, followed below.

Carter's own foreign policy successes had included the consequential and controversial Panama Canal Treaties negotiated in 1977, ratified in 1978; normalization of relations with China; and the monumental Camp David Accords, also in 1978.[5] Attempting to signal support for arms control as he actively pursued agreement with the Soviets for a SALT II, he had cut military spending, wishing to emphasize technology research rather than "hard-target kill capability."[6]

By early 1979, however, this optimistic effort had been shattered by a dismal "international strategic environment" in the Cold War. To the detriment of the U.S., states "either perceived or known to be Soviet proxies," from the Persian Gulf, to East Asia, to the Caribbean, seemed to have gained either "better position" or greater influence in these "areas of high geopolitical value."[7] In addition, deteriorating relations with Iran and revolution that allowed radical students to take over the U.S. embassy in Teheran, destroyed any equanimity for America and "challenged the very essence of Carter's foreign policy."⁸ The terrible year concluded with the Soviet Union's invasion of the nation of Afghanistan in December; after which, the president promptly withdrew the SALT II treaty from the Senate.

Critics later charged that congressional pressure forced the "hardening" of his defense strategy, seen in such moves as the stealth bomber and the Carter Doctrine, U.S. protection for shipping in the Persian Gulf. To the contrary, President Carter had given final approval for a new MX missile system back in June 1979, with plans to reach a final decision on the preferred basing mode the next year. Later creditable analysis has shown that Carter's own internal "evaluation and analysis" prompted the reevaluation and request for increased military spending, including $1.5 billion for MX in the FY 81 (fiscal year 1981) budget.⁹ Whatever the case, it was a change in tone that the Reagan Administration would inherit and claim as its own.

Marshallese Protest

In agreeing to the Hilo Principles, the Carter Administration had found the basis for final settlement of the Trust Territory. After accepting the premise that Micronesia would not remain one monolithic entity, the provisions for choice had resulted in a Federated States of Micronesia (FSM) as well as a separate state of Palau. Each of the new free associations had particular concerns. For Palau, the draft compact covered land issues regarding "harmful substances such as nuclear chemical, gas or biological weapons" that "shall not be used, tested stored, or disposed of…" within its "territorial jurisdiction" without "express approval…."¹⁰

For the Marshall Islands, the free association would mean freely chosen by plebiscite and center on the U.S. military's lease on Kwajalein Island. Also, the looming matter of nuclear testing in the islands after World War II and residual medical effects for the people would be huge. On 14 January 1980, Marshallese and American representatives had initialed a draft compact, which the FSM and Palau also would sign in the fall of that year.

On 16 January 1981, before he relinquished the office, former National Security Advisor Brzezinski received a report for President Carter on the Micronesian Nuclear Claims portion of the draft compact. The language was stark. In Section 177 of the compact, "initialed by Ambassador Peter R. Rosenblatt and Marshall Islands Foreign Secretary Anton deBrum on October 31, 1981, in Washington, D.C.," the U.S. Government "accepts the responsibility for compensation for loss or damage to property and person" resulting from "nuclear testing program in the Northern Marshall Islands between 1946 and 1958." Also, the U.S. agreed to negotiate "a separate (subsidiary) agreement" that would be "subordinate to" the compact for "settling claims arising from the nuclear testing program." With amazing detail, the agreement went on to cover: (1) land claims, with a $10 million ceiling; (2) compensation for personal injury, medical surveillance and treatment, radiological monitoring, with "unspecified cost" and "when approved" by the U.S. Government; and (3) settlement of displaced Marshallese, with "necessary action" and "continued funding."[11]

Clearly, there remained details and definitions to bring finalizing language in the agreement, but this was a major step. Then, ratification by the Marshallese Nitijela (parliament) and the U.S. Congress would be required.[12]

Even before the representatives signed off on the draft, however, in July 1979, adding to President Carter's dreadful year, certain Marshallese had reached the boiling point, expressing their frustration by massive demonstrations designed to block the continued buildup of America's military presence in Kwajalein Atoll. Perhaps, as well, they wished to influence their own new constitutional government in Majuro. *Iroij* Imata Kabua, cousin of Amata, another powerful landowner of Kwajalein Island, and Handel Dribo, an "important" *alab* (clan head), led a large protest against the overcrowding on Ebeye, loss of land leased on the island with inadequate compensation, and limits to free access in the center of the atoll during periods of missile testing. Kabua's action at this time was on Roi-Namur Island, the northern tip of Kwajalein Atoll, with encampment on Dribo's mid-corridor home island. More than thirty indigenes joined in a speedboats disruption, dubbed a "sail-in" by the Army. At the same time, beginning with "approximately" seventy islanders encamped on Kwajalein itself, growing to more than five hundred, until it was finally evacuated on 6 August.[13]

Totally surprised by the unexpected invasion, the military lookout on Roi initially confronted Kabua harshly—an unfortunate response, as Kabua would win a lawsuit charging "assault" by the Army. Resistance by lawsuit also presaged the method Imata Kabua would employ decades later to resist a final Kwajalein Land Use Agreement, as will be seen.

For the immediate future, the sail-in exemplified an effective method to exert new pressures as the possibility of actually signing a compact neared. Attempting organization and strategy for influencing any settlement, a coalition of local leaders including the *Ainiken Dri-Majol* (Voice of the Marshalls), formed back in 1978 to oppose separation of the Marshalls from a united Micronesia, and a new group called the Kwajalein Atoll Corporation (KAC), would build on Kabua's mid-corridor protest. Also, a group of sympathetic volunteers formed the Micronesian Support Committee (MSC), headquartered in Hawaii.[14] Their newspaper editorials and publications, such as "Marshall Islands: A Chronology: 1944–1983" sought to engage the passion of the islanders, as well as to disrupt of U.S. military missile testing—or at least gain more favorable terms in any land use agreement.

After the November election of 1980, progress toward resolution proved impossible for the Carter staff. Control of U.S. policy now would be determined by the Reagan Administration, which needed time to gain some understanding of the complex situation. After taking office in January 1981, the new Secretary of Defense, Caspar Weinberger, issued a nine-month moratorium to study the Marshallese dilemma, thereby relinquishing the momentum gained by the previous administration. That interim would provide superb timing for continued protests.

After that pause, by mid–1981, a professional, tough new High Commissioner of the Trust Territory, Janet McCoy, was in place, as well as a new Ambassador to the Office of Micronesian Status Negotiations, Fred M. Zeder. From 1975 to 1977, Zeder had served in the Department of the Interior as Director of Territorial Affairs, had spent a good deal of time in Saipan, and claimed to have an inside track on the working of the Trust Territory Government.

Zeder had nothing but praise for Janet McCoy. She was "marvelous," he said, "the finest thing that ever happened to the Trust Territory." McCoy would be instrumental in bringing resolution to the current protest spinning out of control with the islanders swamping Kwajalein. One remembers the Marshallese matrilineal culture that may well have been one reason for that success. The other was her own personality. Zeder recalled that McCoy was "strong enough and persuasively and matronly enough" to get "respect and cooperation and be tough enough." She had "the respect, cooperation, and the admiration of everyone out there...."

Zeder also claimed to know the thinking of Reagan and his vice president, George H.W. Bush. Once Zeder was in place as Ambassador and personal representative, the new president wanted to hear the details. Zeder said that his "personal instruction" in a "classified and secret directive" was: "Get it done; conclude the negotiations."[15]

Imata Kabua, Dribo and their cohorts were well aware of timing, in that closing disputes over the exact terms and language of the compact were now in play. To the topic of the Army's presence in the atoll, protesters noted the still-virulent charge against U.S. nuclear testing, as covered in the draft. Later, supporters of Micronesian Support Committee would argue that at the time of negotiations in the 1980s, Americans deliberately withheld information and kept records regarding the tests classified, thus making them unavailable to Marshallese. As they would claim, the impact of that duplicity encouraged the islanders to accept inadequate compensation for the damage of the earlier testing, as well as for the continuing health ramifications caused by radiation exposure.[16]

Even at the time, however, the matter of just compensation for previous American testing was justification for a strong Marshallese position. Equally clear from documentary evidence was U.S. acceptance of responsibility for the damage done. As already noted, in the preliminary compact negotiated by Peter Rosenblatt for President Carter, the language was straightforward: "The Government of the United States accepts responsibility for compensation ... resulting from the nuclear testing program..." of the U.S. The amount of "just and adequate" compensation promised, of course, was the issue. Interior had actually used the term "compassionate compensation," even harder to quantify.[17]

The current expressions of anger, interrupting decisions regarding the final language, caused consternation for those looking for closure in both the American government and that of the Marshallese President Amata Kabua. For the U.S. Army, crucial tests for the MX missile, now equipped with multiple-reentry warhead, were scheduled for 20–21 June 1982. In May, Ambassador Fred Zeder met with Tony deBrum, Marshallese Foreign Secretary. Eager for resolution, deBrum and Zeder signed a Memo-of-Understanding (MOU) calling for a hasty plebiscite to get the required public approval, even granting the yes/no option for either free association or Marshallese independence. DeBrum insisted on the latter, even blustering that the Marshallese, if necessary, would end the Trust Territory by their own declaration.

This bravado was a non-starter for U.S. military officials, who had no intention of relinquishing the unique location of the Marshalls in mid–Pacific or American strategic-denial rights, deemed by even the State Department the "most significant U.S. interest" in the relationship. Without the heavy endorsement for a Kissinger "spike" as noted with the same topic of exchange in 1972, more now than then, the Pentagon would have none of it and quickly squelched the option of self-proclaimed independence. Officials cancelled the August plebiscite, claiming a "program of voter education" would be needed to validate a choice by the people.[18] Furthermore, undeterred by the threat of protests, missile testing continued, though with a modified target location, the Army fearing any actual endangerment. Again, American officials reminded all that safety of the islanders had been the initial reason for the mid-corridor evacuation order, the order that had caused controversy back in the 1960s.

In June 1982, "notwithstanding the provisions ... to noninterference with KMR operations," agreed upon with obstinate resistance, the islanders initiated Operation Homecoming, a larger and stronger sail-in with almost one thousand persons occupying Roi again and Kwajalein Island for a time, attempting to disrupt the tests. With both sides recalcitrant, the military played hardball, cutting sanitary facilities and barring indigene workers from services on the island and from customary eating accommodations, to discourage their passing food to protestors. Trust Territory High Commissioner McCoy sent her personal envoy to induce calm with a more palatable civilian face. A U.S. court order would be needed to lift the draconian military measures and restore water and sanitary conditions.[19]

It would be difficult to argue that the courageous protestors were not effective. After years of negotiations, these demonstrations reminded the world again of the essential truth: the islanders claimed only to control their own homes on their own land. Reports of the standoff led to congressional voices critical of such harsh treatment used to combat peaceful assembly; "and yet we're in their country," sounded one, "a pretty sad spectacle." Alerted to the issue of influencing terms in the new compact, voices from the Protestant World Council of Churches added additional international support for the Marshallese. Even if "the Kwajalein people were after more money ... they were thoroughly justified in doing so...." These published comments from the World Council and "intrusion" into the fray infuriated Ambassador Zeder, according to one report. Further, issues of earlier nuclear testing and continuing American responsibility for the ramifications of those tests again surfaced in the conversations. *The Pacific Daily News*, a Guam tabloid, claimed in headline: "Kwajalein Protest Outlasts Pressure."[20]

Basics of the compact under consideration were well understood, going back to the earlier Hilo Principles: the U.S. military would lease Marshallese land and retain control over security and defense with continued strategic denial to other countries; America would recognize islanders self-government and national sovereignty; a UN sponsored plebiscite would confirm acceptance by the people.

Both sides in the negotiations attempted in various ways to control the remaining details. The U.S. demanded an end to Operation Homecoming, while the Marshallese won additional funds for improvements on Ebeye, where Kwaj workers lived in overcrowded, some said "slum" conditions. As already noted, the financial aspects would include not only annual payment for leasing Kwajalein, but sums related to dislocation of the islanders for nuclear tests and residual health problems caused by exposure to radiation. The matter of access to U.S. Courts for redress still remained on the table, but the possibility of claims based on new circumstances "which in the future may arise" was a clause already in the 1980 draft. Americans floated terms of a fifty-year commitment; the Marshallese offered a fifteen-year agreement. The compromise draft initialed on 1 October 1982, gave the U.S. a thirty-year control of Kwajalein Atoll, an initial fifteen years with a guaranteed option for another fifteen-year renewal.

Even with this agreement, internal political dissent among the Marshallese mounted and threatened the terms of compromise. In the summer, President Amata Kabua made a fruitless trip to Kwajalein, attempting to personally appeal to protesters to end their campaign. Not persuaded by the president, his critics derisively dubbed the negotiators "comprised mainly of Majuro-based national government officials" (who else?). While the Hilo Principles clearly required dealing "government to government," landowners saw themselves as the appropriate and affected party. Disgruntled owners forced even the KAC to acknowledge some had been excluded from their landowner group. These discontents and divisions were a harbinger of the ongoing dilemma facing American occupiers: "land in the Marshall Islands is privately owned. Our use rights on Kwajalein are derived from the *Iroij* Kabua…." Settlement of the controversial Kwajalein Land Use Agreement remained in the distant future.[21]

In 1983, Marshallese efforts to influence the potential compact continued. The opportunity was now. Displaced Bikini islanders reminded the administration of their need for land, with the result that six of the outer islands were returned for resettlement. In Kwajalein Atoll, the Army restored community services and attempted "normalized relations" with the Ebeye residents who worked on the island, both sides establishing Community Relations Committees for the effort.[22]

Amata Kabua, now sometimes with belligerent tone but intent on final resolution, travelled to the United States, visited the Army's BMD Systems Command in Huntsville, Alabama, and then Washington to meet with American officials. Among his entourage, Kabua replaced the abrasive Tony deBrum with Oscar deBrum, another of his key advisors. It should be noted, however, that this would not be a permanent demotion. Tony deBrum would continue to play a major role in the Marshallese government, at Kabua's side until his death, and beyond his term well into the next century.

The Marshall Islands Interim Use Agreement of 20 October 1982 had guaranteed American lease of Kwajalein Atoll while promising $1.5 billion "in economic assistance and services" over thirty years, including "$9.05 million in 1983, $11.06 million in 1984, and $11.06 million in 1985." Changes in the revised rendering signed by Kabua and Zeder on 25 June 1983 in Majuro included an annual Nuclear Compensation Fund of $150 million, specifying money for a "national radiological survey." The U.S. agreed to a Nuclear Claims Tribunal, but sought to limit any "additional liability" that would require further compensation. This hope was weakened by a clause already in the Hilo language admitting that "changed circumstances" might potentially lead to additional compensation, as it so proved. The United States could/would never remove the stain of culpability for its past actions.[23]

Through the United Nations, with the effort of U.S. Ambassador Zeder and Trust Territory High Commissioner McCoy, a new plebiscite was scheduled for the fall of 1983. The result: by a sixty percent margin of approval, the Marshallese people voted to accept a Compact of Free Association with the United States. Under this patronage, the Republic of the Marshall Islands would hold independence in internal government and economic policy. The U.S. would maintain strategic entry rights and military responsibility for protection. On 30 March 1984, in a message to Congress, President Reagan proposed legislation to approve the Compact. The next hurdle was the American lawmakers.

Ambassador Zeder took credit for steering the Compact through the U.S. Congress and would later remember that, with the help of Janet McCoy, it turned out that dealing with the Marshallese was "not the hard part." Dealing with the U.S. Congress was "the hard part." "That was a battle," with "a lot of opposition in the House of Representatives." Others stated less kindly regarding the Compact, reporting that the Congress "tore it apart," with endless amendments and questions.[24]

The resistance included those on "extreme right and extreme left." The right raised again the old dictum of belligerent occupation. They "felt that we had won these islands fairly and squarely during the war and a lot of blood had been shed out there; that's right, and we own them. These were the people that said we stole the Panama Canal fair and square so we ought to keep it." "The extreme left [was] represented most clearly in the person" of a congressman from Akron, Ohio, a "very liberal legislator who doesn't believe in the military at all." Representative John Seiberling

(D–OH), who headed a House subcommittee on public lands and national parks, "had a great idea for Kwajalein. He was going to make it a park and put it in the park service. That was actually a recommendation of his." Of course, he was "very sympathetic" toward the people of Bikini, "those people who felt they had a trust betrayed...." He felt "that we weren't doing enough for them and we need to give them more money and do a lot more things for them."[25]

Zeder recounted thirty-two hearings in the U.S. House of Representatives and two in the Senate. "In addition ... I had twenty-eight different agencies of the federal government and departments of agencies that we had to satisfy and sign off on this job. In addition to that, we had the United Nations to contend with." Within the administration, he noted "good relations with the State Department...." They "were very helpful, but above all I had marvelous support from the Defense Department who recognized what our obligations were and were tremendously supportive." Not surprisingly, given previous recalcitrance, the Ambassador felt he "had no help at all from the Department of the Interior, which was a terrible block." The officials in that department "saw their empire vanishing. That was the worst political battle you have ever seen."[26]

The timing of the final debate could not have been more propitious. The controversy over BMD basing mode had been a subliminal concern in the 1980 election. Then, after taking office, Reagan had his own woes with indecision and resistance from congressional districts that would be impacted by a new idea for basing missiles in "dense pack." Though the intended mission was to bring increased fear to Soviets facing American competition, even the Joint Chiefs were divided in their support for the new MX and its complexities.[27] Changing the name to PEACEKEEPER missile did little to ease the pain. In these years, the uncertainty had a direct impact on the Army's BMD program and the ongoing debate with the Marshallese. The embarrassing publicity over protests in Kwajalein Atoll made the Compact a significant background issue in need of resolution.

Strategic Defense Initiative

Reagan was ready for a new strategic vision. Frustrated by his inability to achieve consensus on the MX basing mode, he sought a "way out" of the dilemma. Moreover, the "nuclear freeze" movement reflected a public finally awakening to the horror of offensive nuclear weapons and the potential for a devastating war. From the summer of 1982, the Joint Chiefs of Staff and National Security Advisors to the president struggled to present a new national defense strategy.[28]

Earlier, President Reagan had asked Lieutenant General Brent Scowcroft (USAF Retired) for a comprehensive overview of existing weapons worthy of support. The Scowcroft Report, which would be published in April 1983, began voicing a "deep abhorrence for both nuclear war and war itself," though recognizing the threat of "aggressive totalitarianism" that might require a defensive response. The report underscored the importance of strategic force and called for a balanced triad of weapon options. These included: (1) the Trident II (D-5) submarine missile; (2) bomber and cruise-missile programs; and (3) vigorous research in anti-submarine warfare and in ballistic-missile defense.[29] At issue here was the question of movement toward actual deployment of a defensive missile, or for only continued research at the present.

In fact, the continuing secret talks would go well beyond these recommended offensive weapons. NSC Advisor Robert McFarland was convinced that the U.S. could never compete with the superiority of Soviet technology in this arena; that would always be a catch-up endeavor. In February 1983, Dr. Richard D. DeLauer, Under Secretary of Defense for Research and Engineering, held strategy sessions with Army personnel, admitting that Secretary Weinberger had challenged him: "Get me a BMD system."[30]

At the time of need, new players gained credibility—new to this generation of advisors, but long in the wings yearning for another chance to replace Mutual Assured Destruction with Assured Survival. Even in the first year of the Reagan Administration, believers in a new space-based missile defense, including various congressional and military persons, sought opportunity to influence Reagan, preempting the president's advisors and White House readiness.[31] Chief among them were two significant persons. First was physicist Dr. Edward Teller, who will be discussed below. Second was Lieutenant General Daniel Graham (USA Retired), among the members of the Committee on the Present Danger, early "neo-cons" back in the 1970s, who feared the superiority of Soviet technology, some would say, with a "paranoid" style of crisis defense. This Committee on the Present Danger had become the "scourge" of President Carter's defense and foreign policies. The influence of that Committee actually included one of the architects of America's paranoid style, Paul H. Nitze, who had worked closely with former Secretary of State Dean Acheson after World War II to define the Cold War. It was the Acheson State Department that penned the momentous NSC-68 blueprint that served "to militarize U.S. foreign policy" in the Truman Administration.³²

Jeopardizing the High Frontier group's attempt to influence Reagan, Graham insisted on making public their concept of space-based defense. After meeting with the president only briefly in January, in February 1982, Graham defied his colleagues and published: "The High Frontier: A New National Strategy," with exaggerated expectations of that frontier, among them satellite-based lasers. Not content with merely weapons, Graham added another controversial element. Beyond the military advantage, which was the selling point for a majority of the group, was the expanded allure of a "space industrialized" with nuclear waste disposal, solar energy, and deep-space transportation.³³ Graham's scheme envisioned an alliance reminiscent of the mercantile imperialists of the McKinley era at the turn of the twentieth century, that of military protection for economic expansion in the Pacific. The exotic extent of Graham's scheme was breathtaking: global "spaceborne" missile defense; "spaceplanes" with human pilots; space-based transportation and energy systems; and multiple orbiting "spacetrucks," with more than forty "kill vehicles."³⁴

Critical of Graham's entrepreneurship that might jeopardize Reagan's acceptance of space-based missile defense, but eager to be a part of a new fantastic scientific venture, the father of the hydrogen bomb, Edward Teller ("Crazy Edward Teller") had been a part of the planning from the outset. It would be Teller's task to convince the president that the military side of the idea was reasonable and doable. Teller, who had been bitterly disappointed that the U.S. abandoned the hydrogen bomb's destructive force, now saw a new opportunity in laser technology.³⁵

It will be remembered that after World War II, President Truman had made the crucial decision to test atomic/nuclear weapons, as previously recounted. Operation Crossroads, two tests at Bikini Atoll in the Marshalls, occurred in 1946. Between 1954 and 1958, the deadly Bravo series unleashed more than twice the powerful explosion than had been anticipated, and raised the intense opposition that brought atmospheric nuclear testing to a halt. The U.S. continued, however, with sixteen more tests until 1958, when Edward Teller then lost his argument with the Eisenhower Administration to proceed.³⁶

J. Robert Oppenheimer, Director of the original Manhattan Project to develop the atomic bomb, had long before taken the high road in opposition to nuclear warfare. Oppenheimer's famous later quote from Hindu sacred scripture, the *Bhagavad Gita*, "Now I Have become Death, the Destroyer of Worlds," in his mind even with the first successful wartime test in July 1945, epitomized American ambivalence toward the power unleashed by the new technology. Determined to continue research, Teller had left the control necessary for the Manhattan Project to found the Lawrence Livermore Laboratory in California, where he worked to develop the next generation of cutting-edge weaponry. Perhaps Reagan could be persuaded.[37]

Clearly, the president's advisors were divided on support for the new concept and certainly on the timing for making it public. Both Secretary of State George Schultz and Secretary of Defense Weinberger had reservations.[38] Nevertheless, Reagan was taken with the breathtaking concept of a space-based strategic program using directed energy to provide a balanced offense/defense—all with nonnuclear intent. On 23 March 1983, he gave his famous TV speech that changed the entire debate.

> The subject I want to discuss with you, peace and national security, is both timely and important. Timely, because I've reached a decision which offers a new hope for our children in the 21st century.... At the beginning of this year, I submitted to the Congress a defense budget.... It is part of a careful, long-term plan....
>
> Since the dawn of the atomic age, we've sought to reduce the risk of war by maintaining a strong deterrent and by seeking genuine arms control. "Deterrence" means simply this: making sure any adversary who thinks about attacking the United States ... concludes that the risks to him outweigh any potential gains....
>
> In recent months, however, my advisers, including in particular the Joint Chiefs of Staff, have underscored the necessity to break out of a future that relies solely on offensive retaliation for our security....
>
> Wouldn't it be better to save lives than to avenge them?
>
> Let me share with you a vision of the future which offers hope.... with measures that are defensive....
>
> What if ... we could intercept and destroy strategic ballistic missiles before they reached our own soil or that of our allies? ...
>
> I call upon the scientific community in our country, those who gave us nuclear weapons, to turn their great talents now to the cause of ... world peace, to give us the means of rendering these nuclear weapons impotent and obsolete....
>
> Our only purpose—one all people share—is to search for ways to reduce the danger of nuclear war.[39]

Initially sold to the president with its intriguing non-nuclear promise and with the catchy phrases: "wouldn't it be better to save lives than to avenge them," and "we could intercept and destroy strategic ballistic missiles before they reached our own soil," Under Secretary of Defense DeLauer was shocked that the concept was made public before his careful strategic advice could be fully developed. He reportedly "went ballistic," and wondered how nuclear policy could be created "with such a 'half-baked political travesty.'"[40]

DeLauer had thought that the White House Coordinating Group would have more time to prepare. The directive had asked that the presentation highlight "a policy of deterrence" not "depending solely upon the threat of effective nuclear retaliation." It should "make clear the risks" the U.S. faces from "the vigorous Soviet ballistic missile defense program." But even the "Congressional and Allied consultations" were not to be returned to the White House Coordinating Group until 14 December 1983.[41]

But Reagan was in a hurry. He had clearly directed the DOD, "working closely with the Department of State and the Director of Central Intelligence," to prepare a "coordinated presentation." The inclusion of Reagan's covert manager William J. (Bill) Casey, an "original Cold Warrior," who headed the CIA and exerted great influence in foreign policy decisions, perhaps was significant. As one of Reagan's inner circle, some would see that he often was "out of control," using dubious and "contrived means." Casey would be a prime advisor in such high-risk ventures as the Iran-Contra scandal, that could have resulted in impeachment.[42]

Nonetheless, DeLauer was correct that the name already given, Strategic Defense Initiative, had not been publically released before the president's speech and the reaction was swift. The next day, on 24 March, *The New York Times* splashed the media definition of Reagan's "Star Wars" defense, as the speech unleashed a future of controversy. Actually, of course, the derisive "Star Wars stuff" label had been used first by military skeptics when Graham had published "High Frontier" the previous year.[43]

After the speech, the media and skeptics in the U.S. Senate adopted the term in deriding criticism of the president. Scrambling to regain credibility and give the proper name for the new concept, DeLauer gave to the president his report in March 1984. This was promptly endorsed on 16 April by Reagan's National Security Decision, Directive Number 119: "The technology plan identified by the Defensive Technologies Study" would serve as the "general guide for initiating this bold, new program," which would have "three aspects as its hallmark: innovation, focused technology programs, and technical demonstration milestones." It would be a "comprehensive program" to:

(1) "develop and demonstrate key technologies" associated with BMD;
(2) coordinate with other "strategic defensive programs";
(3) allow creation of a specific Strategic Defense Initiative Organization management structure under DOD;
(4) place "principal emphasis" on "nonnuclear kill concepts";
(5) protect options for changing threats or security interests; and
(6) include SDI in FY 85 budget request.

Perhaps in recognition of the maelstrom of negative media, the directive discreetly ended with a warning: Keep statements regarding SDI "low key and closely coordinated to ensure that an accurate picture of the nature and scope of this R&D effort is presented to the public." On 24 April 1984, the Secretary of Defense issued an interim charter making it official: the Strategic Defense Initiative (SDI), would be administered by the SDI Organization (SDIO).[44]

For the Army's existing program, the Scowcroft Report had sounded the death knell for the SENTRY missile, but its endorsement of continuing research made the U.S. Army's effort a perfect fit for the president's dream of a viable defensive strategy. While the emphasis in Teller's scheme entailed utilizing reflective laser beams in space, the Army saw an opening for new respect by offering the first leg of SDI in a land-based missile, with a layered-defense approach.

The Army's Homing Overlay Experiment (HOE) would provide the first success claimed for the new national defense program that would define the Reagan years, as well as the backdrop for the final phase in a workable definition for self-determination for the Marshall Islands. Conducted on the Kwajalein Missile Base, HOE was a series of tests designed to resolve "developmental issues in homing and intercept technology for potential use in a nonnuclear system." After partial success in the first three tests of the series, the fourth was spectacular with an impressive intercept above the atmosphere. With "nonnuclear, homing and kill," the HOE device destroyed the ICBM launched from California.[45]

This final test came on 19 June 1984, perfect for displaying U.S. military might and the significance of Kwajalein. By suspicious coincidence, the president's message in March of that year, requesting ratification of the Compact of Free Association with the Marshall Islands, now lay before the U.S. Congress for ratification. Was the HOE series fixed for inevitable success? Later critics would claim the intercept was a little too impressive and not a test at all.[46]

Undeterred by skeptics, the Army claimed its rightful part of the president's Initiative and restructured its BMD program, renaming it the U.S. Army Strategic Defense Command (USASDC). With headquarters in D.C., under the command of Lieutenant General John F. Wall and program office in Huntsville, Alabama, under Major General Eugene Fox, the new USASDC would combine advanced technology and system design within a single organization. For FY 86, the Army's program would be thirty percent of the SDI budget.[47] The corresponding necessity of testing new weaponry again put the spotlight on the requirement for stability in the islands, providing regained leverage in the conclusive legislative effort to end the Trust Territory of the Pacific Islands and gain independence for Micronesian peoples.

After the rigorous debate and numerous final modifications, to which the Marshallese agreed, the U.S. Congress authorized the Compact of Free Association in December 1985. The bill included a thirty-year contract, with the fifteen-year renewal timeframe, negotiated for control of the Kwajalein Missile Range in support of missile testing and Reagan's SDI. The U.S. recognized the sovereignty of the Republic of the Marshall Islands (RMI), but retained the right of "strategic denial" to other foreign nations and American military protection. The details included health and food support for the outer islands that suffered most from the atomic testing, economic aid of $2.6 billion, and certain trade and tax concessions.[48] Future negotiations for the fifteen-year renewal would review and supplement these details. There would be time enough ahead for that battle. On 14 January 1986, President Reagan signed the bill as passed by the Congress to create a Compact of Free Association between the Republic of the Marshall Islands and the United States. It was done.

In the 1980s, the confluence of three—sometimes conflicting—perspectives may be seen in the final agreement. The first perspective is that of American civilian policy makers. At the height of the Cold War, the Reagan Administration gained hegemonic pressure against the Soviet Union, claiming the necessity of testing land-based defensive missiles as part of his Strategic Defense Initiative. The president could also claim credit for terminating the Trust Territory of the Pacific Islands. The Department of the Interior would handle the financial disposition for the islands, while the Department of State would now be relieved of pressure from the United Nations to grant independence to the long-delayed "betrayed trust," a violation of American democratic idealism.

The second perspective has been that of the U.S. Military seeking security for the nation through hegemony in the central Pacific. From the perspective of the Department of Defense, the U.S. Army had secured its base on Kwajalein Island and essential testing in Kwajalein Atoll, now in conjunction with the U.S. Air Force. The promise of the "strategic trust" was secure, "strategic denial" recognized, and protection of the Marshall Islands guaranteed in the Compact of Free Association.

The third perspective is that of the Marshallese people. Even as America sealed the claim on Kwajalein, it still remained their own homeland. The leadership of *Iroij* Amata Kabua had been crucial in determining the settlement won in the final language of the Compact. One would recall the profound statement offered in 1969 by the Congress of Micronesia, Future Political Status Commission Report. It had recognized:

> two inescapable realities: the need for Micronesian self-government and the fact of long-standing American interest in this area....
>
> In recommending free association with the United States we seek not an end but a re-definition, renewal and improvement of this partnership....
>
> How, then, will America benefit by entering into association with Micronesia? How can Micronesia hope to reward continued American contributions to its development? ...
>
> There was an element of trust, of moral obligation, involved then when the United States undertook responsibility for these islands, and such an obligation, which was begun when these islands were in ruins, should not be ended when they are reaching for political maturity.
>
> Yet there is one item of material value which Micronesians can offer the United States—an item which is most precious in Micronesia and to Micronesians: the use of their land. Micronesians recognize that their islands are of strategic value, that the United States may require the use of some areas for purposes of military training and defense. We have seen the strategic value of these islands, have seen them used for nuclear experiments and missile testing. Our experience with the military has not always been encouraging. But as a self-governing state in free association with the United States, we would accept the necessity of such military needs and would feel confident that we could enter into responsible negotiations with the military, endeavoring to meet American requirements while protecting our own interests.[49]

The years of stubborn negotiation had achieved this desired result for future status. With the Trust Territory retired and independence achieved, the Republic of the Marshall Islands would be recognized as a sovereign nation, in control of its own economic and political life. Yet, even with terms of the financial agreement seemingly satisfactory, still the protesters, disgruntled Kwajalein landowners, would hold the key to resolution for the last outstanding issue. Reauthorizing the Compact in 2003 and the final Kwajalein Land Use Agreement will be the subject of the concluding segment of the story. This unique "partnership" even now would require a more complete definition and resolution.

Ten

To the Twenty-First Century

Under the Compact of Free Association, everything would change—or would it? As a Freely Associated State, the Republic of the Marshall Islands (RMI) would have autonomy over domestic decisions. The realization of actual sovereignty, however, included the troublesome issues of reliance on American patronage and the enormous dominating presence of the U.S. Army in the Kwajalein Atoll. In the creation of the Trust Territory of the Pacific Islands (TTPI), the United Nations had granted the United States the one and only "strategic trust." Under the Compact, in U.S. protection of the Marshalls, the significance of "strategic denial" was yet to be adequately defined.

Republic of the Marshall Islands (RMI)

The U.S. Congress had passed the legislation authorizing the Compact of Free Association in December 1985. In January 1986, President Reagan signed the bill into Public Law 99–239. What remained was enactment: "Placing into Full Force and Effect ... the Compact[s] of Free Association with ... the Republic of the Marshall Islands." While prelude to official action by the UN Security Council, Presidential Proclamation in November 1986 outlined the specifics, relishing the fact that on 28 May 1986, "the Trusteeship Council of the United Nations concluded that the Government of the United States had satisfactorily discharged its obligations as the Administering Authority under the terms of the Trusteeship Agreement...." Therefore,

> I determine that the Trusteeship Agreement for the Pacific Islands is no longer in effect as of October 21, 1986, with respect to the Republic of the Marshall Islands.... The Compact of Free Association with the Republic of the Marshall Islands is in full

force and effect as of October 21, 1986.... I am gratified that the people of ... the Republic of the Marshall Islands, after nearly forty years of Trusteeship, have freely chosen to establish a relationship of Free Association with the United States.¹

Reminiscent of the long disputes over jurisdiction in the Marshalls, on 16 October 1986, the president's executive order had spelled out the responsibilities for management under the Compact. The Secretary of State would have authority in "the establishment and maintenance of representative offices in Freely Associated States and supervision of the United States representatives and their staff," as well as "authority and responsibility" in actions of the Compact and "in its related agreements ... as they relate to the conduct of government-to-government relations...."

On the other hand, the Secretary of the Interior would be "responsible for seeking the appropriation of funds for ... economic and financial assistance appropriated...." Interior would "coordinate and monitor any program or any activity by any department or agency" of the U.S. and "coordinate and monitor related economic development planning." Noteworthy was the clear exclusion: "This Section shall not apply to services provided by the Department of Defense...."²

For RMI, while autonomous government had been claimed as far back as the initial Marshallese constitution in 1979, international acknowledgment of its freely associated status with the United States was a major achievement. Fittingly, Amata Kabua became the first president of the new republic. Kabua's preeminent leadership, from his role in the Congress of Micronesia through negotiations for land use and then independence, would continue for another decade, until his death in 1996. Those years would serve to identify both the future of the relationship and unintended consequences that would be addressed through the debate over reauthorization of the Compact in the early 2000s.

As seen in previous years, the Executive in the White House defined a great deal of the association. Also noted, President Reagan had chosen to leverage American foreign policy through the Strategic Defense Initiative (SDI). At the same time, the administration had continued to negotiate missile-defense issues with the Soviet Union.

Amid the tension of that seeming standoff, the president went on to agree with Soviet Premier Mikhail Gorbachev for an amazing "double-zero" strategy, the elimination of both intermediate- and long-range missiles. In December 1987, the leaders signed this Intermediate-Range Nuclear Forces (INF) Treaty in Washington, D.C., and then in Moscow in May 1988. While there were surely other factors, some would credit the huge American defense buildup and the threat of overwhelming force with the eventual end of the Cold War.³ Whatever the case, stepping back from the brink of nuclear destruction for both superpowers granted the entire world a sigh of relief.

In the Marshalls, in 1986, the Kwajalein Missile Range had become the U.S Army Kwajalein Atoll (USAKA). In FY87, continuing the usual, the range conducted "thirteen flight test operations" using missiles launched from Vandenberg Air Force Base in California.⁴ Knowing the key role played by Kwajalein and the Strategic Defense Command (USASDC) in the U.S. show of strength, the Marshallese waited for any revised assessment of their role.

One reflection of the new status included the work of the USASDC Provost Marshal to establish authority for enforcement such as:

(1) "removing unauthorized persons from islands which are required to remain unoccupied" during testing; identifying those "boundaries of the mid-atoll corridor";
(2) expanding the "customs/immigration role," with the RMI "assuming customs inspections" and assisting in renovation of a "dock security check point facility." This would make a "secure holding area or 'international terminal' between Kwajalein and other areas within" the RMI; and
(3) supporting the RMI Nitijela (parliament) in passing a proposed Treason and Sedition Act, requiring "Limited Access Authorization (LAA) programs."

These programs would allow granting "limited security clearances to Marshallese employees of USAKA" and thus "open up more positions for Marshallese employment and advancement."⁵

Subsequently, the Nitijela did pass the Treason and Sedition Act, with the president signing it into law in March 1988. The RMI government made every effort to signal a positive working relationship to reflect their new status. Illustrative of that effort, in February 1989, "USASDC received [the gift of] 50 dwarf palm trees from President Amata Kabua."⁶

Perhaps in a test of "strategic denial," a naval ship of the USSR made an appearance within the republic's three-mile sea barrier. Exerting its claim of sovereignty, in April 1988, the RMI government sent a letter of protest to the Soviet Embassy stating that "a Soviet vessel, 'of a type normally associated with intelligence gathering,'" had been sighted well within RMI territorial limits, off Majuro Atoll, where the "national capital is located."⁷ Understood in the brave objection was an America presence to ensure enforcement of the barrier.

In May 1986, in a three-to-one vote, the UN Trusteeship Council had passed the resolution with "recommendation for concurrence," that the U.S. had "fulfilled 'all obligations' in its trusteeship." Then, in December 1990, the Security Council recognized the termination of the Trust Territory of the Pacific Islands, thus officially ending U.S. trusteeship of the Marshall Islands. President Amata Kabua was quoted declaring it the "greatest Christmas present" the Marshalls ever had. "People will now understand that we are a nation."[8]

Thus, in 1991, without opposition, the Republic of the Marshall Islands was granted full membership in the General Assembly of the United Nations. Happily, the termination of the Soviet Union, "self-dissolved" in December 1991, emboldened American President George H. W. Bush to declare the end of the Cold War.

Having achieved international recognition of the republic's self-determination, President Kabua turned to other issues. Agent membership in the World Bank, the International Monetary Fund (IMF), and the Asian Development Bank would assist in economic development.[9] Paramount among other concerns was the viability and health of his citizens, still dealing with the residual harm caused by the U.S. nuclear testing of the 1950s. Under the language of the Compact, America had accepted responsibility for the possible effects and had allowed for a Nuclear Claims Tribunal to consider charges of "changed circumstances."

In 1992, the election of President William Jefferson "Bill" Clinton brought an Executive who was willing to tackle past reluctance to uncover unflattering American culpability from the past. The Clinton Administration would declassify not only those of interest to RMI, but massive numbers of Cold War documents, allowing for invaluable research into past administrative secrets.

Further, in 1994, noting the fortieth anniversary of the Bravo tests, President Clinton authorized his Independent Advisory Committee on Human Radiation Experiments (ACHRE), which would delve into the primary concerns of the Marshallese, namely that the U.S. had deliberately used the islanders as expendable subjects in tests for radiation effects. This charge had punctuated the protests of the islanders in the 1980s and throughout deliberations regarding the Compact. In 1995, Marshallese former foreign minister, Tony deBrum, brought additional charges of American duplicity.[10] In the next century, deBrum, again foreign minister, would lead an attempt to sue the United States for past mistakes, bringing similar charges before the International Court of Justice against the U.S. and other nuclear powers. Fearful of jeopardizing their relationship with

America, RMI citizens would be of mixed opinion on the subject of deBrum's efforts.

While these claims would never be satisfied for some, the ACHRE did conclude that there "was no evidence that the initial exposure ... constituted a deliberate human experiment." Not so conclusive was the look at one secondary test. While the Committee gave the best positive motive that a "tracer dose" used might have been seen as beneficial for the upcoming Bravo test, it was forced to admit that: "No documentation addressing whether consent was sought is available for either experiment." Also, the ACHRE acknowledged that "thyroid abnormalities," as well as "one fatal case of leukemia have been the most significant late effect of radiation among the Marshallese."[11] There would be others. Already there were increasing numbers of additional cases before the Nuclear Claims Tribunal. Fortunately, the less-than-brilliant idea of making into an international nuclear dump those outer islands already contaminated, received little support in either RMI or the U.S.[12]

In retrospect, one is forced to admit the most likely: Americans had been largely ignorant of what the nuclear age would mean, as Einstein feared and Oppenheimer had predicted. Put more harshly in regard to the Bravo tests, even with the best of intentions granted, it is a "cautionary tale about hubris and incompetence in the nuclear age...."[13] For the Republic of the Marshall Islands, the repercussions of that ignorance would be felt in the lives of its citizens for generations.

Reauthorizing the Compact of Free Association

Language of the Compact of Free Association (CFA) signed in 1986 had been exact in describing the "renewal" or "reauthorization" process. The initial period of operation would be fifteen years, with a right of extension for "fifteen additional years." Specifically, "not later than the thirteenth anniversary of the effective date," October 21, 1986, the "Government of the United States shall elect whether to exercise this extension." After such action, the U.S. would begin "annual grant payment" and "continuing for each subsequent year," with "fixed amount of $1.9 million." That thirteenth anniversary would be in October 1999, with a "provision for a two-year extension to funding authority" if the parties "were continuing to negotiate in good faith."[14]

In the late 1990s, internal politics of the Marshalls complicated the imminent issue of Compact extension. One constitutional problem was the continuing clash between the president and the Nitijela (parliament) jeopardizing an independent judiciary. Within four years, there was removal or resignation of several chief justices, who cited "continued interference with the judiciary by the executive and legislative branches of the Marshall Islands government."[15] Many of these court cases involved land ownership claims, to be discussed below.

In fact, the leadership of the abrasive Tony deBrum, heading the party in opposition to President Kabua, some said "changed forever the political environment" of RMI. While the effort failed to limit consecutive presidential terms by constitutional amendment, there was lingering resentment roused by earlier decisions regarding the judiciary. Given this tone of the discourse, it was perhaps surprising that the 1995 presidential election was a "peaceful campaign," with Kabua winning reelection for a fifth term, along with wins for eight of ten cabinet positions and twenty-five of thirty-three incumbents in the Nitijela.[16] And perhaps not, considering the deep affection and regard with which the majority of Marshallese held their "father of the country." The death of President Amata Kabua in December 1996 brought a landslide of grief and appreciation for the decades of his distinguished leadership in the Marshall Islands.

The contentious political environment, however, would only intensify after Kabua's death. In January 1997, following the dictates of the Marshallese constitution, the Nitijela elected the successor president— in the person of his cousin Imata Kabua, then sitting senator from Kwajalein. President Amata Kabua, long a supporter of the Free Association relationship with the United States and the Compact of Free Association, had notably stated, there was "no such thing as this Compact finally ending."[17] On the other hand, remembering the role of Imata in the opposition protests of the 1980s, the pressing question of renewal could be at risk.

In the very first year in his new position, President Imata Kabua did little to create a positive image in the United States. The *New York Times* reporter Nicholas Kristof found Imata "in his customary place in the hotel bar, apparently inebriated and enjoying yet another pre-dinner drink...." Kristof, asking the obvious question regarding Marshallese–U.S. relations, wrote: "'You know, I was arrested by the United States,' the President, Imata Kabua, slurs proudly," explaining his protest back in 1982. Then, "repeating over and over: 'I don't like America, I don't like America.'"

Not the best first impression. Kristof went on to elaborate on the contradiction considered even in the present study. What is America's appropriate "place" in the Pacific? This reporter defined the paradox of foreign aid: There is no place in the world where America, as America sees it, has been so generous as the Marshall Islands, a collection of coral atolls between Japan and Hawaii. Yet the local economy remains a shambles and the United States is broadly resented. Something went badly wrong for usually it is possible to be resented without paying $1 billion for the privilege.[18]

Unfortunately, this assessment made no mention of the third aspect of the problem, found in the dictates of the U.S. military, though he did go on to mention a "base in Kwajalein." The offensive description of "a collection of coral atolls" and "foreign aid" bears little resemblance to the military's demand for the Marshals, as prime location in strategic planning, Kristof claiming instead that Kwajalein had "lost its strategic advantage." Nevertheless, his point continued with the matter of renewal of the Compact of Free Association, and the charge that from "the perspective of the Marshalls," the U.S. "has been bullying this little country for decades...." Kabua, glad for an American forum, declared: "I don't like it. It shouldn't be renewed. It should be renegotiated, that's right. Renegotiated not renewed."[19] Thus the dilemma. One scholar would describe America's quandary as "colonial constitutionalism."[20]

For many Marshallese, the new president was an embarrassment. In fairness to Kabua, it should be noted that later in the year, perhaps in a more sober moment, the president had spoken of "hopes raised" for "positive discussions" with U.S. officials regarding renewal.[21] Still, the next two years would see "constitutional chaos," low morale, complaints, and multiple votes of "no-confidence" against the Kabua government.[22] In September 1999, the United States did exercise "its option to unilaterally extend its agreement with the RMI for an additional fifteen years," while negotiations for the terms of that agreement were to begin later in the fall.[23]

Anticipating that crucial set of talks, a United Democratic Party finally ousted Imata Kabua, making 2000 a "year of reform" for RMI. For the first time in its constitutional history, a "commoner," not of the Iroij class, would become president. Following the November elections, in January 2000, the now-Democratic Nitijela unanimously elected its Speaker Kessai Note to be president on a platform of "anti-corruption, transparency, and accountability." Noteworthy was the defeat of Tony deBrum, Kabua's Finance Minister, and Foreign Affairs Minister Philip Muller.[24] There would be challenges, of course, as the ousted president did not go quietly. In 2001, in a significant victory for Note, Imata Kabua's attempt at a "no-confidence" vote failed. Though the following year he seemed to accept the new regime, in the next decade Kabua would again attempt to sabotage the Compact. As for Note, he survived his first year with some criticism, but with high marks for reform efforts, gaining an amount of financial stability, and importantly, the Compact renegotiations were "finally on track."[25] In November 2001, Note visited the United States in person, confirming his "readiness to present" the RMI "proposal on Compact assistance" and its "commitment" to "uphold good governance, transparency, and accountability."[26]

The United States faced its own set of challenges. First, in the controversial election of November 2000, a divided Supreme Court named as president George W. Bush, who had received fewer popular votes and with a contested electoral count. With neoconservative Vice President Dick Cheney at his back, the new and inexperienced president would rely on Cheney for guidance.

Second, and probably related, immediately after taking office, the new administration resurrected the concept of Reagan's SDI and arming space. Updated versions of space defense included chemical lasers and "nearly every major element of the original program back in the center" of "a national missile shield." Recurring language speculated about intercepting offensive missiles "in the boost phase"—which essentially would be preemptive strike.[27] This administration would attempt to justify its definition of offense to be defense: preemptive attack to be preventive, reminiscent of Japanese logic before Pearl Harbor.

Third, in a blinding strike, the Jihadist Islamic sect known as al Qaeda attacked the U.S. mainland on 11 September 2001, changing forever American international policy and plunging the nation into more than a decade of war focused in Afghanistan and in Iraq. What would be the impact of this new aggressive militarism on those evaluating the significance of BMD and Kwajalein Atoll?

In November 1998, President Clinton had endorsed the "close, unique and mutually beneficial" relationship between the United States and the Marshall Islands, one that the U.S. "takes very seriously." In May 1999, Secretary of State Madeleine Albright then created the Interagency Group on the Freely Associated States, appointing Allen P. Stayman to the position of Special Negotiator, reporting to the Assistant Secretary of State for East Asian and Pacific Affairs. The work must include the necessary buy-in of representatives from Departments of State, Defense, and the Interior, familiar adversaries.

Anticipating the first of four negotiating rounds, the U.S. Army had detailed to the State Department Dr. John Fairlamb, who would become the Army's Advisor to the Office of Compact Negotiations, remaining there for four years, late 1999–2004. After returning to serve at the USASMDC

Headquarters, he would lead the crucial discussion of the Military Use and Operating Rights Agreement (MUORA) and the Status Of Forces Agreement (SOFA) with the RMI.[28]

In June 2001, before the September terrorist attack, Dr. Fairlamb presented the essential U.S. position paper at the Island Security Conference in Honolulu, aptly titled, "Compact of Free Association Negotiations: Fulfilling the Promise." Fairlamb underscored the primary achievement of the Compact in ending the Trust Territory and granting "sovereign self-government," while at the same time "protecting U.S. security and political interests." He went on to outline strong resolve that would justify continuing economic assistance for the freely associated states such as RMI. Chief among these was "strategic denial," as insurance for U.S. security in the Pacific. U.S. Army installations at Kwajalein Atoll remained important for "missile tracking, testing and U.S. space operations."[29]

The principal elements for successful negotiations, therefore, would include: first, financial assistance, newly defined to "cease transfer funding" to be replaced by grants with "well-defined accountability procedures." These would be targeted to "Health, Education, Infrastructure and Maintenance, Private Sector Development, Capacity Building and the Environment." Each would have "specific objectives," as well as "regular planning, monitoring and reporting requirements."[30]

Second, program and services such as postal and "assuring safe air transportation" would be directed toward the "goal of economic self-reliance." In this regard the Department of the Interior should be given "sufficient authority to require other departments" to cooperate. Third, one primary goal would be creation of a Trust Fund targeted for the "termination of annual U.S mandatory payments" by the end of the next term of the Compact. The U.S. proposed that the fund receive $7 million in 2004, with "increasing U.S. annual contributions from this amount through FY 2023."[31]

A fourth element for review had been necessitated by initial language of the Compact, allowing for a citizen of RMI to "enter into, lawfully engage in occupations, and establish residence as a nonimmigrant in the United States." (PL99–239) The unintended consequence of this liberty had been "substantial impact" on "adjacent jurisdictions of the State of Hawaii, Guam and the Commonwealth of the Northern Mariana Islands." Change should include "basic admissibility requirements under existing immigration law."[32] In a major way, the fear of impending terrorist attacks on the U.S. also would increase concern for this unrestricted access.

Bringing Congress into the loop, in December 2001, Albert V. Short, who had replaced Allen Stayman as the Chief Compact Negotiator when the Bush Administration took office, made his "Pacific Report" to the U.S. Senate Committee on Energy and Natural Resources. In the overview, Short set out the same priorities of the new administration, explaining that "the relationship of free association is not up for renegotiation." Neither the U.S. right of "strategic denial" nor the "agreement to use Kwajalein" would be in question. Sections for renegotiation included financial payment, "effecting the economic transition toward increased budgetary self-reliance" and the important "so called 'defense veto' and provisions regarding additional base rights."[33] Echoing the same strategy as Fairlamb's review, Short clarified financial assistance to include "economic stability," with the expectation of continuing multiple support for the republic from the Asian Development Bank and the International Monetary Fund, as well as other American allies such as Japan and Australia. Thus, the amount of continued U.S. assistance would be on the table.[34] He underlined the essential goal of maintaining U.S. "strategic interests," to be defined in a continuing commitment to the American presence in Kwajalein Atoll.

After this encouraging beginning in 2001, in 2002, the U.S. Government General Accounting Office (GAO) blindsided the negotiating effort with a somewhat inconsistent assessment. First was a laudatory title: "Kwajalein Atoll is the Key U.S. Defense Interest in Two Micronesian Nations," well and good. Then, in explaining the context, the text noted that in December 2001, the new president had given notice that the United States would withdraw from the Anti-Ballistic Missile (ABM) Treaty negotiated by the Nixon Administration in 1972. The "Ballistic Missile Defense Organization has proposed to increase the operational realism of missile defense testing by developing new or expanded facilities. These facilities will be used in conjunction with Kwajalein Atoll as part of an integrated missile defense test bed." Despite this, in seeming contradiction, the report went on to conclude that although "Kwajalein Atoll has become the home to sophisticated radar, optics, and telemetry equipment," from "a more regional or global point of view," RMI "currently" played "no role in the execution of the U.S. defense and security strategy."[35] How could both be accurate?

In a post–Cold War era, GAO questioned the "contribution to U.S. security" represented by the concept of "strategic denial." It added dismissive language regarding another of the Freely Associated States, the Federated States of Micronesia (FSM) and its interlocking importance in close proximity to the Marshalls. It even went on to question the value of any support FSM and RMI afforded for American "positions in the United Nations."[36]

Response to the GOA report was swift. Letters of rebuttal from the Department of Defense, the Embassy of FSM, and the RMI Ministry of Foreign Affairs all claimed great significance for the relationship between the U.S. and these Freely Associated States. While agreeing that the American base in Kwajalein Atoll held "strong defense interest," Assistant Secretary of Defense Peter W. Rodman disagreed that strategic denial was not essential. Rodman underlined the American commitment to defense of the Marshallese "in perpetuity," even as for U.S. citizens.[37]

Ambassador Jesse B. Marehalau from the Embassy of the Federated States of Micronesia (FSM) affirmed the GAO's effort to show interrelationship between political, economic, and defense aspects, while strongly disagreeing with the thought that the FSM itself "lacks any strategic importance." Marehalau focused on the uncertainty of security in light of the recent al Qaeda attack against the United States and an uncertain future for the Asia-Pacific arena. In multiple pages, he took grave issue with the conclusion that "security interests" for the Pacific had been overstated. In a rather lame return, the GAO commented that neither the Departments of State nor Defense had provided specifics to make their case.[38] Minister of Foreign Affairs Gerald M. Zackios gave an even stronger response from the Marshall Islands. With a positive beginning, he welcomed the opportunity to respond. Then, with a large "however," he stated that RMI could "not concur" with the report's mere "opinions." The GAO had "ignored" history and needed to be "refreshed" on the facts; the report was a "litany of oversimplification," amounting to "historical revisionism." The "defense veto" had not been invoked because it had not been needed—the threat had worked; there had been no "outside threats" because strategic denial had worked. And the Compact certainly had not been a greater "defense burden" than the NATO alliance. The GAO denied that it had used the word "burden."

Foreign Minister Zackios proceeded with a passionate, rather idealized paean to the relationship between the United States and the Marshall Islands, crediting the Reagan Administration for finalizing the Trust Territory of the Pacific Islands. In fact, termination of the TTPI "was itself important to the Reagan Administration's efforts to develop the Strategic Defense Initiative…." Discounting the stormy debates between 1960 and 1980, he then claimed that through the long years of trusteeship, the Marshallese and Americans had developed real "friendship." Despite the deadly "hardship and injury inflicted on us during nuclear testing," because of "decades of common experience," somehow "a residual mutual respect and understanding grew between our peoples and government." Even with the horrors, remarkably:

> The compassion Americans showed even as they created the conditions of hardship required that the Marshall Islanders learn to live with the contradictions and paradoxes of the modern world in a way that perhaps no other culture ever has. It speaks volumes about who the Marshallese people are that we seek justice with forgiveness in our hearts and that we choose to become allies with the U.S. based on all that we knew about Americans instead of just what we suffered from nuclear testing.

Understandably, the American goal of Micronesian unity at the end of the trust had not been possible, given the high and long-sought goal of "self-determination" for each island entity. Further, in order to recognize national sovereignty, the Military Use and Operating Rights Agreement (MUORA) must exist "government to government." Thus, the U.S. had "honorably ended its role in administering power," creating a superior relationship of "an ally to democratic governments." Clearly, the GAO had not understood the subtleties of the situation, their so-called "analysis" was "both simplistic and ahistorical."[39] Amazing! Amata Kabua himself could not have said it better. All three responders agreed that the GAO had overestimated the role of Soviets in ending the trusteeship, as well as an anticipated relaxed post–Cold War atmosphere that would make unnecessary their part in strategic defense.

As the deadline for reauthorization of the Marshallese Compact loomed in September 2003, the Bush Administration was engaged in full-court press to gain public support for American military action against Saddam Hussein, unrelated to the 9/11 terrorist attack but used as justification. After extensive congressional debate and with furious division and opposition, on 19 March 2003, the U.S. invaded Iraq, placing the nation on war footing and dramatically changing the American mood.

In the wake, on 30 April 2003, the RMI government negotiating team, headed by Zackios, signed the draft agreement for renewal of the Compact of Free Association with the U.S. Conspicuously absent from the signing ceremony, held in the Nitijela, were members of the Kwajalein Negotiation Commission (KNC). This group, representing the landowners, clearly registered dissent by their absence. On 23 June, President Bush sent to Congress the proposed reauthorization package. The summer brought additional debate in House and Senate hearings on the value of missile defense and Compact renewal, addressing remaining issues of concern for the Marshallese.[40]

In July 2003, Dr. Fairlamb returned to the Island State Security Conference in Honolulu to report the details. In his paper entitled "Where Are We Now?," Fairlamb repeated the areas for concern in renewal outlined at the outset in 2001. The U.S. offer extended Title Two economic assistance to $35.7 million in FY 2004 (beginning October 2003), providing "declining annual assistance from these amounts through FY 2023." The reductions would be paid into the trust funds to be created for future termination of annual payments. The RMI government, with future president Christopher Loeak at the table, also agreed to make contributions "to jump-start" the trust funds. As anticipated, the U.S. annual payments would be targeted to areas of health, education, and infrastructure. In awareness of special needs for the communities of the Kwajalein Atoll, the amount of $5 million would go: first, $3.1 million to Ebeye; and second, $1.9 million in the MUORA.[41]

The matter of this Military Use Agreement for Kwajalein Atoll had been the focus of "contentious" debate within the RMI throughout the year of negotiations with the U.S. The sum of $16.9 million to landowners, with further increase to $19.9 million in 2014, initialed by RMI Foreign Affairs Minister Gerald Zackios in January 2003, had been wildly different from that of those organized to speak for the disgruntled Kwajalein landowners, the KNC. The U.S. had rejected out of hand their demand for $2 billion. Thus, with the signoff from the Note Administration to the agreed contract, the details of the MUORA had brought an angry walkout from the landowners.[42] Without their participation, and just ahead of the deadline, the Congress would authorize and the president sign reauthorization of the Compact of Free Association in September 2003.

Kwajalein Land Use Agreement

After two centuries of indigenous islanders having resisted Western imperialism, it is perhaps sufficiently ironic that the last hurdle for complete settlement of the Compact renewal would be another landowner dispute. Critics would say the disaffected group only wanted more money, not untrue. One remembers, however, the big guns and German scheme to relocate workers to copra plantations; or, the racist Japanese attempt at culture makeover, the claim of state-owned land, and forced labor; or, the American trade routes and weapons testing designed for economic and military hegemony. What exactly is just compensation for colonial constitutionalism? And who is the worthy recipient of the obligatory largesse?

The "landowners" of *Iroij* class did not represent one unified group. The present study has only hinted at the complexity of land claims that existed in the Marshalls and noted the numerous times Americans sought the "final solution" for leasing land in the Kwajalein Atoll. As previously noted, back in 1962, one baffled U.S. congressman had complained: "there is no analogy between the common American idea of an absolute owner and the Marshallese idea of a holder of any one of the levels of rights in common kinds of landownership in the Marshalls."

Evident here, the most obvious dispute among the landowners themselves has been among the cousins Kabua, Amata having been accused by his own *jowi* (clan) of benefitting most from American lease of his land on Kwajalein. In 1990, Kabua Kabua, Paramount *Iroij,* had filed case against both Amata and Imata Kabua, "concerning the ownership of the northern lands, including Kwajalein," though the suit later was dismissed.[43] The Kwajalein Atoll Corporation (KAC) of Ebeye never felt adequately compensated. Divisions in the Nitijela and land claims in the courts have ever been a part of governing in RMI.

The Marshallese constitution adopted in 1979 recognized the primal significance of land ownership, a concept infused into the very core of this matrilineal culture. In their history, the mystic of land was inalienable to the individual, "never regarded as a mere commodity."[44] Beginning with the claim of "our rightful home on these islands," the constitution adopted a parliamentary government, "subscribing to the principles of democracy," to "achieve fair and democratic government."[45] It created a "Council of *Iroij,*" with power to request "reconsideration" of any bill passed by the Nitijela "affecting the customary law, or any traditional practice, or land tenure, or any related matter...." In form similar to the American system, it effected legislative, executive, and judicial branches, adding to the standard judiciary a Traditional Rights Court to include the complex "fair representation of all classes of land rights...."[46]

While these special courts clearly were designed to deal with hopelessly entangled land claims, still the Traditional Rights section underlined again that "nothing" in Article II, spelling out certain individual rights, should "be construed to invalidate the customary law or traditional practice concerning land tenure or any related matter" involving the *Iroij* land powers. Further, no person with land claim "under the customary law or any traditional practice" would be allowed to make "any alienation or disposition of that land, whether by way of sale, mortgage, lease, license or otherwise, without the approval" of the *Iroij* class landowners, "who shall be deemed to represent all persons having an interest in that land."[47] Point taken: under the RMI constitution, approving the lease of Kwajalein Atoll to the United States was the prerogative of the landowners.

This point, of course, had been well understood by negotiators of the first compact, including Amata Kabua, back in 1979 during the breakthrough conference in Hawaii. The first of the Hilo Principles was negotiations on a "government-to-government basis" prior to termination of the Trust Territory. In principle five, anticipating the landowner problem, the text stated that the U.S. would have "full authority and responsibility" for security and defense. The renegotiation for leasing land would be between governments; that is, the RMI government would need to settle with the Kwajalein landowners. The lease payment from the U.S. would go through the RMI government offices, not directly to the landowners.

One of the continuing landowner complaints against this government-to-government arrangement had occurred in the late 1980s, after the initial Compact of Free Association law. In a poignant letter, the Committee on Interior and Insular Affairs in the U.S. House of Representatives had informed the Secretary of the Interior Donald Paul Hodel that more than 800 landowners had issued a petition requesting fairer distribution of lease funds. The "problem" the petitioners cited was that "many of the senior ranking landowners, or *iroij*, do not share the payments that they receive ... with the lower-ranking landowners." The charge was that this conflicted with "traditional Marshallese custom" and did not comport with "the spirit of the law," instead creating "hardships among the vast majority of the landowners while making millionaires out of a few." With the overcrowding of the dispossessed on Ebeye, these concerns would inevitably only grow.[48]

After an exhaustive investigation of this issue, the Army came to the unambiguous conclusion that it would be neither "appropriate or constructive" for the U.S. to be involved in adjudicating traditional land claims. The RMI "is in full compliance with its obligations to provide land use rights at Kwajalein Atoll...." Those "not satisfied" with "current land use payment distribution have available to them both customary and legal remedies under RMI law." Clearly, the Americans would have "hands off" on this "matter of internal RMI law and politics." There simply were "no facts" and "no provisions of the Compact or U.S. law" which would require any involvement. The CFA provides a "framework" for "government to government" consultation only.[49]

Testing this judgment, in June 2000, the first year of the Note presidency, anticipating compact renewal negotiations, a group of landowners under the rubric of the Kwajalein Atoll Development Authority (KADA), filed a civil lawsuit against the RMI government. After Compact negotiations, RMI had failed to recognize the legitimacy of the initial Kwajalein Atoll Corporation (KAC), thus necessitating this new KADA. With the hire of a Mississippi legal firm, they claimed that they should be the legitimate negotiators in the renewal process, the government having "'failed or refused' to obtain fair market value for the Kwajalein Defense sites" in the original Compact. Their attorney reiterated that RMI "had no ownership interest" in Kwaj; without redress, they would be "left with no alternative but to begin proceedings … to remove the United States from Kwajalein." The group of forty named included Senators Ataji Balos and Imata Kabua, charging the "unconstitutional and unlawful taking of land." Scrambling for evidence that payments had been just in the 1986 transaction, the RMI Justice Minister contacted the U.S. State Department. While the RMI High Court dismissed the case, it served as harbinger of what lay ahead.[50]

In 2003, therefore, to contest another settlement without their approval and signature, the walkout had occurred, noted above. Even with the pact signed "government to government," the U.S. must then satisfy the Military Use and Operating Rights Agreement (MUORA) and Status of Forces Agreement (SOFA) for leasing Kwajalein Atoll. It would be difficult to operate as usual with the ongoing "rift" between the RMI government in Majuro and the contentious landowners. Even after the signing, organized protests attempted to "turn up the heat" on the Note Administration, disrupting the opening of the Nitijela August session with a "Buck Stops Here Rally."[51]

In 2005, former president Imata Kabua wrote to the U.S. Ambassador Greta Morris a blistering letter repeating again his contention that the "RMI government owns no land." For "legitimate use of Kwajalein beyond 2016, a Land Use Agreement between RMI and the people of Kwajalein is required by law and by the Constitution. No such agreement exists and we have proclaimed our intention not to agree to a new one and to return to our lands in 2016." The U.S. intent to remain after that date marks "a remarkable display of colonial audacity."[52]

Thus it would be for the remainder of the Note tenure, with continuing economic problems and seasons of opposition and angry division within the Nitijela. Speaker Litokwa Tomeing, who abandoned Note's United Democratic Party, condemned the administration as "a dismal failure." In July 2007, the Minister of Foreign Affairs, Gerald Zackios, who had been RMI Chief Negotiator during Compact renewal negotiations, resigned his office. Then, in November, a contentious and disputed election ended the Note regime in an unusually botched election process requiring recounts after disputed results. In January 2008, in multiple close votes, the Nitijela named Speaker Tomeing himself as President of the RMI. Future president and "perennial incumbent" Christopher Loeak, survived to become Minister in Assistance, while Tony deBrum reemerged as Minister of Foreign Affairs. Yes, and former president Imata Kabua, who had supported Tomeing, envisioned more lawsuits.[53]

As one of the landowners, *Irioj* Imata Kabua had not forgotten protests in the 1980s and still maintained that he, representing "the landowners," had not signed off on the first Compact of Free Association. This time his suit would be against the RMI government that had signed the renewal Compact, again without his signature, violating the Marshallese constitution. Also included, his argument would be that any agreement for years beyond the obligatory fifteen ending in 2016 would require his signature. The MUORA and SOFA for Kwajalein Atoll held the key for resolution.

In the years leading up to the reauthorization debate, Kwajalein had undergone another round of name changes. In 1992, USASDC had merged with the Army's Space Command to become the U.S. Army Space and Missile Defense Command (USASMDC). Under that command, the USAKA had become the Kwajalein Missile Range (KMR). Then, in 1999, it would include the Ronald Reagan Ballistic Missile Defense Test Site (RTS). Clearly, the atoll's new name recognized the role President Reagan had played in terminating the Trust Territory and in finalizing the first Compact of Free Association. Somewhat intriguing, without the Army's prior knowledge, the Marshallese themselves suggested the revision and effected the change through the U.S. Congress. Representative Roscoe Bartlett (R–MD) first introduced HR 3554 in January 2000, with Senator Bob Smith (R–NH) following with companion measure for the Senate in March 2000. The name change was incorporated in HR 4205, the Floyd D. Spence National Defense Authority Act for FY2001 and became PL 106–398. Bartlett's legislative director, who visited USAKA, first heard the request; thus, the Army learned secondhand.[54]

With changes in operation, the U.S. Army had reduced the number of American personnel on Kwajalein as well as Marshallese workers. These reductions in employment, combined with continuing growth on already-crowded Ebeye Island, whose population had doubled since the 1980s, only exacerbated the "already tense" relationship. The reality was a debilitating dependency of the Marshallese economy on the American presence, despite all effort to develop self-sufficiency.

With no Land Use Agreement (LUA) between the Kwajalein land-owners and the RMI Government in place after the 2003 renewal, the U.S. and RMI Government had kept in escrow $20 million for rental payments, with a deadline for settlement to claim the fund in December 2008. Public bickering, euphemistically called "dialogue," between RMI President Tomeing and U.S. Ambassador Clyde Bishop did not assist in resolution of the conflict. Weary of the never-ending complaints, Bishop spoke darkly of seeking a plan to "provide for the return of assets to the landowners in 2016. Private talks between Tomeing and Bishop, however, yielded a different tone. Before the end of the prescribed deadline, outgoing U.S. President Bush "granted Tomeing's request for an indefinite extension in order to produce a new Land Use Agreement," while the rent money would be kept in escrow" after all.[55]

Another American president would offer new personnel and a fresh perspective. Optimism came with the election of Barrack Obama, who had campaigned on "hope" and "change you can believe in." Effective slogans notwithstanding, the new administration needed the usual breaking-in, fact-finding period to fully appreciate the issues of the Freely Associated States. In August 2009, President Obama's appointment of career diplomat Martha Campbell as Ambassador to the Marshall Islands signaled an attempt to reestablish a positive community-exchange atmosphere.

Secretary of State Hillary Clinton expected to visit Kwajalein. Unfortunately, a deadly earthquake in Haiti required her presence and changed the schedule already announced. Secretary Clinton, however, did travel extensively in the Asia Pacific area and visited the Cook Islands to attend the Pacific Islands Forum in August 2012. She became, thereby, the first U.S. Secretary of State to make a public statement in a Pacific Islands Forum-Post Forum Dialogue. In her remarks, Clinton took a broad approach, noting that in 2011, President Obama had met with Pacific Island leaders in Hawaii, "America's own bridge to the Pacific." Further, she claimed that the "Obama Administration has made a major push to increase our engagement across the Asia Pacific." She emphasized the "shared values, a shared history, and shared goals for our future" with American allies.

In the face of an aggressive Chinese move to control the South Sea area, some would see the secretary's extensive Pacific travel as intended to ensure an awareness of U.S. presence and commitment to the region. She mentioned, with specifics: (1) "a sound economic agenda"; (2) "maintaining peace and security in the Pacific"; and (3) "supporting the women of the Pacific." Secretary Clinton's strong statement of recognition of significance for Oceania was framed in a memorable affirmation: "We too, of course, are a Pacific nation."[56]

In the meantime, in July 2007, Tony deBrum had appeared before the Foreign Affairs Subcommittee of Asia, the Pacific and the Global Environment in the U.S. House of Representative making the case for the new Land Use Agreement. He repeated the dictum that the RMI did not own land; the landowners must sign off on any American lease in Kwajalein Atoll. DeBrum added the charge that the U.S. had "waived off" any involvement in resolving this "internal" matter, adding: "We submit this is not so." There was truth in the statement that the landowners tangle was more than internal to the islanders. For example, the new administration would realize that cordial relations between the personnel at the Kwaj base and people on Ebeye were essential.[57]

With that lead, what followed was the expected: requisite lawsuit. In October 2009, former president Imata Kabua filed the case before the High Court that the RMI government "took the lands and gave them to the United States of American to occupy and use exclusively...." The charges concerned the extended use of Kwajalein Atoll beyond the 2016 time agreed to in the Compact renewal. Again Kabua claimed it was "not money I'm after," but "my rights under the Constitution." The RMI government's agreement with the U.S. had been "one-sided," not offering "just compensation" for use of his land. Also, it should be noted, in the next year the withheld escrow account would grow to more than $32 million. Perhaps it was time to settle.[58]

By 2010, the demand included U.S. acceptance of a $3 billion trust fund with interest payments to landowners and the appointment by RMI president of a Kwajalein Atoll Development Authority. Not guaranteed, but there was talk of $570 million "proposal for infrastructure in Ebeye and the Kwajalein Islands."[59] By the fall of that year, the agreement was struck.

The Office of the President of RMI issued the official word from Majuro. The "longstanding impasse between the Republic of the Marshall Islands Government and the Kwajalein Landowners has finally been resolved...." In a "ceremony on May 10, 2011, held in Ebeye, Kwajalein Atoll, the RMI Government and the Kwajalein Landowners signed the Kwajalein Land Use Agreement (LUA) which now extends the use of lands in Kwajalein by the United States to the year 2066, with an option for 20 years extension." The signing of the LUA "now triggers the release" of the now over-$32 million Joint Escrow Account "for distribution to the Kwajalein Landowners in accordance with the provisions of the agreement."[60] Kwajalein Atoll was now "America's place" in the Pacific.

For the military, the U.S. Army Space and Missile Defense Command/Army Forces Strategic Command operated with its Program Office on Redstone Arsenal, Alabama. Within Kwajalein Atoll, the DOD Major Range and Test Facility Base now included the U.S. Army's Ronald Reagan Ballistic Missile Defense Test Site, with its mission: "to provide a Major Range Test Facility Base (MRTFB) activity on Kwajalein Atoll and Wake Island...." The command reveled in the claim of its "unquestioned value," which was "based upon its strategic geographical location, unique instrumentation, and unsurpassed capability to support ballistic missile testing and space operations." On the ground, the base designation became the U.S. Army Garrison—Kwajalein Atoll. It counted as its mission to conduct:

> base operations and installment management functions in support of a diverse community of military, Department of Army Civilians and contract personnel and their families, while also fulfilling U.S. Ambassador's Military Liaison Office requirements with RMI ... at this geographically strategic location.[61]

Conclusion

In 2012, the Republic of the Marshall Islands celebrated twenty-five years of independence under the Compact of Free Association. In January of that year, the Nitijela elected a new president, longstanding leader and landowner *Iroij* Christopher Loeak. President Loeak's Foreign Minister, Philip Muller, would meet with U.S. Assistant Secretary of State for East Asia and the Pacific, Kurt Campbell, who visited the Marshall Islands. They joined "in pushing a button to 'reset' and improve the relationship between the two nations." Having embarked on the "second quarter century of free association between our two nations," the reset would "signify a shared hope for better relations." Acknowledging one key interaction between his indigenous citizens and Americans, in October 2013 and again in the summer of 2014, Loeak visited Kwajalein Atoll and held a "Town Hall" meeting in outreach to islanders who worked on the base.[62]

Through his three-year tenure, the new U.S. Ambassador to RMI, Thomas Armbruster, would continue positive interaction with the Marshallese. Underlining the effort to connect, Secretary of the Interior Sally Jewell chose Esther Puakela Kia'aina to be Assistant Secretary of Interior for Insular Areas. Assistant Secretary Kia'aina was born in Guam of Hawaiian parents and clearly held a "strong connection to Pacific islands...."

In 2014 in New York, RMI President Loeak and his wife would meet with the U.S. President and Mrs. Obama in a cordial exchange. The American reception for heads of state at the opening of the United Nations General Assembly was the perfect photo op to underline the new attempt at civility in common purpose.

In that same setting U.S. Secretary of State John Kerry also met with Loeak for discussion of climate issues and the crises the Marshalls face from rising seas. Administration officials were well aware of increasing dangers to islanders and to Americans. The U.S. Army Kwajalein base had experienced catastrophe in 2008 when a tidal wash flood destroyed freshwater supplies. This climate reminder required desalination machines and

President and Mrs. Barack Obama and President and Mrs. Christopher Loeak, United Nations, New York, 2012.

"heavy-duty seas walls" constructed with "fortified granite" of the sort "used in hydraulic engineering." In 2013, when the Marshalls hosted the Pacific Forum, one action was to create and support the Majuro Declaration for Climate Leadership.[63]

As president, Loeak gave greater international visibility to RMI. He traveled to other nations such as Japan, which included an audience with the Emperor and a stop in Hiroshima. RMI saw increasing patronage from Japan and also from the Republic of China in the form of Taiwan, both establishing embassies with resident ambassadors in Majuro. Multiple exchange programs and visits underlined the history of their Pacific linkage. Still, the economy of the Marshalls was inextricably bound to the United States through the financial payments under the Compact of Free Association and the future Trust Fund.

The balance between the principle of democratic idealism and the reality of power well may be seen in America's history with the Marshall Islands. President Obama has made the proclamation that the twenty-first would be the "century of the Pacific" for the United States. What hegemony would that intend broadly, and what role would Kwajalein play, America's unique place. The challenges seem vast with: aggressive Asian neighbors; signs of global warming already evident in the islands; and questions of U.S. culpability for nuclear testing remaining. As President Loeak has stated with classic understatement: the United States and the Republic of the Marshall Islands sustain a "very special relationship."[64]

Epilogue

With the challenges of the twenty-first century before them, the citizens of the Republic of the Marshall Islands inevitably would have differences of opinion. Since 1979, living with a constitutional government created by democratic principles, they enjoyed a healthy political life of debate and rule by majority vote.

While striving for a positive relationship, and acknowledging the interdependency of RMI and the United States, still the Christopher Loeak Administration included various Cabinet members who proved divisive. Former Foreign Minister Tony deBrum returned to that familiar role and continued in his combative style. In two particular cases he became the international face of the Marshalls.

The first was the lawsuit against the U.S and other nuclear countries, through which deBrum seemed tireless in his determination to excoriate the United States for past mistakes. In 2014, he had filed suit that claimed the U.S. had not taken appropriate action for nuclear disarmament required by the UN Nuclear Non-proliferation Treaty. That treaty, negotiated in 1968 and put in force in 1970, had been "extended indefinitely" in 1995 with 190 signatories, "including the five nuclear-weapons States," of which the United States was one. In the U.S., after various arguments regarding standing, a lower Federal Count dismissed the RMI case, saying that U.S. courts "have no jurisdiction to review the executive branch's conduct of its foreign and treaty relations." That ruling would be appealed to the U.S. Ninth Circuit Court of Appeals.[1]

In the publicity over the case and continuing headlines, deBrum himself had mixed reviews. The Nuclear Age Peace Foundation applauded the attempt to castigate the nations who still held nuclear weapons. In RMI, on the other hand, radio host Fred Pedro roundly denounced deBrum. Pedro recalled that when the TTPI ended, President Reagan had said "you will always be family to us." Pedro urged RMI officials to remember that sentiment, to "set aside our prejudices," and to "rejuvenate" the amity of alliance with the United States. Other voices ruled that the lawsuit was illegal in any case without a Nitijela endorsement, as required by the RMI Constitution.[2]

Second was the climate issue, with global warming having direct and visible effect in the Marshalls, a nation of low-lying islands. President Obama had long considered the threat of climate change a major issue for the United States and the world. He and Secretary of State John Kerry had already taken a leading role in addressing climate issues with Marshallese officials. Back in 2009, at the Climate conference held in Copenhagen, then Secretary of State Hillary Clinton had made a controversial proposal that "rich countries would mobilize $100 billion annually by 2020 to help poor countries."

The UN Climate Change Conference in Paris, France, held 30 November–12 December 2015, drew world attention. President Obama himself visited Paris and addressed attendees in the opening session. By the end of the conference, the resulting Paris Agreement proved an historic document of consensus, with representatives of 196 entities signing onto the goal of limiting global warming to fewer than two degrees (Celsius) as "compared to pre-industrial levels," though one serious flaw in the language of the agreement was "exclusion of the rights of indigenous people," which many had expected.[3]

A delegation of forty-four persons from RMI, headed by President Christopher Loeak, traveled to Paris and took part in the conference. Marshallese Foreign Minister Tony deBrum became the outspoken "poster child" for climate concerns. Interviewed on National Public Radio (NPR), deBrum quipped that the island nations needed more than a two-degrees commitment to limit warming, but a "one-point-five to stay alive." Then, in a front-page article of *The New York Times*, deBrum was in the spotlight again. With the headline: "Rising Seas are Claiming a Vulnerable Nation," reporter Coral Davenport quoted deBrum and expounded on ways in which the Marshalls exemplify the world crisis. Citing the need for migration to the U.S. as their islands disappear, the article pointed to communities of thousands of Marshallese already in towns such as Springdale, Arkansas, and Salem, Oregon. There were other communities as well, of course, for climate and other reasons. One 2014 statistic had estimated that already thirty percent of RMI citizens lived in Guam, Hawaii, and the mainland United States.[4]

Later, President Loeak would claim regarding the conference: "We took our message of hope and leadership to the world and they listened."[5] Returning to the Marshalls, however, the international travelers faced a "no-confidence" vote from critics of the administration in the RMI national election held in November.

In a surprisingly high turnout and clear demand for change, nine "government-aligned" incumbents lost seats in the Nitijela, including Foreign Minister Tony deBrum, Speaker Donald Capelle, and Health Minister Phillip Muller. Christopher Loeak retained his seat, but would not be elected for a second term as president.

In January 2016, the new Nitijela, composed of many first-time candidates, chose one of their own: a fresh face in young Marshallese leader, Casten Nemra. But in the thirty-three person assembly, an excruciatingly close vote of seventeen to sixteen promised that his term as president would not be smooth sailing. While Nemra spoke of a coalition cabinet with competing elements working for cooperation, various power factions would continue the contentious politics the Republic had often faced in the past. Quickly, the coalition would be challenged by a no-confidence vote.[6]

In eight previous no-confidence votes in RMI legislative history, only one had been successful in overturning a president. This would be the second, as Nemra's victory had been fragile and his term lasted less than two weeks. The coalition did not hold, but in a strong confidence vote, the Nitijela reached a new historical milestone with the election of Dr. Hilda Heine, who had been Minister of Education in the Loeak administration, was respected as a strong leader, and founder of Women United Together in the Marshall Islands. Dr. Heine, the first Marshallese person to hold a doctoral degree, also became the first female president of any independent nation of the Pacific islands. Her election as president quickly became an international news story.[7]

With the politics of both nations volatile, in November 2016, the American presidential election would determine the follow-on to President Obama's leadership, notably on the thirty-year anniversary of the Compact of Free Association between the U.S. and RMI in 1986. The challenges of the twenty-first century would be faced, and the postscript for this chronicle would be written, by the people of the Marshall Islands—and by American voters—who would decide in what way: "We too, of course, are a Pacific nation."

Chapter Notes

Introduction

1. Thomas K. Magstadt, *An Empire If You Can Keep It: Power and Principle in American Foreign Policy* (Washington, D.C.: CQ Press, 2004). Magstadt gives a succinct, astute discussion of the issue. He modifies the Franklin quote for his title.
2. Francis Hezel, *Making Sense of Micronesia: The Logic of Pacific Island Culture* (Honolulu: University of Hawai'i Press, 2013), 33; Niccolo Machiavelli, *The Prince* (Oxford: Oxford University Press, 2005). Machiavelli noted "…[one] must abstain from the property of others; because [people] sooner forget the death of [a parent] than the loss of their property."

Chapter One

1. David Hanlon, *Remaking Micronesia: Discourses Over Development in a Pacific Territory, 1944–1982* (Honolulu: University of Hawai'i Press, 1998), 189. Hanlon sees Kwajalein as one example where "colonialism had free rein," and as a "stage for empire revealed."
2. Tadao Yanaihara, *Pacific Islands Under Japanese Mandate*. International Research Series, Institute of Pacific Relations (Westport, CT: Greenwood Press, 1940), 1–2, 20; William Alkire, *An Introduction to Peoples and Cultures of Micronesia*. 2nd ed. (Menlo Park, CA: Cummings, 1977), 7–12; Robert F. Rogers, *Destiny's Landfall: A History of Guam* (Honolulu: University of Hawai'i Press, 1995), 22–23.
3. Donald Denoon, ed., *The Cambridge History of the Pacific Islanders* (Cambridge: Cambridge University Press, 1997), 8–9.
4. David Stanley, *Micronesia Handbook: Guide to an American Lake* (Chico, CA: Moon Publications, 1985); Yanaihara, 1–2; Bell Labs, *ABM Research and Development at Bell Laboratories: Kwajalein Field Station* (Whippany, NJ: Bell Labs for the U.S. Army Ballistic Missile Defense Systems Command, 1975), 5–6. Note: Marshallese spelling of Kwajalein would be *Kuwajleen*; spelling of Ebeye: *Ebeje*.
5. Neil M. Levy, *Micronesia Handbook*. 5th ed. Moon Travel Handbook (Emeryville, CA: Avalon Travel Publishing, 2000), 47; Laurence Marshall Carucci, *In Anxious Anticipation of Kuwajleen's Uneven Fruits: A Cultural History of the Significant Locations and Important Resources of Kuwajleen Atoll* (Huntsville, AL: U.S. Army Strategic Defense Command, 1996), 7–8.
6. Kate Galbraith, Glenda Bendure, and Ned Friary. *Micronesia*. 3rd ed. A Lonely Planet Survival Kit (Oakland, CA: Lonely Planet, 2000), 150; Alkire, 15.
7. E.J. Kahn, Jr., *A Reporter in Micronesia* (New York: W.W. Norton, 1966), 136; Winkler, *Report of the Sea Captain,* File no. 488. German Documents Relating to Micronesia, 1898–1910, trans. Stewart Firth and Paula Mochida. University of Hawai'i Archives (hereafter referred to as UHI Archives), 1986; *The Marshall Islands Journal* (hereafter referred to as *MI Journal*) 8 August 2014.
8. Giff Johnson, *Don't Ever Whisper—Darlene Keju: Pacific Health Pioneer, Champion for Nuclear Survivors* (CreateSpace Independent Publishing Platform, 2013), 154ff, 194–95, 273, 432–33, 437; *MI Journal* 24 July 2015: 22.
9. Carol Curtis, Interview with Author (September 1987); Norm Smith, Interview with Author (September 1987); Leonard Mason, ed., *The Laura Report*. An East-West Center Book (Honolulu: University of Hawai'i Press, 1967), 8–10; Carucci, *In Anxious Anticipation,* 22; Francis X. Hezel, *The New Shape of Old Island Cultures: A Half Century of Social Change in Micronesia* (Honolulu: University of Hawai'i Press, 2001), 47–48; Johnson, *Don't Ever Whisper,* 423; *MI Journal* 23 September

2013; Tobolar Ad: "Copra Products from the Marshall Islands," *MI Journal* 21 November 2014. Note: Other legends using the name *Tobolar* include "Tobolar, Coconut Boy." Note: See Epilogue for mention of "Women United Together in the Marshall Islands."
 10. Mason, *The Laura Report*, 8–10; See Carucci for more modern evidence in oral tradition.
 11. *MI Journal* 26 October 2012 and 15 November 2013; Natalie Nimmer, Interview with Author (May 2008); Hezel, *New Shape of Old Island Cultures*.
 12. Kahn, 75; Mason, *The Laura Report*, 15; Carucci, *In Anxious Anticipation*, 411.
 13. Daniel J. Boorstin, *The Americans: The National Experience* (New York: Vintage, 1965), 5, 7, 21–22; Nathaniel Philbrick, *Sea of Glory: America's Voyage of Discovery, The U.S. Exploring Expedition, 1838–1842* (New York: Viking, 2003). Philbrick modifies to: "the sea was a highway that led to just about anywhere in the world," xvi. Philbrick's fascinating chronicle of the voyage gives the entire story of Wilkes' personality and medical disasters on the expedition. This account follows only the part related to the Marshalls.
 14. Boorstin, 52, 244, 247.
 15. Ibid., 258, 266.
 16. Philbrick, *Sea of Glory*, xvi; "John Adams to John Jay, 1785." *Works of John Adams, Vol. 8*, 343–44, quote in Arthur Power Dudden, *The American Pacific: From the Old China Trade to the Present* (New York: Oxford University Press, 1992), 4; Boorstin, 7.
 17. Dudden, *The American Pacific*, 16; Philbrick, 24, 29, 31.
 18. Philbrick, *Sea of Glory*, 4, 32–33, 41, 45.
 19. Philbrick; William Reynolds, *The Private Journal of William Reynolds: United States Exploring Expedition, 1838–1842*, eds. Nathaniel Philbrick and Thomas Philbrick (New York: Penguin, 2004). Note: Artifacts from the Wilkes voyage became the origin of the Smithsonian Collection.
 20. Boorstin, 258; Norman A. Graebner, "James Polk," in *The American Empire in the Pacific: From Trade to Strategic Balance, 1700–1922*. The Pacific World: Lands, Peoples and History of the Pacific, 1500–1900. Vol. 9. ed. Arthur Power Dudden (Burlington, VT: Ashgate Variorum, 2004), 105–138.
 21. Francis X. Hezel, *First Taint of Civilization: A History of the Caroline and Marshall Islands in Pre-Colonial Days, 1521–1885*. Pacific Islands Monograph Series, Book 1 (Honolulu: University of Hawai'i Press, 2000), 23, 34, 197ff; Rogers, 17. Note: Routes of the Spanish Galleons tracked north of the Marshalls.
 22. Hezel, *First Taint of Civilization*, 200; *MI Journal* 30 August 2013.
 23. Dudden, *The American Pacific*, 50–52; Hezel, *First Taint of Civilization*, 63–65; *MI Journal* 19 September 2014. Note: Some argue that the Marshall Islands should deny their Western appellate and reclaim their indigenous name, *Aelon Kein*, "Our Islands." This name was taken by "Aelon Kein Ad," or the Kabua Party, which became part of controversial politics in the twenty-first century.
 24. Dudden, *The American Pacific*, 3ff; Carol Curtis, *Handicrafts*, Alele National Archives, Library, and Museum, Majuro, Marshall Islands, 7; Harold F. Nufer, *Micronesia Under American Rule: An Evaluation of the Strategic Trusteeship (1947–77)* (Hicksville, NY: Exposition Press, 1978), 4.
 25. Tom Coffman, *Nation Within: The Story of America's Annexation of the Nation of Hawai'i* (Honolulu: EpiCenter Press, 1998); Dudden, *The American Pacific*, 56.
 26. Hezel, *First Taint of Civilization*, 201; Francis X. Hezel and M.L. Berg, eds., documents in *Micronesia Winds of Change: A Book of Readings on Micronesian History* (Saipan, Mariana Islands: Omnibus Program for Social Studies Cultural Heritage, 1979); Document 11, 257; George Pierson, "Missionary Herald, March 1858," quoted in *The Friend*, Honolulu 1 May 1863: 20–38, 1, document in Gerard R. Ward, ed., *American Activities in the Central Pacific, 1790–1870: A History, Geography, and Ethnography Pertaining to American Involvement and Americans in the Pacific Taken from Contemporary Newspapers, etc*. Vol. 7 (Upper Saddle River, NJ: Gregg Press, 1967), 435ff.
 27. Hezel, *First Taint of Civilization*, 203, 207.
 28. Ward, 438.
 29. Hezel, *First Taint of Civilization*, 201; Hezel and Berg, eds., *Micronesia Winds of Change*, 262; Ward, 435–37.
 30. Ward, 328, 445.
 31. Hezel, *First Taint of Civilization*, 203–04.
 32. Hezel, *First Taint of Civilization*, 207; Francis Hezel, *Strangers in Their Own Land: A Century of Colonial Rule in the Caroline and Marshall Islands*. Pacific Islands Monograph Series 13 (Honolulu: University of Hawai'i Press, 2003), 51, 125. Note: Disease reduced the population by thirty percent. "Retro 1974" *MI Journal* 5 December 2014. Native Population "before Western contact," estimated in 1974 at 25,000. Nimmer, Interview with Author (May 2008): Nimmer reflected that casual sex and babies were "no big deal."
 33. Hezel, *First Taint of Civilization*, 206–07; Hezel, *Strangers in Their Own Land*, 25–27, 34–39, 89ff.
 34. Hezel, *First Taint of Civilization*, 207–09; Ward, 442.
 35. Junius B. Wood, "Japan's Mandate in

the Pacific." *Asia* XXI.9 (September 1921): 747–53.

Chapter Two

1. Stewart Firth, "German Firms in the Pacific Islands, 1857–1914," in *Germany in the Pacific and Far East, 1870–1914*. eds. John A. Moses and Paul M. Kennedy (Brisbane, Australia: University of Queensland Press, 1977), 4, 6, 21.
2. Francis X. Hezel, *Strangers in Their Own Land: A Century of Colonial Rule in the Caroline and Marshall Islands*. Pacific Islands Monograph Series 13 (Honolulu: Hawai'i University Press, 2003), 48.
3. Quoted in Hezel, *Strangers in Their Own Land*, 46, 50–51.
4. Mary Evelyn Townsend, *The Rise and Fall of Germany's Colonial Empire, 1884–1918* (New York: Macmillan, 1930), 58; A.J.P. Taylor, *Bismarck: The Man and the Statesman* (New York: Vintage, 1967), 227–28.
5. Taylor, 215; Townsend, 66–67.
6. Richard G. Brown, "The German Acquisition of the Caroline Islands, 1898–99," in *Germany in the Pacific and Far East, 1870–1914*, eds. John A. Moses and Paul M. Kennedy, 138; Francis X. Hezel, *First Taint of Civilization: A History of the Caroline and Marshall Islands in Pre-Colonial Days, 1521–1885*. Pacific Islands Monograph Series, Book 1 (Honolulu: University of Hawai'i Press, 2000), 300–301; Akira Iriye, *Japan and the Wider World: From the Mid-Nineteenth Century to the Present* (London: Longman, 1997); Mark R. Peattie, *Nan'yō: The Rise and Fall of the Japanese in Micronesia, 1885–1945*. Pacific Islands Monograph Series, No. 4 (Honolulu: University of Hawai'i Press, 1988).
7. Tadao Yanaihara, *Pacific Islands Under Japanese Mandate*. International Research Series, Institute of Pacific Relations (Westport, CT: Greenwood Press, 1940), 18–19; Brown, 138; Townsend, 68; Jeannette Keim, "Forty Years of German-American Political Relations" (dissertation, University of Pennsylvania, 1919), 128.
8. Brown, 138; Yanaihara, 18.
9. Hezel, *First Taint of Civilization*, 299; Firth, "German Firms in the Pacific," 6–7; Taylor, 208.
10. German Document #19 "Stuckhardt, District Officer, Jaluit, 2 February 1909." German Documents Relating to Micronesia, trans. Stewart Firth and Paula Mochida. University of Hawai'i Archives (hereafter referred to as UHI Archives), 1986, 2–4.
11. Francis Hezel, *Strangers in Their Own Land*, 45–52.
12. "Treaty of Friendship Between the Marshallese Chiefs and the German Empire (1885)." *Marshall Islands History Sources No. 18 in the series Kirchen-und Schulsachen* 2h no 3. File no RKA2606. National Library of Australia, Canberra. Microfilm no. G8557, UHI Archives.
13. Leonard Mason, ed., *The Laura Report*. An East-West Center Book (Honolulu: University of Hawai'i Press, 1967), 15–16, 23; Carol Curtis, *Handicrafts*, Alele National Archives, Library, and Museum, Majuro, Marshall Islands, 20; German Document #24 *"Merz, for the District Officer, Jaluit, 16 September 1910,"* UHI Archives, 1986, 1.
14. Hezel, *Strangers in Their Own Land*, 124.
15. German Document #13 *"Sigwanz, Actiing Governor, Jaluit, 12 November 1907,"* 2–3; German Document #24 *"Merz, for the District Officer, Jaluit, 16 September 1910,"* UHI Archives, 1986.
16. German Document #17 "Stuckhardt, District Officer, Jaluit, 30 September 1908," 51; German Document #18 "Ahlert, 'Condor,' Truk, 27 October 1908," UHI Archives, 1986, 1.
17. German Document #20 "Hahl, Governor, Herbertshöhe, 30 March 1909," UHI Archives, 1986, 1–2.
18. William Reynolds, *The Private Journal of William Reynolds: United States Exploring Expedition, 1838–1842*. eds. Nathaniel Philbrick and Thomas Philbrick (New York: Penguin, 2004).
19. Charles Wilkes, "Narrative IV," quoted in Willis Edward Snowbarger, "The Development of Pearl Harbor" (dissertation, University of California, Berkeley, Graduate Division, Northern Section, 1950), 42.
20. *United States Senate Executive Documents, 52nd. Cong., 2d. sess., Document Number 77*, document in Arthur Power Dudden, *The American Pacific: From the Old China Trade to the Present* (New York: Oxford University Press, 1992), 58–59.
21. United States. Department of State. *Foreign Relations of the United States (FRUS), 1894: Affairs in Hawaii: Appendix II*, 39–41; William Michael Morgan, *Pacific Gibraltar: U.S.-Japanese Rivalry Over the Annexation of Hawai'i, 1885–1898* (Annapolis, MD: Naval Institute Press, 2011), 12–13; Edward P. Crapol, *James G. Blaine: Architect of Empire*. Biographies in American Foreign Policy, 4 (Washington, D.C.: Rowman and Littlefield, 1999), 7.
22. Morgan, 16ff; Jonathan K. Osorio, *Dismembering Lahui: A History of the Hawaiian Nation to 1887* (Honolulu: University of Hawai'i Press, 2002), quoted in Morgan, 50.
23. Morgan, 20; Crapol, 77.
24. Foster Rhea Dulles, *America in the Pacific: A Century of Expansion* (Boston: Houghton

Mifflin, 1938), 100–103; Hezel, *First Taint of Civilization*, 211.
25. Dulles, 104, 107.
26. Crapol, 12, 45, 115, 117; Dulles, 109.
27. Hezel, *First Taint of Civilization*, 306, 311–12.
28. Taylor, 202, 208, 212.
29. Great Britain would remain in Germany's corner, having signed another treaty of reciprocity, 6 April 1886, dividing Western Pacific (Samoa exempt), noted below in the text. Keim, 154; Dulles, 113. Dulles calls this "South Pacific." In exchange for German support of British colonial ventures in New Guinea, Egypt, and Africa. Dulles, 121–23; Keim, 192–93.
30. Hezel, *First Taint of Civilization*, 312–13.
31. Dulles, 113.
32. Holger H. Herwig, *Politics of Frustration: The United States in German Naval Planning, 1889–1941* (New York: Little, Brown, 1976), 15.
33. Marcus Jones, "Strategy as Character: Bismarck and the Prussian-German Question, 1862–1878," in *The Shaping of Grand Strategy, Policy, Diplomacy, and War*. eds. Williamson Murray, Richard Hart Sinnreich, and James Lacey (Cambridge: Cambridge University Press, 2011), 86; Taylor, 228.
34. Dulles, 126; Crapol, 116; Morgan, 25–26; Document in Keim, 195; Keim, 194.
35. Firth, "German Firms in the Pacific," 3, 17; Morgan, 167–69.
36. Dudden, *The American Pacific*, 66; Adams quote in Walter LaFeber, *The New Empire: An Interpretation of American Expansion 1860–1898* (Ithaca, NY: Cornell University Press, 1998), 54; Bayard quoted in Snowbarger, 68.
37. Dudden, *The American Pacific*, 66–67; Morgan, 15ff. Morgan makes the struggle for political control the subject of his entire book.
38. Dudden, *The American Pacific*, 67–68; Morgan, 118–23. Morgan dismisses Cleveland's effort as "his own obscure reasons."
39. Snowbarger, 61; Crapol, 78; Morgan, 27, 40–41.
40. A.T. Mahan, "A Twentieth-Century Outlook," *Harper's New Monthly Magazine* (September 1897): 525.
41. Morgan, 169–70.
42. Thomas K. Magstadt, *An Empire if You Can Keep It: Power and Principle in American Foreign Policy* (Washington, D.C.: CQ Press, 2004), 57–59; Morgan, 178; LaFeber, *The New Empire*, 303–04.
43. Richard E. Welch, *Response to Imperialism: The United States and the Philippine-American War, 1899–1902* (Chapel Hill: University of North Carolina Press, 1987), 8; LaFeber, *The New Empire*, 413–16; Evan Thomas, *The War Lovers: Roosevelt, Lodge,* *Hearst, and the Rush to Empire, 1898* (New York: Back Bay Books, 2011); Morgan, 172ff.
44. Morgan, 201; Ronald Spector, *Eagle Against the Sun: The American War With Japan* (New York: Vintage, 1985), 44.
45. Morgan, 44–45, 112.
46. LaFeber, *The New Empire*, 408–10; Morgan, 206–17; Brown, 140–41.
47. Welch, 4–5; Herwig, 28–29.
48. Welch, 6.
49. Brown, 143–48; Keim, 222–23, 230–33.
50. Jackson to Hay, 29 December 1898, document in Brown, 148.
51. Brown, 149.
52. Quoted in Townsend, 197.
53. Welch, 17–18; LaFeber, *The New Empire*, 416.
54. Herwig, 33–34; Brown, 148.
55. Publicado en el numero 180 dl la GACETA DE MADRED, Tomo II, pagina 151 el dia 29 de Junio de 1899, translated by Sarah Bradham.
56. Keim, 212; Document in Keim, 195.
57. Dulles, 135; Document in Keim, 212. In July 1900, indigenous chiefs formally ceded Tuituila to the United States, while in 1929, the U.S. Congress formally accepted American Samoa as a U.S. territory under administrative control of the U.S. Navy Department. Dulles, 131.
58. Hay to Joseph H. Choate, quoted in Keim, 213.
59. Townsend, 196; Hezel, *First Taint of Civilization*, 304.

Chapter Three

1. Eric T. Love, *Race Over Empire: Racism and U.S. Imperialism, 1865–1900* (Chapel Hill: University of North Carolina Press, 2004); Howard Jones, *Crucible of Power: A History of American Foreign Relations from 1897* (Washington, D.C.: Rowman and Littlefield, 2008), 24; Willis Edward Snowbarger, "The Development of Pearl Harbor" (dissertation, University of California, Berkeley, Graduate Division, Northern Section, 1950), 119–23. Note: Final dredging of Pearl Harbor in 1903 and celebration of the occasion, 14 December 1911.
2. United States. Department of State. *Foreign Relations of the United States (FRUS), 1901: Affairs in China: Appendix*, 12; 372; Walter LaFeber, *The Clash: U.S.–Japanese Relations Throughout History* (New York: W.W. Norton, 1998), 69–70.
3. Akira Iriye, *Pacific Estrangement: Japanese and American Expansion, 1897–1911*. Harvard Studies in American-East Asian Relations (Boston: Harvard University Press, 1972), *preface*, 18.

4. Mark R. Peattie, *Nan'yō: The Rise and Fall of the Japanese in Micronesia, 1885–1945*. Pacific Islands Monograph Series, No.4 (Honolulu: University of Hawai'i Press, 1988), 9–12, 322, 362; Sketches in "Taiheiyo Gakkai shi," (22 April 1984): 59. See Peattie, 362.
5. Francis X. Hezel, *Strangers in Their Own Land: A Century of Colonial Rule in the Caroline and Marshall Islands*. Pacific Islands Monograph Series 13 (Honolulu: University of Hawai'i Press, 2003), 5, 75–76; Peattie, *Nan'yō*, preface, note *xviii*. Note: Use of Nanyo-"South Seas" used for mandated islands for simplicity and consistency despite its ambiguity in Japanese usage for islands north of the equator.
6. Akira Iriye, *Japan and the Wider World: From the Mid-Nineteenth Century to the Present* (London: Longman, 1997), 14.
7. Iriye, *Pacific Estrangement*, 20.
8. Peattie, *Nan'yō*, 10, 12.
9. Stewart Firth, "German Firms in the Pacific Islands, 1857–1914," in *Germany in the Pacific and Far East, 1870–1914*. eds. John A. Moses and Paul M. Kennedy (Brisbane, Australia: University of Queensland Press, 1977); Hezel, *Strangers in Their Own Land*, 45ff; Peattie, *Nan'yō*, 25.
10. Peattie, *Nan'yō*, 1.
11. Iriye, *Pacific Estrangement*, 84; Yano Toru, Nihon ... [Japan's historical view of the South Seas], 1979, quoted in Peattie, *Nan'yō* , 37, 367.
12. Iriye, *Pacific Estrangement*, 85; LaFeber, *The Clash*, 57, 62.
13. Peattie, *Nan'yō*, 34; Iriye, *Japan and the Wider World*, 16–17.
14. Paul H. Clyde, *Japan's Pacific Mandate* (New York: Macmillan, 1935), 21.
15. LaFeber, *The Clash*, 82; W.G. Beasley, *The Rise of Modern Japan: Political, Economic, and Social Change Since 1850* (New York: St. Martin's Press, 1995), 151; Iriye, *Pacific Estrangement*, 103.
16. Charles E. Neu, *The Troubled Encounter: The United States and Japan* (Malabar, FL: Krieger, 1979), 53–55.
17. Walter LaFeber, *The American Search for Opportunity, 1865–1913*. The Cambridge History of American Foreign Relations Volume II (Cambridge: Cambridge University Press, 1998), 98–99; LaFeber, *The Clash*, 44–47, 85–87; Iriye, *Japan and the Wider World*, 16; Iriye, *Pacific Estrangement*, 80, 83; James Bradley, *The Imperial Cruise: A Secret History of Empire and War* (New York: Back Bay, 2010), 208.
18. Pettie, *Nan'yō* , 39; LaFeber, *The Clash*, 76; Bradley, 210.
19. Margaret MacMillan, *Paris 1919: Six Months That Changed the World* (New York: Random House, 2001), 312.
20. Sachiko Hatanaka, *Culture Change in Micronesia Under the Japanese Administration*. Programme of Participation, No. 4 (Paris: UNESCO, 1973), 1–4; Peattie, *Nan'yō*, 39–44.
21. Hatanaka, 1–4; Peattie, *Nan'yō*, 25.
22. Mark R. Peattie, "The Nan'yō: Japan in the South Pacific," in *The Japanese Colonial Empire, 1895–1945*. eds. Mark R. Peattie and Ramon H. Myers. (Princeton, NJ: Princeton University Press, 1987), 181; Peattie, *Nan'yō*, 44–47; Jackson Treat Payson, *The Far East: A Political and Diplomatic History* (New York: Harper, 1928); LaFeber, *The Clash*, 113; Samuel Flagg Bemis, "The Yap Island Controversy," *The Pacific Review* 2 (September 1921): 312. Note: In common usage *haole* usually refers to American whites.
23. LaFeber, *The Clash*, 112–14.
24. David Hunter Miller, *My Diary at the Conference of Paris* (New York: G.P. Putnam's Sons, 1928), 100. "We had sent 7,000 troops to Siberia and they promised to send about the same number but had sent 70,000 and had occupied at the strategic points as far as Irkutsk..." Miller's account of the entire conference refutes Throntveit's charge that Wilson remained "isolated" and "kept his own counsel." Trygve Throntveit, "The Fable of the Fourteen Points: Woodrow Wilson and National Self-Determination," *Diplomatic History* 35.3 (June 2011): 445–81.
25. Bemis, "Yap"; Memorandum, Breckinridge Long, Third Under Secretary of State, 14 December 1918, in *FRUS, 1919: The Paris Peace Conference, Vol. II*, 512; 514.
26. Miller, *My Diary*, 151.
27. Huntington Gilchrist, *Imperialism and the Mandates System*. Published for the League of Nations Non-Partisan Association by the Margaret C. Peabody Fund (New York: Margaret C. Peabody Fund, 1928), 636; Miller, *My Diary*, 100.
28. David Hunter Miller, *The Drafting of the Covenant*. 2 vols. (New York: G.P. Putnam's Sons, 1928), 45; LaFeber, *The Clash*, 80; Bradley, 193, 242–43.
29. Miller, *My Diary*, 204; LaFeber, *The Clash*, 114.
30. Miller, *My Diary*, 184, 187–88.
31. LaFeber, *The Clash*, 109, 123; Bemis, 315–16.
32. Miller, *My Diary*, 132–33, 143, 161.
33. Iriye, *Pacific Estrangement*, 103.
34. Miller, *My Diary*, 188; LaFeber, *The Clash*, 123–24.
35. A.T. Mahan, "A Twentieth-Century Outlook," *Harper's New Monthly Magazine* (September 1897): 525; Bradley; LaFeber, *The Clash*, 79–80; Thomas G. Dyer, *Theodore Roosevelt and the Idea of Race* (Baton Rouge: Louisiana State University Press, 1992).
36. Love, 200; Jeffrey A. Keith, "Civilization,

Race, and the Japan Expedition's Cultural Diplomacy, 1853–1854," *Diplomatic History* 35.2 (April 2011): 179–202; William Michael Morgan, *Pacific Gibraltar: U.S.-Japanese Rivalry Over the Annexation of Hawai`i, 1885–1898* (Annapolis, MD: Naval Institute Press, 2011).
37. Miller, *My Diary*, 361.
38. Wilson's State of the Union Speech to Congress, December 1913, document in Erez Manela, *The Wilsonian Moment: Self-Determination and the International Origins of Anticolonial Nationalism*. Oxford Studies in International History (Oxford: Oxford University Press, 2009), 31.
39. Manela, 31, 60–61, 219.
40. Miller, *My Diary*, 188; Manela, 222.
41. Miller, *The Drafting of the Covenant*, 36; LaFeber, *The Clash*, 125–26; Noriko Kawamura "Wilsonian Idealism and Japanese Claims at the Paris Peace Conference," *Pacific Historical Review* 66.4 (November 1997): 503–26.
42. Throntveit, 445–81; Erez Manela, "Woodrow Who?" *Diplomatic History* 35.1 (27 December 2010): 76, review of *Reconsidering Woodrow Wilson: Progressivism, Internationalism, War, and Peace*. ed. John Milton Cooper (Baltimore, MD: Johns Hopkins University Press, 2008); Kawamura, 19. The Washington Conference finally ended the Anglo-Japanese Alliance, noted below in the text.
43. Miller, *The Drafting of the Covenant*, 589.
44. Miller, *My Diary*, 103.
45. Transcript of the hearing found in Bemis, 318–19.
46. LaFeber, *The Clash*, 140–42.
47. Peattie, *Nan'yō*, 60–61.
48. The League of Nations, *Official Journal, First Year No. 1*. Geneva, Switzerland, February 1920, 9; *Official Journal, Second Year No. 1*. Geneva, Switzerland, 1921, 1. Allen J. Greenberger, "Japan as a Colonial Power: The Micronesian Example," *Asian Profile* 2.2 (April 1974): 151–63.
49. The League of Nations. *Annual Report to the League of Nations on the Administration of the South Sea Islands Under Japanese Mandate for Year 1922*. Prepared by the Japanese Government. Geneva, Switzerland. PAC DU29 S59a 1922, University of Hawai'i Archives (hereafter referred to as UHI Archives); Felix Moos and Grant Kohn Goodman, eds., *United States and Japan in the Western Pacific: Micronesia and Papua New Guinea* (Boulder, CO: Westview Press, 1981), 1–2; 4.
50. Leonard Mason, "A Marshallese Nation Emerges from the Political Fragmentation of American Micronesia," *Pacific Studies* 13.1 (1989): 16; Greenberger, 152–61; *Annual Report to the League of Nations for Year 1922*, UHI Archives, 3.
51. *Annual Report to the League of Nations on the Administration of the South Sea Islands Under Japanese Mandate for Year 1925*. Prepared by the Japanese Government. Geneva, Switzerland. 19270 1933, UHI Archives; *Annual Report to the League of Nations for Year 1922*, UHI Archives; Junius B. Wood, "Japan's Mandate in the Pacific," *Asia* XXI.9 (September 1921): 749.
52. Greenberger, 159; Hatanaka, 10; Greenberger, 157.
53. Ella Theodora Crosby Bliss, *Micronesia Fifty Years in the Island World: A History of the Mission of the American Board* (Ann Arbor: University of Michigan Press, 2009), 1906; Microfilm, Reel no. 0282, Frame no. 47, Trust Territory of the Pacific Islands Archives, University of Hawai'i Archives (hereafter referred to as TTPI Archives, UHI Archives).
54. Moos, 15; Interviews with Author: Oscar de Brum (September 1987), 7; Norm Smith (September 1987), 7; Carol Curtis (September 1987), 9; Greenberger, 155.
55. Greenberger, 156; Thomas Gilliland, Land Title Officer, *Concepts of Land Ownership and Riparian Rights in the Marshall Islands*, 2; 8 March 1959, Microfilm, Reel no. 0003, Frame no. 198, 2: A, TTPI Archives, UHI Archives.
56. David Stanley, *Micronesia Handbook: Guide to an American Lake* (Chico, CA: Moon Publications, 1985), 55; Norm Smith, Interview with Author (September 1987).
57. *The Marshall Islands Journal* (hereafter referred to as *MI Journal*), reports documented throughout 2014 and 2015.
58. Moos, 9.
59. Jack A. Tobin, "Land Tenure in the Marshall Islands." 1952. Microfilm, 28ff, Reel no. 32, Frame no. 150, TTPI Archives, UHI Archives.
60. *Annual Report to the League of Nations for Year 1922*, 15; Hatanaka, 12.
61. Greenberger, 153.
62. Moos, 10; Hatanaka, 5.
63. Wood, 748; Mason, 16.
64. Wood, 762, 766; Naomasa Yamasaki, *Micronesia and Micronesians*. Preliminary Paper Prepared for Second General Session of the Institute of Pacific Relations. Honolulu, 15–29 July 1927. UHI Archives, 9; Moos, 5, 9.
65. Yamasaki, 5; *Annual Report to the League of Nations for Year 1922*, UHI Archives, 6; *Civil Affairs Handbook. Marshall Islands Statistical Supplement. OPNAV 50E-18. Office of the Chief of Naval Operations, 20 May 1944* (Washington, D.C.: U.S. Government Printing Office, 1944); *Annual Report to the League of Nations on the Administration of the South Sea Islands Under Japanese Mandate for Year 1926*. Prepared by the Japanese Government. Geneva, Switzerland, 103; Hatanaka, 6.
66. Hatanaka, 7; Peattie, "The Nan'yō," 197;

Greenberger, 155; Hatanaka, 8; *Annual Report to the League of Nations for Year 1926.*
   67. Mark R. Peattie, "The Nan'yō," 199–201.
   68. Hezel, *Strangers in Their Own Land,* 217; LaFeber, *The Clash,* 176.
   69. Oscar de Brum, Interview with Author (September 1987), 4–7.
   70. *Annual Report to the League of Nations for Year 1922,* UHI Archives, 7; Wood, 1–4; Hezel, *Strangers in Their Own Land,* 218.
   71. Mason, 18; Greenberger, 151, 164.

Chapter Four

   1. Eri Hotta, *Japan 1941: Countdown to Infamy* (New York: Knopf, 2013), 21. Hotta feels it "utterly inadequate" to say "inevitable" in the decision of Yamamoto, who against the war, would favor the attack at Pearl Harbor and risk a "national gamble."
   2. Warren F. Kimball, *Forged in War: Roosevelt, Churchill, and the Second World War* (Chicago: Ivan R. Dee, 1997), 30.
   3. Mark D. Roehrs and William A. Renzi, *World War II in the Pacific,* 2nd ed. (New York: Routledge, 2003), 25; Francis Pike, *Hirohito's War: The Pacific War, 1941–1945* (London: Bloomsbury, 2015), 80.
   4. Roehrs and Renzi, 16; Walter LaFeber, *The Clash: U.S.-Japanese Relations Throughout History* (New York: W.W. Norton, 1998), 153–59.
   5. LaFeber, *The Clash,* 168ff.
   6. Roehrs and Renzi, 30; LaFeber, *The Clash,* 186–88.
   7. Ronald Spector, *Eagle Against the Sun: The American War With Japan* (New York: Vintage, 1985), 55–59; Pike, 187.
   8. Spector, 78–81; Pike, 406.
   9. Spector, 79; Pike, 164.
   10. Pike, 164–68, 182–84; Spector, 79.
   11. LaFeber, *The Clash,* 192–93; Pike, 407; Roehrs and Renzi, 32.
   12. Spector, 60–61.
   13. Kimball, 13, 23, 31; LaFeber, *The Clash,* 194.
   14. LaFeber, *The Clash,* 186–213.
   15. Spector, 84.
   16. Burton Wright, *Eastern Mandates: The U.S. Army Campaigns of World War II.* Publication 72–23 (Washington, D.C.: Center of Military History, 1993), 3; Walter R. Borneman, *The Admirals: Nimitz, Halsey, Leahy, and King—The Five-Star Admirals Who Won the War at Sea* (New York: Back Bay, 2013), 223, 231–33.
   17. LaFeber, *The Clash,* 223–24.
   18. Wright, 8; Philip A. Crowl and Edmund G. Love, *U.S. Army in World War II. The War in the Pacific: Seizure of the Gilberts and Marshalls* (Center of Military History, U.S. Army, Washington, D.C.: U.S. Government Printing Office, 1955), 7–9; Pike, 618, 794.
   19. Pike, 327; Borneman, 241; Spector, 73–74.
   20. Pike, 327; Wright, map, 4–5.
   21. Crowl and Love, *vii,* 14, 17.
   22. Wright, 3, 6–7; Borneman, 325; Crowl and Love, 17.
   23. Pike, 794; Spector, 267–68; Borneman, 230.
   24. Crowl and Love, 101, 125–26.
   25. Joseph H. Alexander, *Utmost Savagery: The Three Days of Tarawa* (Annapolis, MD: Naval Institute Press, 2008); Pike, 810.
   26. Crowl and Love, 157, 159–61, 165; Borneman, 347–48; Pike, 800, 810–12.
   27. Wright, 7–8.
   28. Pike, 376; Wright, 9–10.
   29. Crowl and Love, 302.
   30. Crowl and Love, 212, 216; Gordon L. Rottman, *The Marshall Islands 1944: Operation Flintlock, the Capture of Kwajalein and Eniwetok.* Campaign 146 (Oxford: Osprey, 2004), 9, 12, 27. Note: Commanding the operation: Vice-Admiral Raymond A. Spruance commanded the Fifth Fleet; Rear-Admiral Richmond Kelly Turner commanded the Fifth Amphibious Force; Marine Corps Major General Holland M. Smith commanded the V Amphibious Corps, the principal landing force; Army Major General Charles H. Corlett commanded the Army 7th Infantry Division.
   31. Crowl and Love, 173; Wright, 12–15; Rottman, 56.
   32. Pike, 816–17; Crowl and Love, 177.
   33. Wright, 14–16; Pike, 818–20. See photo: Plaque on Japanese ruin-defense fortification, east coast of Kwajalein Island.
   34. Wright, 20–24; Rottman, 18; Crowl and Love, 366.
   35. Ian W. Toll, *The Conquering Tide: War in the Pacific Islands, 1942–1944.* Pacific War Trilogy (New York: W.W. Norton, 2015), 397.
   36. Pike, 820; "Lieutenant General, Robert C. Richardson," 1–2, Center of Military History Archives (hereafter referred to as CMH Archives).
   37. "Lieutenant General, Robert C. Richardson," CMH Archives, 2; Dorothy E. Richard, *United States Naval Administration of the Trust Territory of the Pacific Islands. Vol. 1, The Wartime Military Government Period,* Office of the Chief of Naval Operations (Washington, D.C.: U.S. Government Printing Office, 1957), 338.
   38. G. H. Matsinger, Major Sanitary Corps; James H. Reid, 1st Lieutenant, COE, "Sewage Disposal, Kwajalein Island," 1, Annex 7, typed manuscript, CMH Archives; Bell Labs. *ABM Research and Development at Bell Laboratories:*

Kwajalein Field Station (Whippany, NJ: Bell Labs for the U.S. Army Ballistic Missile Defense Systems Command, 1975), 60.

39. Matsinger and Reid, 4, 8; CMH Archives; Richard, 350.

40. Oscar de Brum, Interview with Author (September 1987), 9–10, 15–16.

41. Oscar de Brum, Interview with Author, 17; Richard, 338.

42. Richard, 335, 338–39, 344–45, 359, 363, 366.

43. Richard, 335–36, 339.

44. Richard, 16.

45. Richard, 15A; Admiral Radford, Chairman of the Joint Chiefs of Staff, foreword in Richard, vi; Richard E. Welch, *Response to Imperialism: The United States and the Philippine-American War, 1899–1902* (Chapel Hill: University of North Carolina Press, 1987), 13–18, 163–64.

46. Richard, 2, 74; United States. Department of the Navy, *Military Government Handbook. OPNAV P22–1 (Formerly OPNAV 50E-1): Marshall Islands. Office of the Chief of Naval Operations, 17 August 1943* (Washington, D.C.: U.S. Government Printing Office, 1943); Richard, 760.

47. Richard, 17–19, 62–63; 79; United States. Department of the Navy. *Handbook on the Trust Territory of the Pacific Islands: A Handbook for Use in Training and Administration. Office of the Chief of Naval Operations.* Prepared at the School of Naval Administration, Hoover Institute, Stanford University (Washington, D.C.: U.S. Government Printing Office, 1948); Richard, 760.

48. Richard, 62–63, 355, 358.

49. Quoted in Richard, 339.

50. Majuro Field Order No. 7, 11 March 1944, signed: V.F. Grant, Captain, United States Navy, Island CMD, Majuro Subu, "Establishing Buying Prices for Articles of Native Handiwork." Microfilm, Reel no. 0001, Frame no. 83, TTPI Archives, UHI Archives ; E.A. Cruise, Captain U.S. Navy, no date, Microfilm, Reel no. 0001, Frame no. 84.

51. Richard, 370–71.

52. Richard, 336; "Proclamation No. One, Appendix No. 2," Richard, 651–52.

53. Richard, 376. Italics added.

54. Richard, 374–77; R.J. Umhoefer, Acting High Commissioner, 27 May 1957. Microfilm, Reel no. 452, Frame no. 81, TTPI Archives, UHI Archives.

55. Richard, Appendix 7. Excerpt from Special Order No. 1.

56. Richard, Appendix 7, 71.

57. Richard, Appendix 7, 11; Majuro Ordinance No. 3, 1 March 1944, Microfilm, Reel no. 0001, Frame no. 84, TTPI Archives, UHI Archives; Richard, 350.

58. *Majuro Order No. 4, 11 March 1944*, Microfilm, Reel no. 0001, Frame no. 83, TTPI Archives, UHI Archives.

59. Richard, 382–83, 408–09; David Hanlon, *Remaking Micronesia: Discourses Over Development in a Pacific Territory, 1944–1982* (Honolulu: University of Hawai'i Press, 1998), 29. Note: In the twenty-first century, handicrafts would regain value as means for self-respect. See Giff Johnson, *Don't Ever Whisper—Darlene Keju: Pacific Health Pioneer, Champion for Nuclear Survivors* (CreateSpace Independent Publishing Platform, 2013); *The Marshall Islands Journal*, 2014. Hanlon sees the Navy's effort as economic imperialism. Perhaps better would be his example in Yap in western Micronesia, where the islanders furiously resisted resort tourism development in the 1970s. See Hanlon, 124–25.

60. Richard, 403; Jack A. Tobin, "Ebeye Village: A Typical Marshallese Community, 18 February 1954," 3ff, Microfilm, Reel no. 0282, Frame no. 173, TTPI Archives, UHI Archives.

61. Richard, 403–04.

62. Richard, 405–06.

63. Tobin, "Ebeye Village," 3, TTPI Archives, UHI Archives.

64. Maynard Neas to D.H. Nucker, 10 January 1955, Microfilm, Reel no. 452, Frame no. 8, TTPI Archives, UHI Archives.

65. Richard, Appendix 2; Proclamation No. 5, 661; Richard, 424.

66. "Narrative History of the Negotiations for the Acquisition by the Trust Territory Government of Roi-Namur for Defense Use by the United States." Typed manuscript, October 1970. Microfilm, Reel no. 506, Frame no. 105, TTPI Archives, UHI Archives; *TTPI History, 1949*, TTPI Archives, UHI Archives; 1954 letter and list dated 1953, "Islands … Kwajalein Atoll occupied…"

67. Richard, 425.

Chapter Five

1. Quoted in Walter LaFeber, *The American Age: United States Foreign Policy at Home and Abroad, Vol. 2: Since 1896* (New York: W.W. Norton, 1994), 434.

2. United Nations, "History of the United Nations, 1941–1950," http://www.un.org.

3. Ronald Ian Heiferman, *The Cairo Conference of 1943: Roosevelt, Churchill, Chiang Kai-shek and Madame Chiang* (Jefferson, NC: McFarland, 2011), 43, 59, 99, 103, 112, 120–22, 169.

4. Cordell Hull, *The Memoirs of Cordell Hull*. 2 Vols. (New York: Macmillan, 1948).

5. United States. Department of State. *Foreign Relations of the United States (FRUS)*,

1945: Conferences at Malta and Yalta, 859, 993.
 6. Hal M. Friedman, *Arguing Over the American Lake: Bureaucracy and Rivalry in the U.S. Pacific, 1945–1947*. Williams-Ford Texas A&M University Military History Series No. 126 (College Station: Texas A&M University Press, 2009), 129.
 7. *FRUS: Conferences at Malta and Yalta*, 993.
 8. Hull, 1235, 1706; Leland M. Goodrich and Marie J. Carroll, eds. *Documents on American Foreign Relations, Volume VI: July 1943–June 1944* (Boston: World Peace Foundation, 1945), 442; *FRUS, Conferences at Malta and Yalta*, 844.
 9. Walter LaFeber, *The Clash: U.S.-Japanese Relations Throughout History* (New York: W.W. Norton, 1998) 239; Thomas G. Patterson, *American Foreign Policy: A History* (Lexington, MA: D.C. Heath, 1977), 413.
 10. *FRUS: Conferences at Malta and Yalta*, 94.
 11. Friedman, *Arguing Over the American Lake*, 129.
 12. *Memorandum from James Clement Dunn, Assistant Secretary of State and Chairman of the Coordinating Committee to Cordell Hull*, in *FRUS: Conferences at Malta and Yalta*, 93–95.
 13. Stephen C. Schlesinger, *Act of Creation: The Founding of the United Nations* (New York: Basic Books, 2004), 63, 167–68.
 14. Friedman, *Arguing Over the American Lake*, 139–67. Friedman follows the debate between delegates.
 15. *FRUS: Conferences at Malta and Yalta*, 311–12.
 16. *FRUS: Conferences at Malta and Yalta*, 314.
 17. *FRUS: Conferences at Malta and Yalta*, 315.
 18. *FRUS: Conferences at Malta and Yalta*, 319, 451.
 19. *FRUS: Conferences at Malta and Yalta*, 350; Harry S. Truman, *Memoirs by Harry S. Truman, Vol. 1: Year of Decisions* (New York: Doubleday, 1955), 60.
 20. Francis B. Sayre, "American Trusteeship Policy in the Pacific." *Foreign Policy XXII.4* (January 1947): 406–16. Thanks to Caitlin McQueen for her assistance in accessing United Nations documents for this section.
 21. Donald F. McHenry, *Micronesia, Trust Betrayed: Altruism vs. Self Interest in American Foreign Policy* (Washington, D.C.: Carnegie Endowment for International Peace, 1975), 35–36; Schlesinger.
 22. *FRUS: Conferences at Malta and Yalta*, 844; Document in Patterson, 413 from Gabriel Kolko, *The Politics of War: The World and United States Foreign Policy, 1943–1945* (New York: Pantheon, 1990), 465.
 23. *United Nations Charter, Chapter XI, Article 73*; *Chapter XII, Article 77*. *United Nations Charter, 26 June 1945* (New York: United Nations, 1945).
 24. *United Nations Charter, Chapter XI, Article 73*.
 25. Dorothy E. Richard, *United States Naval Administration of the Trust Territory of the Pacific Islands. Vol. 1, The Wartime Military Government Period*, Office of the Chief of Naval Operations (Washington, D.C.: U.S. Government Printing Office, 1957), *Appendix III*, 52.
 26. *United Nations Charter, Chapter XIII, Article 86*.
 27. *Draft Statement, United Nations Trusteeship Agreement*.
 28. Richard, *Appendix III*, 52.
 29. Fred M. Zeder, Interview with Author (15 February 1988), USASDC Historical Office; Friedman, *Arguing Over the American Lake*, 137.
 30. Richard, 42; McHenry, 33–34.
 31. Robert C. Kiste, "Overview of U.S. Policy," in *History of the Trust Territory of the Pacific Islands: Proceedings of the Ninth Annual Pacific Islands Conference*. Ed. Karen Knudsen. Working Papers (Honolulu: University of Hawaii at Manoa, 1985), 5; U.S. Army Ballistic Missile Defense Organization (BMDO). *Annual History, 1967, 1970*.
 32. Richard, 38.
 33. BMDO. *Annual History 1967*, 5; *Memorandum, Judge Advocate General to the Chief of Naval Operations, 11 May 1950*, TTPI Archives, University of Hawai'i Archives (hereafter referred to as TTPI Archives, UHI Archives).
 34. United Nations. *Trusteeship Agreement for the Former Japanese Mandated Islands, Article 5*.
 35. McHenry, 32.
 36. *FRUS, 1946: Council of Foreign Ministers, Volume II*, 545. The Preparatory Commission of the United Nations met in London, 24 November–22 December, 1945 and prepared a resolution for the General Assembly to invite states holding mandates under the League of Nations to plan under United Nations international trusteeship.
 37. *Coordinating Committee to the Joint Chiefs of Staff, 19 September 1946*, in *FRUS: Council of Foreign Ministers*, 627–28.
 38. Harry S. Truman, *First Annual Report to Congress, 19 March 1946* (Independence, Missouri, Harry S. Truman Presidential Library), 8; Hal M. Friedman, "The Beast in Paradise: The United States Navy in Micronesia, 1943–1947," *The Pacific Historical Review* 62.2 (May 1993): 183.
 39. *FRUS: Memorandum, Act of 18 July 1947, 61, Stat. 397*.
 40. United States. Office of the President. *Executive Order 10265. Transfer of the Administration of the Trust Territory of the Pacific*

Islands from the Secretary of the Navy to the Secretary of the Interior, 29 June 1951 (Washington, D.C.: U.S. Government Printing Office, 1951).
  41. Ruth G. Van Cleve, *The Office of Territorial Affairs*. Praeger Library of U.S. Government Departments and Agencies (New York: Praeger, 1974), 176, 179.
  42. Emil J. Sady, "The Department of the Interior and Pacific Island Administration." *Public Administration Review* (Winter 1950): 13.
  43. Harold L. Ickes, "The Navy at Its Worst." *Collier's Weekly* 118 (31 August 1946): 22–23.
  44. Harold F. Nufer, *Micronesia Under American Rule: An Evaluation of the Strategic Trusteeship (1947–77)* (Hicksville, NY: Exposition Press, 1978), 41.
  45. Fred Zeder, Interview with Author (15 February 1988), 14–15, 57.
  46. "By Order of Elbert D. Thomas, High Commissioner," *Basic Information, Trust Territory of the Pacific Islands, 1951,* TTPI Archives, UHI Archives.
  47. Sady, 18; Philip Drucker, "Anthropology in Trust Territory Administration." *The Scientific Monthly* 72.5 (May 1951): 306–312. Note: In defining military role, the Naval Handbook set the standard for military government in Micronesia.
  48. Nufer, 43, 46, 49, 51, 121.
  49. Sady, 13; U.S., Office of the President. *Executive Order 9875, 18 July 1947.*
  50. Richard; Drucker, 308.
  51. David Hanlon, *Remaking Micronesia: Discourses Over Development in a Pacific Territory, 1944–1982* (Honolulu: University of Hawai'i Press, 1998), 5.
  52. Note: In 1952, Truman transferred Saipan and Tinian back to the Navy. In 1953, Eisenhower returned to the Navy all Northern Marianas except Rota. In 1962, John F. Kennedy gave the entire TTPI to the Department of the Interior. Van Cleve, 10.
  53. McHenry, 9. Note: After the creation of the Federated States of Micronesia, Ponape became Pohnpei, Truk became Chuuk.
  54. U.S., Office of the President. *Executive Order 10265, 29 June 1951.*
  55. Francis Pike, *Hirohito's War: The Pacific War, 1941–1945* (London: Bloomsbury, 2015), 10, 64–70; Einstein telegram in Simon Winchester, *Pacific: Silicon Chips and Surfboards, Coral Reefs and Atom Bombs, Brutal Dictators, Fading Empires, and the Coming Collision of the World's Superpowers* (New York: Harper, 2015), 39.
  56. Winchester, 53–64; Byron S. Miller, "A Law is Passed: The Atomic Energy Act of 1946," *The University of Chicago Law Review* 15.4 (Summer 1948): 799–821.
  57. Alice Buck, *The Atomic Energy Commission*, United States Department of Energy. Office of Management. Office of the Executive Secretariat. Office of History and Heritage Resources, July 1983. http://www.energy.gov, 1–3, 24.
  58. *Atomic Energy Commission Report, 18 Jan 1955*. Document quoted in Giff Johnson, *Don't Ever Whisper—Darlene Keju: Pacific Health Pioneer, Champion for Nuclear Survivors* (CreateSpace Independent Publishing Platform, 2013), 393–94.

Chapter Six

  1. Jack Tobin, *Ebeye Village: A Typical Marshallese Community, 18 February 1954*. Microfilm, 3ff, Reel no. 0282, Frame no. 173, 4–6. Thomas Gilliland, Land Title Officer, Office of Land and Management, 1 Marshall Islands District. *A Briefing on Land Problem in the Marshalls, 1–12. 20 October 1959*. Microfilm, Reel no. 493, Frame no. 136; Al Gergely, Wiles-Aiken & Company, to Chief Counsel, 1957. Microfilm, Reel no. 052, Frame no. 51. Trust Territory of the Pacific Islands Archives, University of Hawai'i Archives (hereafter referred to as TTPI Archives, UHI Archives).
  2. Tobin, *Ebeye Village*, 19–20, TTPI Archives, UHI Archives.
  3. Oscar de Brum, Interview with Author (15 September 1987), 31–32.
  4. Maynard Neas, Acting District Administrator, to Nat Logaer Smith, Director of Personnel, TTPI, 6 May 1954. Microfilm, Reel no. 452, Frame no. 93; William C. White, District Land and Title Officer to Nucker, Acting High Commissioner, 28 November 1955. Microfilm, Reel no. 452, Frame no. 94–45; White to Nucker, 1 December 1954. Microfilm, Reel no. 452, Frame no. 86. TTPI Archives, UHI Archives.
  5. Tobin, *Ebeye Village*, 13–14, TTPI Archives, UHI Archives.
  6. Tobin, *Ebeye Village*, 17–19, TTPI Archives, UHI Archives; D.H. Nucker, High Commissioner, to Anthony T. Lausi, Office of Territories, Department of the Interior, 8 August 1960. Microfilm, Reel no. 452, Frame no. 83, TTPI Archives, UHI Archives.
  7. *The Marshall Islands Journal* (hereafter referred to as *MI Journal*), 2013–2014; "Study by the U.S. National Institutes of Health," *MI Journal* 9 August 2013: 8; Giff Johnson, *Don't Ever Whisper—Darlene Keju: Pacific Health Pioneer, Champion of Nuclear Survivors* (CreateSpace independent Publishing Platform, 2013), 180, 292, 432.
  8. Jack A. Tobin, *Land Tenure in the Marshall Islands*. 1952. Microfilm, 28ff, Reel no. 32, Frame no. 150; William C. White, District Administrator to Alfred N. Hurt, Executive Office, TTPI, 13 August 1954. Microfilm, Reel no. 452, Frame no. 59; Jack A. Tobin, District

Anthropologist, Marshall Islands District, "Turn Ebeye Over to the Navy," 23 December 1954. Microfilm, Reel no. 452, Frame no. 92–93; Jack A. Tobin, "Ebeye Village: A Typical Marshallese Community"; Tobin to McConnell, "Islands Guide," 1. TTPI Archives, UHI Archives.

9. Maynard Neas, May 1954. Microfilm, Reel no. 4452, Frame no. 79; Tobin, Turn Ebeye Over to the Navy; Paul C. Atkin, 3 August 1966. Microfilm, Reel no. 452, Frame no. 62. TTPI Archives, UHI Archives.

10. Maynard Neas to D.H. Nucker, December 1954, 10 January 1955. Microfilm, Reel no. 452, Frame no. 86, TTPI Archives, UHI Archives.

11. R.J. Umhoefer to D.H. Nucker, 6 November 1956. Microfilm, Reel no. 452, Frame no. 78, TTPI Archives, UHI Archives.

12. Chief Counsel, J.C. Putnam, to the High Commissioner, 18 July 1957. Microfilm Reel no. 452, Frame no. 54, TTPI Archives, UHI Archives.

13. Thomas Gilliland, Notice, February 1957; J.C. Putnam to the High Commissioner, February 1957. Microfilm, Reel no. 452, Frame no. 54. TTPI Archives, UHI Archives.

14. Maynard Neas to the Deputy High Commissioner, 9 July 1957. Microfilm, Reel no. 452, Frame no. 54, TTPI Archives, UHI Archives.

15. R.J. Umhoefer, 23 December 1957. Microfilm, Reel no. 452, Frame no. 87; Gilliland, Notice, February 1958, Microfilm, Reel no. 452, Frame no. 54. TTPI Archives, UHI Archives.

16. R.J. Umhoefer to D.H. Nucker, 14 August 1958. Microfilm, Reel no. 452, Frame no. 66, TTPI Archives, UHI Archives.

17. Anthony T. Lausi to the High Commissioner, 20 January 1959. Microfilm, Reel no. 452, Frame no. 88; R.J. Umhoefer to the High Commissioner, 17 February 1959. Microfilm; District Representative of Ebeye to the High Commissioner, 16 April 1959. Microfilm, Reel no. 452, Frame no. 64. TTPI Archives, UHI Archives.

18. Chief Counsel, J.C. Putnam, to the High Commissioner, 18 July 1957. Microfilm Reel no. 452, Frame no. 5, TTPI Archives, UHI Archives.

19. Thomas Gilliland, A Briefing on Land Problem in the Marshalls; William C. White to Alfred M. Hurt, 31 August 1954. Microfilm, Reel no. 452, Frame no. 59, TTPI Archives, UHI Archives.

20. Linda Hunt, *Secret Agenda: The United States Government, Nazi Scientists, and Project Paperclip, 1945–1990* (New York: St. Martin's Press, 1991); "Project Paperclip," Walter LaFeber, *The American Age: United States Foreign Policy at Home and Abroad, Vol. 2: Since 1896* (New York: W.W. Norton, 1994), 462; Annie Jacobsen, *Operation Paperclip: The Secret Intelligence Program That Brought Nazi Scientists to America* (Boston: Little, Brown, 2014).

21. *United States Air Force Space and Missile Systems Organization: A Chronology, 1954–1979* (Washington, D.C.: U.S. Government Printing Office), 1.

22. Ruth Currie-McDaniel (hereafter Currie), *The U.S. Army Strategic Defense Command: Its History and Role in the Strategic Defense Initiative* (Huntsville, AL: Historical Office, U.S Army Strategic Defense Command, 1986), 2; Bell Labs, *ABM Research and Development at Bell Laboratories: Kwajalein Field Station* (Whippany, NJ: Bell Labs for the U.S. Army Ballistic Missile Defense Systems Command, 1975), 24.

23. Donald R. Baucom, *The Origins of SDI, 1944–1983* (Lawrence: University Press of Kansas, 1992), 11.

24. Bell Labs, 25.

25. Currie, 2; Bell Labs, 31, 36, 39, 43.

26. U.S. Army, Ballistic Missile Defense Organization (BMDO). *Annual History, 1967*, 10–11.

27. Bell Labs, 38–39; *Narrative History of Negotiations for Acquisition by the Trust Territory Government of Roi-Namur for Defense Use by U.S.*, typed manuscript, Microfilm Reel no. 506, Frame no. 105, TTPI Archives, UHI Archives.

28. Bell Labs, 44, 63. See Map no. 5: Drawing of Zeus Corridor.

29. BMDO, *Annual History, 1967*, 26–27, 47.

30. Baucom, 17; Bell Labs, 55–56; Currie, 2.

31. United States. House of Representatives. 87th Cong., 2d sess. Subcommittee on Territorial and Insular Affairs. Report No. 2054, 30 July 1962.

32. House of Representatives. 87th Cong., 2d sess. Subcommittee on Territorial and Insular Affairs. Report No. 2054, 30 July 1962.

33. M.W. Goding, High Commissioner to Richard Taitane, Director of the Office of Territories, Department of the Interior, 20 December 1962. Microfilm, Reel no. 0452, Frame no. 47, TTPI Archives, UHI Archives.

34. Attorney General R.K. Shoecraft to the High Commissioner, "Discussion at Majuro, Regarding Kwajalein Land Settlement," 17 December 1962. Microfilm, Reel no. 0452, Frame no. 47; "Use and Occupancy Agreement for Land in the Trust Territory of the Pacific Islands Under the Administrative Responsibility of the Department of the Interior," 22 March 1963. Microfilm, Reel no. 452, Frame no. 63; Attorney General, R.K. Shoecraft, "Minutes of Meeting with Representatives of the People who will be Relocated from the Mid-Atoll Corridor," 12 December 1964. Microfilm, 7, refers to "signing of the Kwajalein Land Use Agreement" after February 10th or 11th, 1963, TTPI Archives, UHI Archives.

35. Currie, 2.
36. BMDO, *Annual History, 1967*, 26; Currie, 5; Micronesian Support Committee, *Marshall Islands, A Chronology: 1944–1983*, 3rd ed. (Honolulu: Maka'ainana Media, 1983), 31; Brian J. Auten, *Carter's Conversion: The Hardening of American Defense Policy* (Columbia: Missouri University Press, 2008), 43.
37. Bell Labs, 59–60, 67; *Marshall Islands, A Chronology*, 31.
38. Bell Labs, 68.
39. *Marshall Islands, A Chronology*, 31; BMDO, *Annual History, 1970*, 1; Bell Labs, 63. See Map no. 5.
40. BMDO, *Annual History, 1967*, 27.
41. Udall's memo quoted in MOU, John A. Carver, Assistant Secretary of the Interior, to Paul R. Ignatious, Under Secretary of the Army; cc High Commissioner Goding, 10 Jun 1964, TTPI Archives, UHI Archives.
42. Peter T. Colemen, District Administrator to the High Commissioner, "Confusion Concerning Erection of Building on Ebeye for Shelter," 13 February 1963. Microfilm, Reel no. 454, Frame no. 214, TTPI Archives, UHI Archives.
43. BMDO, *Annual History, 1967*, 29.
44. Shoecraft, Minutes (12 December 1964), TTPI Archives, UHI Archives.
45. Shoecraft, Minutes (12 December 1964), 3–4, TTPI Archives, UHI Archives.
46. Shoecraft, Minutes (12 December 1964), 5–6, TTPI Archives, UHI Archives.
47. Shoecraft, Minutes (12 December 1964), 8, TTPI Archives, UHI Archives.
48. BMDO, *Annual History, 1967*, 30–31; U.S. Army. BMDO, "Summary of the Events and Circumstances Concerning Acquisition of the Kwajalein Mid-Atoll Corridor," as of 31 May 1970, 9–11.
49. BMDO, "Summary," 9.
50. BMDO. "Summary," 9–11.
51. BMDO, *Annual History, 1970*, 9–11; Baucom, 20ff.
52. Auten, 43; Currie, 7–9.
53. Typed, "To the High Command of the Trust Territory of the Pacific Islands from the Iroijlaplaps (Kings) of the Marshall Islands," April 1968, cc of the Original Kept at Headquarters, Lands and Surveys with Signatures, 19 May 1972. Microfilm, TTPI Archives, UHI Archives.

Chapter Seven

1. United Nations Resolution 1541, 14 December 1960.
2. United Nations General Assembly Resolution 1541, 21 December 1960, document in Donald F. McHenry, *Micronesia, Trust Betrayed: Altruism vs. Self Interest in American Foreign Policy* (Washington, D.C.: Carnegie Endowment for International Peace, 1975), 37; Masahiro Igarashi, *Associated Statehood in International Law* (The Hague: Kluver Law International, 2002), 5.
3. McHenry, 13; Howard P. Willens and Deanne C. Siemer, *National Security and Self-Determination: United States Policy in Micronesia (1961–1972)* (Westport, CT: Praeger, 2000), 17–18; Norman Meller, *The Congress of Micronesia: Development of the Legislative Process in the Trust Territory of the Pacific Islands* (Honolulu: University of Hawai'i Press, 1969), 195.
4. McHenry, 14; Willens and Siemer, 18.
5. John F. Kennedy, Speech in the United Nations, 25 September 1961.
6. McHenry, 19.
7. Willens and Siemer, 8; Timothy P. Maga, *John F. Kennedy and a New Pacific Community, 1961–63* (New York: Saint Martin's Press, 1990), x, 16.
8. John F. Kennedy, Speech. Remarks at the America Cup Dinner Given by the Australian Ambassador. Newport, Rhode Island, 14 September 1962.
9. Maga, 16–17; Willens and Siemer, 19.
10. United States. Office of the President. National Security Council. National Security Action (NSA) Memo No. 145, 18 April 1962.
11. *Annual Report of the High Commissioner of the Trust Territory of the Pacific Islands to the Secretary of the Interior, 1963* (Washington, D.C.: U.S. Government Printing Office, 1963), 1; United States. House of Representatives. House Resolution Bill. Note: It is questionable that the TTPI was eligible for these funds because it was neither a foreign country nor integral part of the United States; see Willens and Siemer, 38.
12. David M. Lynch, "United States Policy Toward Micronesia, 1945–1972" (dissertation, West Virginia University, 1973), 56; McHenry, 192, 198.
13. Ruth Currie-McDaniel (hereafter Currie), *The U.S. Army Strategic Defense Command: Its History and Role in the Strategic Defense Initiative* (Huntsville, AL: Historical Office, U.S Army Strategic Defense Command, 1986), 1–2; Bell Labs, *ABM Research and Development at Bell Laboratories: Kwajalein Field Station* (Whippany, NJ: Bell Labs for the U.S. Army Ballistic Missile Defense Systems Command, 1975), 25, 31, 36, 43.
14. Currie, 7; Micronesian Support Committee, *Marshall Islands, A Chronology: 1944–1983*, 3rd ed. (Honolulu: Maka'ainana Media, 1983), 8.
15. *The New York Times* 19 July 1962; Bell Labs, 55; Currie, 2. Note: "Successful intercept" was within lethal range of the nuclear warhead ZEUS was designed to carry.

16. Bell Labs, 55; *The New York Times* 20 July 1962; NSA Memo No. 191, 1 October 1962; Currie, 8. Note: Amata Kabua visited Saipan, TTPI government, October 1962. ZEUS had two more successful hits, December 1962.
17. Willens and Siemer, 38.
18. NSA Memo No. 229, 21 March 1963.
19. *Report by the United States Government Survey Mission to the TTPI (Solomon Report) 1963.* Summary and 2 Vols. (Honolulu: University of Hawai'i, Hamilton Library, Hawaiian and Pacific Collection).
20. David Nevin, *The American Touch in Micronesia* (New York: Norton, 1977), 124.
21. Summary, *Solomon Report.*
22. McHenry, 16, 18.
23. Summary, *Solomon Report.*
24. Quoted in Nevin, 126.
25. *NSA Memo No. 268, 25 October 1963.*
26. Nevin, 123; McHenry, 14; Willens and Siemer, 47.
27. James A. Bryan, III, et al., "Poliomyelitis in an Isolated Population: Report of a Type I Epidemic in the Marshall Islands, 1963," *American Journal of Epidemiology* 82.3 Johns Hopkins University (1966): 283; Dr. James Bryan, Interview with Author (July 2012).
28. Francis Hezel, *Strangers in Their Own Land: A Century of Colonial Rule in the Caroline and Marshall Islands.* Pacific Islands Monograph Series 13 (Honolulu: University of Hawai'i Press, 2003), 301.
29. Memorandum in Willens and Siemer, 71, 74.
30. McHenry, 191; Willens and Siemer, 72.
31. Willens and Siemer, 69–74; Ambassador Fred Zeder, Interview with Author (15 February 1988), 15.
32. Ruth G. Van Cleve, *The Office of Territorial Affairs.* Praeger Library of U.S. Government Departments and Agencies (New York: Praeger, 1974), 176; Meller, 70.
33. Van Cleve, 178.
34. Willens and Siemer, 70, 79; McHenry, 15–16; *FRUS: Task Force Reports.*
35. Hezel, *Strangers in Their Own Land,* 301, 303.
36. David Hanlon, *Remaking Micronesia: Discourses Over Development in a Pacific Territory, 1944–1982* (Honolulu: University of Hawai'i Press, 1998), 130. Note: See Chapter 4 regarding the Navy's role after the battle.
37. Meller, 181–82.
38. Meller, 182.
39. Meller, 182–83.
40. Hanlon, 133; Meller, 183.
41. Meller, 184–85.
42. Meller, 185; *Annual Report of the High Commissioner of the Trust Territory of the Pacific Islands to the Secretary of the Interior, 1963. tp,* *I, ii, 1–28; 60–67; 82–88* (Washington, D.C.: U.S. Government Printing Office, 1963), 10.
43. Meller, 183–85, 189. Note: The U.S. Constitution gives Congress jurisdiction over "the Territory," Article IV, Sec. 3.
44. *Annual Report of the High Commissioner of the Trust Territory of the Pacific Islands to the Secretary of the Interior, 1965. tp, iii; 1–23; 55–63; 76–93* (Washington, D.C.: U.S. Government Printing Office, 1965), 1, 3, 14, 82; Lynch, 41.
45. Meller, 185–87, 375, 406; Igarashi, 183–85; *Marshall Islands, A Chronology,* 32; Meller, 406.
46. Quoted in Willens and Siemer, 70; Van Cleve, 179.
47. Memorandum, Lyndon Baines Johnson to the Director of Budget, 25 February 1965, Willens and Siemer, 59, *n*87.
48. Willens and Siemer, 75, 78.
49. Van Cleve, 179; Willens and Siemer, 80–81, 85.
50. Van Cleve, 181; McHenry, 28; Willens and Siemer, 84.
51. Willens and Siemer, 83–85, 137, *n*161; *Memorandum, 28 April 1969.*
52. Igarashi, 186; Willens and Siemer, 108, 117.
53. Willens and Siemer, 85, 108–09, 113.
54. *Annual Report of the High Commissioner of the Trust Territory of the Pacific Islands to the Secretary of the Interior, 1968. tp, iii, v–vi; 1–9; 26–27; 30–43* (Washington, D.C.: U.S. Government Printing Office, 1968), 1; Lynch, 43; Willens and Siemer, 122.
55. Willens and Siemer, 112, 115, 117–18, 121–22, 131; Igarashi, 186–87.
56. Willens and Siemer, 118–19, 122–23.
57. *Marshall Islands, A Chronology,* 10; Willens and Siemer, 118, 125.
58. Congress of Micronesia. The Future Political Status Commission of the Marshall Islands. 3rd Cong., 2d sess., "Final Report, Future Political Status Commission," July 1969. Capitol Hill, Saipan, Mariana Islands, 1.

Chapter Eight

1. Congress of Micronesia. The Future Political Status Commission of the Marshall Islands. 3rd Cong., 2d sess., "Final Report, Future Political Status Commission," July 1969. Capitol Hill, Saipan, Mariana Islands, 1–2, 4, 8–9, 27.
2. Walter LaFeber, *The American Age: United States Foreign Policy at Home and Abroad, Vol. 2: Since 1896* (New York: W.W. Norton, 1994), 638; Howard P. Willens and Deanne C. Siemer, *National Security and Self-Determination: United States Policy in*

Micronesia (1961–1972) (Westport, CT: Praeger, 2000), 144.

3. Ruth Currie-McDaniel (hereafter Currie). *The U.S. Army Strategic Defense Command: Its History and Role in the Strategic Defense Initiative* (Huntsville, AL: Historical Office, U.S Army Strategic Defense Command, 1986), 8–12.

4. Henry Kissinger, *The White House Years* (New York: Little, Brown, 1979), 223–25.

5. Kissinger, 223–25; James H. Webb, Jr., *Micronesia and U.S. Pacific Strategy: A Blueprint for the 1980s*. Praeger Special Studies in International Politics and Government (New York: Praeger, 1974), 8; LaFeber, *The American Age*, 638.

6. *The New York Times* 26 July 1969.

7. Quoted in Willens and Siemer, 149.

8. P.F. Kluge, *The Edge of Paradise: America in Micronesia* (Honolulu: University of Hawai'i Press, 1991), 55; Willens and Siemer, 149; Norman Meller, *The Congress of Micronesia: Development of the Legislative Process in the Trust Territory of the Pacific Islands* (Honolulu: University of Hawai'i Press, 1969), 342.

9. United States. Department of State. *The Future Political Status of the Trust Territory of the Pacific Islands*, Office of Micronesian Status Negotiations, Official Records.

10. Carl Heine, *Micronesia at the Crossroads: A Reappraisal of the Micronesian Political Dilemma*. An East-West Center Book (Honolulu: University of Hawai'i Press, 1974), 124; Willens and Siemer, 158; Masahiro Igarashi, *Associated Statehood in International Law* (The Hague: Kluver Law International, 2002), 190–91.

11. Quoted in Willens and Siemer, 148; Kissinger later denied the quote, but admitted to a similar version. Fred Zeder, Interview with Author (15 February 1988). Ambassador Zeder recalled a similar version.

12. Kluge, 55.

13. Heine, 172.

14. Ruth G. Van Cleve, *The Office of Territorial Affairs*. Praeger Library of U.S. Government Departments and Agencies (New York: Praeger, 1974), 176; Willens and Siemer, 159–60.

15. Igarashi, 191–92; Heine, 46.

16. Willens and Siemer, 159; Igarashi, 192.

17. Willens and Siemer, 183, 212.

18. Van Cleve, 3–5, 13; Willens and Siemer, 212–16.

19. Willens and Siemer, 212–13, 218.

20. Igarashi, 193.

21. United States. Department of State. *The Future Political Status of the Trust Territory of the Pacific Islands. Proceedings of the 4th Round of Micronesian Future Political Status Talks. Koror, Palau, 2–13 April 1972* (Washington, D.C.: Office for Micronesian Status Negotiations, 1972), 7.

22. *Proceedings of the 4th Round of Micronesian Future Political Status Talks*, 7–55, 59; Willens and Siemer, 257.

23. *The Future Political Status of the Trust Territory of the Pacific Islands. Proceedings of the 5th Round of Micronesian Future Political Status Talks. Washington, D.C., 12 July–1 August 1972*, 2–3.

24. *Proceedings of the 5th Round of Micronesian Future Political Status Talks*, 7, 16–18.

25. *The Future Political Status of the Trust Territory of the Pacific Islands. Proceedings of the 6th Round of Micronesian Future Political Status Talks. Barbers Point Naval Air Station, Oahu, Hawaii, 28 September–6 October 1972*, 20.

26. *Proceedings of the 6th Round of Micronesian Future Political Status Talks*, 13–14.

27. *Proceedings of the 6th Round of Micronesian Future Political Status Talks*, 7, 31, 33.

28. David Hanlon, *Remaking Micronesia: Discourses Over Development in a Pacific Territory, 1944–1982* (Honolulu: University of Hawai'i Press, 1998), 135–36; March 1997; "Retro, 8 June 1973," 3 August 2012; "Retro, 10 August 1974" 3 January 2014. *The Marshall Islands Journal* (hereafter referred to as *MI Journal*).

29. Congress of Micronesia, *Joint Committee on Future Status. Hearings of the Eastern Districts Subcommittee (Truk, Ponape, and the Marshalls), November 1973* (Saipan, Mariana Islands: Trust Territory Government Press, 1973), 1–81.

30. *FRUS, Henry Kissinger to Richard Nixon, Memorandum No. 306, 9 November 1973.*

31. Igarashi, 196–97; Arnold H. Liebowitz, *Colonial Emancipation in the Pacific and the Caribbean: A Legal and Political Analysis* (New York: Praeger, 1976), 82–83, quoted in Igarashi.

32. United States. TTPI Government. "Trust Territory of the Pacific Islands, Political History, Chronology," 10.

33. Heine, 46, 80, 140, 156, 158, 168–69.

34. "Retro, 8 June 1973," 3 August 2012; "Retro, 10 August 1974," 5 October 2012. *MI Journal.*

35. Kluge, 51–52; Heine, 172.

36. "Retro, 12 October 1974" *MI Journal* 6 December 2013.

37. "Trust Territory of the Pacific Islands, Political History, Chronology," 9–10; Igarashi, 197–98.

38. United States. Office of the President. National Security Council (NSC), Memorandum No. 312, from Charles W. Robinson, Chairman of the National Security Council Under Secretaries Committee, to President Ford, 24 May 1976.

39. NSC Memorandum No. 312, 2.

40. NSC Memorandum No. 312, 3.
41. Quoted in *Marshall Islands, A Chronology* (entry for July 4th, 1976), 14.
42. Article XIII, Section 5, quoted in Igarashi, 198.
43. *NSC Memorandum No. 312*. Note: "Retro, June 1975" *MI Journal* 31 May 2013-"status negotiations going nowhere."
44. Quoted in Igarashi, 198.
45. United States. Department of the Interior. Interior Order No. 2918, "Self Government in the Trust Territory of the Pacific Islands," 27 December 1968, Part II Section 2; Igarashi, 199.
46. Jimmy Carter, *White House Diary* (New York: Farrar, Straus, Giroux, 2010), 353, 429, 497.
47. "Presidential Directive/NSC-11," 5 May 1977, 1–2.
48. "Presidential Directive/NSC-11," 2.
49. "Retro 1977" *MI Journal* 14 March 2014, CIA snooping regarding 200-mile zone brought No-Confidence vote in Nitijela; *Presidential Directive/NSC-11*, 3.
50. Carter, 185.
51. "Retro, 5 August 1977," 2 August 2013: 7; "Retro, 16 August 1977," 6 September 2013: 30, *MI Journal;* Giff Johnson, "Marshall Islands: Politics in the Marshall Islands," in *Micronesian Politics*. ed. Ron Crocombe. Suva, Fiji: Institute of Pacific Studies, University of the South Pacific, 1988), 82.
52. Transcript, Peter Rosenblatt, Oral History Interview, 26 July 1984, by Ted Gittinger, Internet Copy, Lyndon Baines Johnson Library.
53. Igarashi, 200; United States. Department of the Interior. Office of the Solicitor, Memorandum from the Assistant Solicitor of Territories, Division of General Law to the Office for Micronesian Status Negotiations, Attention: A. John Armstrong. Ownership of Real Property in the Marshall Islands, 28 March 1978 (Washington, D.C.: U.S. Government Printing Office, 1978).
54. Igarashi, 200–201.
55. NSC Memorandum from Zbigniew Brzezinski, National Security Council Adviser, to President Carter, 23 May 1979.
56. Memorandum for Zbigniew Brzezinski from Matt Nimetz Chairman of the Micronesia Interagency Group. Revision of Negotiating Instructions, 23 May 1979. Note: Ambassador Zeder recalled that in 1975 attorney George Allen had encouraged landowners to ask for funds never accounted for. Fred Zeder, Interview with Author (15 February 1988), 17–19.
57. NSC Internal Memorandum, Zbigniew Brzezinski, 6 May 1979; Memorandum, Department of State to Zbigniew Brzezinski, 23 May 1979.

58. Armstrong quoted in Igarashi, 202*n*.
59. Giff Johnson, "Marshall Islands: Politics in the Marshall Islands," 72; Giff Johnson, *Don't Ever Whisper—Darlene Keju: Pacific Health Pioneer, Champion for Nuclear Survivors* (CreateSpace Independent Publishing Platform, 2013), *notes*; "Retro, 14 October 1977" *MI Journal* 12 October 2012, Seating Iroij Anjua Loeak at Marshall Islands Constitutional Convention; U.S. Army Ballistic Missile Defense Systems Command (BMDSC), "Kwajalein Missile Range," 32, *Annual Historical Review: 1 October 1979 to 30 September 1980.*
60. *The Virgin Islands Daily News* 12 August 1980: 18.
61. United States. Office of the President. Memorandum, Zbigniew Brzezinski to the Joint Committee, 29 December 1979.
62. NSC Internal Memorandum, Zbigniew Brzezinski, 2 December 1980. Note: Brzezinski added underlined emphasis.

Chapter Nine

1. Donald R. Baucom, *The Origins of SDI, 1944–1983* (Lawrence: University Press of Kansas, 1992), *xiii*; Brian J. Auten, *Carter's Conversion: The Hardening of American Defense Policy* (Columbia: Missouri University Press, 2008), 39–41.
2. Baucom, 53–71.
3. *United States Air Force Space and Missile Systems Organization: A Chronology, 1954–1979* (Washington, D.C.: U.S. Government Printing Office), 233–34, 237; Ruth Currie-McDaniel (hereafter Currie), *The U.S. Army Strategic Defense Command: Its History and Role in the Strategic Defense Initiative* (Huntsville, AL: Historical Office, U.S Army Strategic Defense Command, 1986), 15.
4. Currie, 20–21.
5. Stanly Godbold, Carter biographer, Email correspondence with Author, 2012.
6. Auten, 173.
7. Auten, 272–74.
8. Godbold, Correspondence with Author, 2012.
9. Baucom, 175; Auten, 173, 272, 258–59, 303–08.
10. United States. Office of the President. Draft Compact of Free Association, Article XIII, Section 6; Masahiro Igarashi, *Associated Statehood in International Law* (The Hague: Kluver Law International, 2002), 204.
11. United States. U.S. Army. State Department Interagency Group on Micronesia, Memorandum for Zbigniew Brzezinski from Rozanne L. Ridgway, Chairman of the Micronesian Interagency Group. Micronesian Nuclear Claims, 16 January 1981, 1–5.

12. Roger S. Clark, "Self-Determination and Free Association-Should the United Nations Terminate the Pacific Islands Trust?" *Harvard International Law Journal* 21.1 (Winter 1980): 8, 51ff; Igarashi, 202.
13. Giff Johnson, *Don't Ever Whisper—Darlene Keju: Pacific Health Pioneer, Champion for Nuclear Survivors* (CreateSpace Independent Publishing Platform, 2013), 58–61; U.S. Army Ballistic Missile Defense Systems Command (BMDSC), "Kwajalein Missile Range," 79–82, *Annual Historical Review: 1 October 1978 to 30 September 1979*.
14. Giff Johnson, "Politics in the Marshall Islands," in *Micronesian Politics*. ed. Ron Crocombe (Suva, Fiji: Institute of Pacific Studies, University of the South Pacific, 1988), 72, 82; Johnson, *Don't Ever Whisper*, 91.
15. Bryan Vila and Cynthia Morris, *Micronesian Blues: The Adventures of an American Cop in Paradise* (Boulder, CO: Paladin Press, 2009), 174–80; Fred Zeder, Interview with Author (15 February 1988), 16, 35–36, 43, 47.
16. Johnson, *Don't Ever Whisper*, 416.
17. United States. Office of the President. Draft Compact of Free Association, Section 177, 14 January 1980; United States. Department of the Interior. Statutory Compensation, Public Law 95–134, 15 October 1977, 2. Note: Includes "compassionate compensation" for specific ailments.
18. United States Congress. General Accounting Office (GAO) "Report to Congressional Requesters, 2000," 18; Also see *The Marshall Islands Journal* (hereafter referred to as *MI Journal*) 31 January 2014; Micronesian Support Committee, *Marshall Islands: Chronology, 1944–1983*, 3rd ed. (Honolulu: Maka'ainana Media, 1983), 21; Johnson, "Politics in Marshall Islands": 74–75.
19. U.S. Army BMDSC, "Kwajalein Missile Range," 35, *Annual Historical Review: 1 October 1981 to 30 September 1982*; Johnson, *Don't Ever Whisper*, 109, Frank Quimby, "Kwajalein Protests Outlast Pressure," *Pacific Daily News* 29 July 1982, quoted in Johnson, *Don't Ever Whisper*, 398–99; Vila and Morris, 187–97.
20. *Marshall Islands, A Chronology*, 19–22; Johnson, *Don't Ever Whisper*, 109, 413–14.
21. Johnson, "Politics in the Marshall Islands," 73; *Marshall Islands, A Chronology*, 23; United States. Department of the Interior. Office of the Solicitor, Memo from the Assistant Solicitor of Territories, Division of General Law to the Office for Micronesian Status Negotiations, Attention: A. John Armstrong. Ownership of Real Property in the Marshall Islands, 28 March 1978 (Washington, D.C.: U.S. Government Printing Office, 1978).
22. *Marshall Islands, A Chronology*, 23–24; U.S. Army BMDSC, "Kwajalein Missile Range,"

39, *Annual Historical Review:* 1 October 1982 to 30 September 1983.
23. Currie, 30; U.S. Army BMDSC, "Kwajalein Missile Range," 39, *Annual Historical Review:* 1 October 1982 to 30 September 1983; Johnson, *Don't Ever Whisper*, 126, 404; *MI Journal* 31 January 2014. Note: "Sixty-Years Commemoration of Bravo," ceremony of remembrance held at the Clinton Presidential Library, Little Rock, Arkansas. Japan also held a week-long commemoration. *MI Journal* 28 February 2014.
24. Johnson, "Politics in the Marshall Islands," 76.
25. Fred Zeder, Interview with Author (15 February 1988), 41.
26. Fred Zeder, Interview with Author (15 February 1988), 41–42; House of Representatives Subcommittee on Public Lands and National Parks, Hearings.
27. Baucom, 176–81.
28. Baucom, 184–89.
29. United States. Department of Defense, President's Commission on Strategic Forces, Scrowcroft, Chariman, 6 April 1983, in USASDC Historical Office; Currie, 25.
30. Baucom, 182–83; Currie, 23.
31. Baucom, 141–52.
32. Frances FitzGerald, *Way Out There in the Blue: Reagan, Star Wars and the End of the Cold War* (New York: Simon & Schuster, 2001), 32–33, 84, 126ff. FitzGerald quotes historian Richard Hofstater's classic, *Paranoid Style in American Politics, 1960s*, 95; Walter LaFeber, *The American Age: United States Foreign Policy at Home and Abroad, Vol. 2: Since 1896* (New York: W.W. Norton, 1994), 504; John Prados, "The Wave Maker: Bill Casey in the Reagan Years," in *The Policymakers: Shaping American Foreign Policy from 1947 to the Present*, ed. Anna Kasten Nelson (Washington, D.C.: Rowman and Littlefield, 2009), 135, 141, 145.
33. Daniel O. Graham, *High Frontier: A New National Strategy* (Washington, D.C.: High Frontier, 1982), 18, 45; Baucom, 158–60, 163.
34. Graham, 33–34, 131–33, 135ff; Baucom, 163–64.
35. Baucom, 148–49; 156.
36. Note: The United States continued sixteen more tests after Bravo. See Atomic Energy Commission (AEC) Report, 18 January 1955. Those in the Marshall Islands represented only seven percent of U.S. testing, but eighty percent of atmospheric. Testing continued until 1988. *AEC Report* quoted in Johnson, *Don't Ever Whisper*, 393–94, 408.
37. Note: Spurious charges of espionage used to discredit Oppenheimer were later proven to be false. He was honored for his pioneer work in atomic research and in antinuclear leadership.

38. Baucom, 151, 247–48.
39. President Reagan, television address, *23 March 1983*, Reagan Library files.
40. FitzGerald, 210.
41. NSC. National Security Decision: Directive No. 116, Strategic Defense Initiative, 2 December 1983, 1–2, Reagan Library.
42. NSC. National Security Decision: Directive No. 116; Prados, 135ff.
43. Baucom, 165.
44. "The Strategic Defense Initiative Defensive Technologies Study," March 1984, US-ASDC Historical Office; NSC. National Security Decision: Directive No. 119, 16 April 1984, Reagan Library; Currie, 34.
45. Currie, 30, 44–42.
46. FitzGerald, 489.
47. Currie, 49–51.
48. *The New York Times* 16 December 1985; United States. Congress. *Public Law 99–239: Compact of Free Association Act of 1985 Between the Government of the United States and the Government of the Federated States of Micronesia and the Government of the Republic of the Marshall Islands, 14 January 1986* (Washington, D.C.: U.S. Government Printing Office, 1986).
49. Congress of Micronesia. The Future Political Status Commission of the Marshall Islands. Report. 3rd Cong., 2d sess. Trust Territory of the Pacific Islands. Capitol Hill, Saipan, Mariana Islands. July 1969, 9. Italics added.

Chapter Ten

1. United States. Office of the President. Presidential Proclamation No. 5564, November 1986, Federal Register Vol. 81, No. 216.
2. United States. Office of the President. Executive Order No. 12569, 16 October 1986, Federal Register, Vol. 51, No. 202.
3. State Department, various reports; Walter LaFeber, *The American Age: United States Foreign Policy at Home and Abroad, Vol. 2: Since 1896* (New York: W.W. Norton, 1994), 734. Note: LaFeber's discussion is broad-based and analyzes various other factors, as well.
4. United States. U.S. Army Strategic Defense Command (USASDC). *Annual Historical Review, FY 87*, 285, 298.
5. USASDC, *Annual Historical Review, FY 87*, 298; *Annual Historical Review, FY 88*, 397.
6. USASDC, *Annual Historical Review, FY 89*, "Significant Events," 1.
7. USASDC, *Annual Historical Review, FY 88*, 383.
8. USASDC, *Annual Historical Review, FY 86*, II, 239; "Retro, 28 December 1990," *The Marshall Islands Journal* (hereafter referred to as *MI Journal*) 25 December 2015.
9. Giff Johnson, "Marshall Islands." Political Reviews, Micronesia. *The Contemporary Pacific* (Spring 1993): 143.
10. Michael R. Ogden, "Republic of the Marshall Islands." Political Reviews, Micronesia. *The Contemporary Pacific* (Spring 1996): 166.
11. Document in Giff Johnson, *Don't Ever Whisper—Darlene Keju: Pacific Health Pioneer, Champion for Nuclear Survivors* (CreateSpace Independent Publishing Platform, 2013), 417–18.
12. Ogden, 166.
13. Alex Wellerstein, quoted in George Washington University National Security Archive.
14. *Public Law 99–239: Compact of Free Association act of 1985 Between the Government of the United States and the Government of the Federated States of Micronesia and the Government of the Republic of the Marshall Islands, 14 January 1986* (Washington, D.C.: U.S. Government Printing Office, 1986); John Fairlamb, "Session II: Enduring Issues, Compacts of Free Association, A U.S. Perspective: Where Are We Now?" A paper presented to the Island State Security Conference: Asia-Pacific Center for Security Studies. Honolulu, Hawaii, 15–17 July 2003, 3. Island State Security Conference, July 2003, 3. Note: While reports frequently used the term "renewal," the Compact of Free Association, per se, would not expire, but continue unless one or both parties would decide to terminate. In this chapter, terms "renewal, renegotiate, and reauthorize" are sometimes interchangeable.
15. David M. Strauss, "Marshall Islands Terminates Service of Another Chief Justice," *Pacific Islands Report* (2 July 2000): 1.
16. Jim Hess, "Republic of the Marshall Islands." Political Reviews, Micronesia. *The Contemporary Pacific* (Spring 1997): 211; Johnson, "Marshall Islands." Political Reviews, Micronesia (1993): 143.
17. Quoted in Hess, 211.
18. Nicholas D. Kristof, "Yankee, Go Home. Send Cash," *The New York Times* 30 March 1997.
19. Ibid.
20. E. Robert Statham, Jr., *Colonial Constitutionalism: The Tyranny of United States' Offshore Territorial Policy and Relations* (Lanham, MD: Lexington Books, 2002), 140.
21. *MI Journal* 17 August 1997.
22. Julianne M. Walsh, "Marshall Islands." Political Reviews, Micronesia. *The Contemporary Pacific* (Spring 2000): 205–09.
23. United States Congress. General Accounting Office (GAO) Report, 2003, 7.
24. Julianne M. Walsh, "Marshall Islands." Political Reviews, Micronesia. *The Contemporary Pacific* (Spring 2001): 211.
25. Kristina E. Stege, "Marshall Islands."

Political Reviews, Micronesia. *The Contemporary Pacific* (Spring 2002): 199, 202.

26. "Pacific Islands Report," Political Reviews, Micronesia. *The Contemporary Pacific* (6 December 2001): 3–4.

27. *The New York Times* 22 July 2001: 10; Congressional Research Service, *Missile Defense*, 25 February 2002, 36.

28. John Fairlamb, email note to author, 26 September 2011. Thanks to Dr. Fairlamb for his help in research for this entire section.

29. John Fairlamb, "Compact of Free Association Negotiations: Fulfilling the Promise," a paper presented to the Island State Security Conference at the Asia-Pacific Center for Security Studies. Honolulu, Hawaii (June 2001), 3–4.

30. Fairlamb, "Fulfilling the Promise," 5.

31. Fairlamb, "Fulfilling the Promise," 5–6, 8.

32. Fairlamb, "Fulfilling the Promise," 6.

33. "Pacific Islands Report," Political Reviews, Micronesia. *The Contemporary Pacific* (6 December 2001): 1.

34. "Pacific Islands Report," Political Reviews, Micronesia, 3.

35. GAO Report, January 2002, 14–16.

36. GAO Report, January 2002, 17.

37. GAO Report, 2002, Appendix VI, 51. Note: Rebuttal letters to draft report and GAO comment to letters printed with report as appendices.

38. GAO Report, 2002, Appendix VII, 53–64. Federated States of Micronesia: Islands of Chuuk, Pohnpei, Yap, Kosrae.

39. GAO Report, 2002, Appendix VIII, 65–71.

40. John Fairlamb, "Where Are We Now?" 24–25; Kristina E. Stege, "Marshall Islands." Political Reviews, Micronesia. *The Contemporary Pacific* (Spring 2004): 128; United States. House of Representatives, "Reauthorizing Compacts of Free Association with Micronesia and the Marshall Islands," House Subcommittee on Asia and the Pacific, 18 June 2003; United States. Senate. Committee on Energy and Natural Resources. Hearing to Examine the Recently Renegotiated Compact of Free Association Between the United States and the Republic of the Marshall Islands and the United States and the Federated States of Micronesia Focusing on the Extension of U.S. Financial Assistance to the Republic of the Marshall Islands and the Federated States of Micronesia for Economic Development and Other Purposes, 15 July 2003; Hearings the previous summer: United States. House of Representatives. Committee on Resources. Renewal Hearings on the Compact of Free Association, 17 July 2002; United States. House of Representatives. Hearing before the Committee on International Relations, 23 July 2002.

41. Fairlamb, "Where Are We Now?" 10–12.

42. Fairlamb, "Where Are We Now?" 10–12; John Fairlamb, Interview with Author (14 October 2011); Stege, "Marshall Islands," Political Reviews, Micronesia (2004): 128.

43. Strauss.

44. Francis Hezel, *Making Sense of Micronesia: The Logic of Pacific Island Culture* (Honolulu: University of Hawai'i Press, 2013), 33.

45. Marshall Islands Constitution, Preamble; Article I, Section 3.

46. Marshall Islands Constitution, Preamble; Article VI, Section 4.

47. Marshall Islands Constitution, Preamble; Article X, Section 1.

48. Memorandum, Ronald V. Dellums, Chairman of the Subcommittee on Military Installations and Facilities and Rondo Lugo, Chairman of the Subcommittee on Insular and International Affairs to Donald Paul Hodel, Secretary of the Interior, 4 May 1988; United States. Department of the Interior. Office of the Solicitor, Memo from the Assistant Solicitor of Territories, Division of General Law to the Office for Micronesian Status Negotiations, Attention: A. John Armstrong. Ownership of Real Property in the Marshall Islands, 28 March 1978.

49. "Report on the Implementation of the Military Land Use and Nuclear Claims Settlement Provisions, CFA," March 1988. Prepared for the United States Senate Committee on Energy and Natural Resources and the House Subcommittee on Insular and Internal Affairs, 18–20.

50. United States. Department of State. Memorandum, Scott C. Taylor to Secretary of State, Madeleine K. Albright, et. al., 1 May 2000; Republic of the Marshall Islands High Court, Civil Action No. 2000-133; Department of State Memorandums, U.S. Embassy, Majuro: May 9, June 2, August 29, September 11, 2000. For initial KAC necessitating new KADA, see report on Implementation of Military Land Use, 1988, 5.

51. Stege, (2004): 128.

52. *Iroijlaplap* Imata Kabua to U.S. Ambassador to the Republic of the Marshall Islands, Greta Morris, 4 October 2005, *Yokwe Online*, 9 October 2005.

53. David Kupferman, "Marshall Islands," Political Reviews, Micronesia. *The Contemporary Pacific* 21.1 (2009): 127–29. Note: Zackios later bacame RMI Ambassador to the U.S.

54. Ruth Currie-McDaniel, Claus R. Martel, and James A. Walker, *The U.S. Army Space and Strategic Defense Command: Historic Overview*. 4th ed. (Huntsville, AL: Historical

Office, U.S. Army Strategic Defense Command, 1993) 77; Public Law 106–398, Section 2891*:* "Naming of Army missile testing range at Kwajalein Atoll as the Ronald Reagan Ballistic Missile Defense Site at Kwajalein Atoll"; Memorandum, Albert V. Short to John Fairlamb, 15 September 2014. Thanks to Dr. Fairlamb for his research assistance.

55. Kupferman, "Marshall Islands." Political Reviews, Micronesia (2009): 129–30; David Kupferman, "Marshall Islands." Political Reviews, Micronesia. *The Contemporary Pacific* 22.1 (2010): 141; Giff Johnson, "Quiet Diplomacy," MI Journal 16 September 2016: 14.

56. U.S. State Department, "Remarks at the Pacific Islands Forum, Post-Forum Dialogue," 31 August 2012.

57. Testimony of Senator Tony A. deBrum, Member of the Nitijela for Kwajalein Before the Foreign Affairs Subcommittee on Asia, the Pacific, and the Global Environment, 25 July 2007, 3.

58. Quoted in *MI Journal* 9 October 2009; Tony de Brum, *Statement Before the U.S. House of Representatives, Committee on Foreign Affairs, Subcommittee on Asia, 20 May 2010,* 5.

59. Quoted in *MI Journal* 15 January 2010: 2; "U.S. Military Gets Green Light on Kwajalein Lease," "Pacific Islands Report," Political Reviews, Micronesia. *The Contemporary Pacific* (25 October 2010).

60. "Pacific Islands Report," Political Reviews, Micronesia (25 October 2010).

61. Department of Defense, MRT, Reagan Test Site, *Command Statement,* http://www.smdc.army.mil/RTS (21 January 2016); *Command Statement,* http://www.army.mil/kwajalein (21 January 2016).

62. *MI Journal* 10 August 2012: 1–2; 4 October 2013; 4 July 2014.

63. *MI Journal* 2 September 2013, 7 February 2014, 24 October 2014; Coral Davenport, "Rising Seas are Claiming a Vulnerable Nation," *The New York Times* 2 December 2016.

64. Quote in *MI Journal* 7 February 2014: 18.

Epilogue

1. United Nations. Office for Disarmament Affairs, "Non-proliferation Treaty," January 2016; *The Marshall Islands Journal* (hereafter referred to as *MI Journal*) 25 December 2015.

2. Fred Pedro on Emom Radio, 30 July 2014, quoted in *MI Journal* 8 August 2014; *The New York Times* February 2015; Nuclear Age Peace Foundation, 24 April 2014; *MI Journal* 2 May 2014; 16 May 2014; 5 September 2014; 19 December 2014; 5 February 2016. Note: In recognition of his efforts to hold nuclear nations in contempt, Tony deBrum was nominated for the Nobel Peace Prize.

3. *MI Journal* 18 December 2016.

4. Coral Davenport, "Rising Seas are Claiming a Vulnerable Nation," *The New York Times* 2 December 2015; *MI Journal* March 2014.

5. *MI Journal* 1 January 2016.

6. *MI Journal* 15 January 2016; 22 January 2016.

7. *MI Journal* 29 January 2016; ABC News, 28 January 2016. Note: President Heine's brother was the late Carl Heine.

Bibliography

Primary Sources, Archives and Documents

Carucci, Laurence Marshall. *In Anxious Anticipation of Kuwajleen's Uneven Fruits: A Cultural History of the Significant Locations and Important Resources of Kuwajleen Atoll.* Huntsville, AL: U.S. Army Strategic Defense Command, 1996.
Congress of Micronesia. Records, 1965–1978.
Crowl, Philip A. *Campaign in the Marianas.* Washington, D.C.: Center of Military History, 1993.
____, and Edmund G. Love. *U.S. Army in World War II. The War in the Pacific: Seizure of the Gilberts and Marshalls.* Washington D.C.: Center of Military History, 1955.
Currie-McDaniel, Ruth. *The U.S. Army Strategic Defense Command: Its History and Role in the Strategic Defense Initiative.* Huntsville, AL: Historical Office, U.S. Army Strategic Defense Command, 1986.
____, Claus R. Martel, and James A. Walker, *The U.S. Army Space and Strategic Defense Command: Historic Overview.* 4th ed. Huntsville, AL: Historical Office, U.S. Army Strategic Defense Command, 1993.
Fairlamb, John. "Compact of Free Association Negotiations: Fulfilling the Promise." A paper presented to the Island State Security Conference at the Asia-Pacific Center for Security Studies. Honolulu, Hawaii, June 2001.
____. U.S. Space and Missile Defense Command Representative, Office of Compact Negotiations. "Session II: Enduring Issues, Compacts of Free Association, A U.S. Perspective: Where are we now?" A paper presented to the Island State Security Conference: Asia-Pacific Center for Security Studies. Honolulu, Hawaii, 15–17 July 2003.
Firth, Stewart and Paula Mochida, trans. *German Documents Relating to Micronesia, 1898–1910.* University of Hawai'i Archives (UHI Archives), 1986.
Hezel, Francis X., and M.L. Berg, eds. Documents in *Micronesia Winds of Change: A Book of Readings on Micronesian History.* Saipan, Mariana Islands: Omnibus Program for Social Studies and Cultural Heritage, 1979.
The League of Nations. Records, 1920–1926.
Publicado en el Numero 180 de la Gaceta de Madred, Tomo II. 29 June 1899. Translated by Sarah Bradham.
Trust Territory of the Pacific Islands Archives, University of Hawai'i Archives (TTPI Archives, UHI Archives), 1949–1972.
United Nations Records, 1945–1961.
____. *Report of the United Nations Visiting Mission to the Trust Territory of the Pacific Islands, 1961.* Supplement 20 Official Records, Twenty-seventh Session, 1 June–19 July 1961. New York: United Nations, 1961.
United States Atomic Energy Commission. Records, 1968.

United States Center of Military History Archives (CMH Archives).
United States Central Intelligence Agency. Records, 1949.
United States Congress. *Atomic Energy Act of 1946, Public Law 585. 79th Cong. Excerpted from "Legislative History of the Atomic Energy Act of 1946," compiled by James D. Nuse. AEA Headquarters Library. Vol. 1, Principal Documents.* Washington, D.C.: U.S. Atomic Energy Commission, 1965.

_____. *The Compact of Free Association Amendments Act of 2003. Compilation of Documents. Federated States of Micronesia Joint Committee on Compact Economic Negotiations, Washington Office May 12, 2004.* Washington, D.C.: U.S. Government Printing Office, 2004.

_____. *Public Law 99–239: Compact of Free Association Act of 1985 Between the Government of the United States and the Government of the Federated States of Micronesia and the Government of the Republic of the Marshall Islands, 14 January 1986.* Washington, D.C.: U.S. Government Printing Office, 1986.

_____. *Public Law 99–658: Compact of Free Association Approval Between the Government of the United States and the Government of the Federated States of Micronesia and the Government of the Republic of the Marshall Islands, 14 November 1986.* Washington, D.C.: U.S. Government Printing Office, 1986.

_____. *Public Law 108–188: Compact of Free Association Amendments Act of 2003 Between the Government of the United States and the Government of the Federated States of Micronesia and the Government of the Republic of the Marshall Islands, 17 December 2003.* Washington, D.C.: U.S. Government Printing Office, 2003.

United States Congress, General Accounting Office. *Report by the Comptroller General of the United States. The Challenge of Enhancing Micronesian Self-Sufficiency, 25 January 1983. GAO ID 83–1.* Washington, D.C.: GAO, 1983.

_____. *Report to Congressional Requesters, September 1992. Marshall Islands: Status of Nuclear Claims Trust Fund.* Washington, D.C.: GAO, 1992.

_____. *Report to Congressional Requesters, January 2002. Foreign Relations: Kwajalein Atoll is the Key U.S. Defense Interest in Two Micronesian Nations.* Washington, D.C.: GAO, 2002.

_____. *Compact of Free Association, as Amended, Between the Government of the United States and the Government of the Republic of the Marshall Islands. "Title Two-Economic Relations." Article I, Grant Assistance. 03–890T.* Washington, D.C.: GAO, 2003.

United States. Court of Appeals for the Federal Circuit. *Brief of Defendant-Appellee United States. Appeal From the U.S. Court of Federal Claims in 06-CV-288, Judge Christine O.C. Miller. 2007–5175: The People of Bikini, By and Through the Kili/Bikini/Ejit Local and Government Council, Plaintiffs-Appellants v. United States, Defendant.* Washington, D.C., 4 April 2008.

United States Department of Defense Records, 1945–1983.
United States Department of the Interior Records, 1968–1978.
United States Department of the Interior. Annual Report of the High Commissioner of the Trust Territory of the Pacific Islands to the Secretary of the Interior, 1963, 1965, 1966, 1967, 1968, 1969, 1970, 1971.

_____. 13th Annual Report of the United States to the United Nations on the Administration of the Trust Territory of the Pacific Islands. 1 July 1959–30 June 1960.

_____. 15th Annual Report of the United States to the United Nations on the Administration of the Trust Territory of the Pacific Islands. 1 July 1961–30 June 1962.

_____. 16th Annual Report of the United States to the United Nations on the Administration of the Trust Territory of the Pacific Islands. 1 July 1963–30 June 1964.

United States Department of the Interior. Office of the Solicitor. Vice Admiral Blandy's Press Conference Pertaining to Joint Army-Navy Task Force Number One, Operation Crossroads. "Full Story of Atomic Bomb Tests Will Be Told to Public." Release No. 46, 13 May 1946. Washington, D.C.: U.S. Government Printing Office, 1946.

United States. Department of the Air Force. *United States Air Force Space and Missile Systems*

Organization: A Chronology, 1954–1979. Washington, D.C.: U.S. Government Printing Office.
U.S. Army Ballistic Missile Defense Systems Command. "Annual History," 1967; 1970.
_____. *ABM Research and Development at Bell Laboratories: Kwajalein Field Station*. Whippany, NJ: Bell Labs for the U.S. Army Ballistic Missile Defense Systems Command, 1975.
_____. "Kwajalein Missile Range." *Annual Historical Review: 1 October 1975 to 30 September 1986*.
_____. Kwajalein Missile Range Directorate. *KREMS: The History of the Kiernan Reentry Measurements Site*. Michael S. Holtcamp, 1 October, 1980.
_____. *Summary of the Events and Circumstances Concerning Acquisition of the Kwajalein Mid-Atoll Corridor, as of 31 May 1970*.
U.S. Army in World War II. The War in the Pacific: Seizure of the Gilberts and Marshalls. Washington, D.C.: Office of the Chief of Military History, 1955.
U.S. Army Space and Strategic Defense Command. *Analysis of Existing Facilities. USASDC Kwajalein Atoll Marshall Islands. June 1992*. Facilities Support Division Work Control Department. Contract DASG60–87-C–0115. Prepared by Johnson Controls World Service, Inc.
_____. *Memorandum of Agreement Between the U.S. Army Space and Strategic Defense Command and the Republic of the Marshall Islands*. Signed by the United States, 26 January 1994, and by the Republic of the Marshall Islands, 18 February 1994.
U.S. Army Strategic Defense Command. *Annual Historical Reviews, 1982–1990*.
_____. Information Paper, Kwajalein Missile Range. Public Affairs Office, Kwajalein Missile Range, 28 February 1986.
United States. Department of Defense. *Department of Defense, MRT, Reagan Test Site, Command Statement*, http://www.smdc.army.mil/RTS (21 January 2016), *Command Statement*, http://www.army.mil/kwajalein, 21 (January 2016).
United States. Department of the Navy. *Military Government Handbook. OPNAV P22–1 (Formerly OPNAV 50E-1): Marshall Islands. Office of the Chief of Naval Operations, 17 August 1943*. Washington, D.C.: U.S. Government Printing Office, 1943.
_____. *Civil Affairs Handbook. Marshall Islands Statistical Supplement. OPNAV 50E-18. Office of the Chief of Naval Operations, 20 May 1944*. Washington, D.C.: U.S. Government Printing Office, 1944.
_____. *Handbook on the Trust Territory of the Pacific Islands: A Handbook for Use in Training and Administration. Office of the Chief of Naval Operations*. Prepared at the School of Naval Administration, Hoover Institute, Stanford University. Washington, D.C.: U.S. Government Printing Office, 1948.
Department of State. Bulletins. *Bulletin, Chapter XIII: The Trusteeship Council* (24 June 1945): 1131–1132. Washington, D.C.: U.S. Government Printing Office, 1945.
_____. *Bulletin, Trusteeship and Non-Self-Governing Territories in the Charter of the United Nations*. Ralph J. Bunche. (30 December 1945): 1037–1044. Washington, D.C.: U.S. Government Printing Office, 1945.
_____. *Bulletin, Policy on Japanese Mandated Islands* (27 January 1946): 113. Washington, D.C.: U.S. Government Printing Office, 1946.
_____. *Bulletin, U.S. Position on the Establishment of the Trusteeship System* (23 March 1947): 991- 94. Washington, D.C.: U.S. Government Printing Office, 1947.
_____. *Bulletin, The Inauguration of the Trusteeship System of the United Nations*. Elizabeth Armstrong and William I. Cargo. (23 March 1947): 511–13; 521. Washington, D.C.: U.S. Government Printing Office, 1947.
_____. *Bulletin, Trusteeship Agreement for the Former Japanese Mandated Islands* (4 May 1947): 791- 92. Washington, D.C.: U.S. Government Printing Office, 1947.
United States Department of State. "Contemporary Practice of the United States Relating to International Law." Marian Nash Leich. Digest *of U.S. Practice in International Law. U.S. Digest*. Ch. 2 §6 (1987): 405–10. Washington, D.C.: U.S. Government Printing Office, 1987.

_____. "Contemporary Practice of the United States Relating to International Law." Marian Nash Leich. Digest of U.S. Practice in International Law. *U.S. Digest*. Ch. 4 §1 (1990): 237–48. Washington, D.C.: U.S. Government Printing Office, 1990.

_____. *Bureau of Public Affairs. Office of Public Communication. Background Notes, Marshall Islands*. Washington, D.C.: U.S. Government Printing Office, 1994.

_____. "Contemporary Practice of the United States Relating to International Law." Marian Nash Leich. Digest of U.S. Practice in International Law. *U.S. Digest* (1995): 96–130. Washington, D.C.: U.S. Government Printing Office, 1995.

United States Department of State. Foreign Relations of the United States (FRUS). *FRUS, 1894: Affairs in Hawaii, Appendix II*. Washington, D.C.: U.S. Government Printing Office, 1894.

_____. *FRUS, 1901: Affairs in China*. Washington, D.C.: U.S. Government Printing Office, 1901.

_____. *FRUS, 1919: The Paris Peace Conference, Vols. I and II*. Washington, D.C.: U.S. Government Printing Office, 1919.

_____. *Papers Relating to Foreign Relations of the United States, Vol. 1*. Washington, D.C.: U.S. Government Printing Office, 1921.

_____. *FRUS, 1945: Conferences at Malta and Yalta*. Washington, D.C.: U.S. Government Printing Office, 1945.

_____. *Foreign Relations of the United States, 1946. General: The United Nations Volume 1 (1946)*. "Memorandum on United States Participation in the Administration of the Trust Territories, Briefing Book II: 20 December 1945." Washington, D.C.: U.S. Government Printing Office, 1946.

_____. *FRUS, 1945–1950: Emergence of the Intelligence Establishment*. Washington, D.C.: U.S. Government Printing Office, 1996.

_____. *Foreign Relations of the United States, 1973–1976: China, Volume XVII*. Washington, D.C.: U.S. Government Printing Office, 2006.

United States Department of State. Memoranda, 1918–1969.

_____. Memoranda, Office for Micronesian Status Negotiations, 1969–87. United States. Library of Congress. Congressional Research Service. *CRS Report for Congress*. "Missile Defense: The Current Debate." *Coordinated by Steven A. Hildreth and Amy F. Woolf, Specialists in National Defense, Foreign Affairs, Defense, and Trade Division*. 25 February 2002.

_____. *CRS Report for Congress*. "Report Evaluating the Request of the Government of the Republic of the Marshall Islands Presented to the Congress of the United States of America." Regarding Changed Circumstances Arising from U.S. Nuclear Testing in the Marshall Islands Pursuant to Article IX of the Nuclear Claims Settlement Approved by Congress in Public Law 99–239, November 2004. Order Code RL 32811. Updated 16 May 2005.

United States. Office of the President. National Security Council Bulletins.

_____. *Bulletin Vol. 86. No. 2117. Compact of Free Association with Pacific Islands* (16 October 1986): 74–75. Washington, D.C.: U.S. Government Printing Office, 1986.

_____. Office of Compact Negotiations. *Compact of Free Association Negotiations Update, 1 July 2003*. Washington, D.C.: U.S. Government Printing Office, 2003.

_____. Embassy of the United States, Majuro, Marshall Islands. *"Compact 2023: What Next?" Ambassador Martha L. Campbell, College of the Marshall Islands. Majuro, Marshall Islands, 22 April 2010*. Washington, D.C.: U.S. Government Printing Office, 2010.

United States. Office of the President. National Security Council. National Security Archives, 1963–2005.

_____. *National Security Council Memorandums, 1976–2001*.

Wright, Burton. *Eastern Mandates: The U.S. Army Campaigns of World War II*. Publication 72-23. Washington, D.C.: Center of Military History, 1993.

Interviews

Bryan, Dr. James A., III. Interview with Author. June 2012, July 2012.
Curtis, Carol. Interview with Author. September 1987. For *U.S. Army Strategic Defense Command*. (USASDC).
deBrum, Oscar. Interview with Author. September 1987. For USASDC.
Fairlamb, John. Email correspondence with Author. September 2011 to September 2014.
_____. Telephone Interview with Author. 14 October 2011.
Godbold, Stanly. Email correspondence with Author. 2012 to 2015
Lindsey, Art. Interview with Author. 20 December 2015.
Nimmer, Natalie. Interview with Author. May 2008.
Smith, Norm. Interview with Author. September 1987. For USASDC.
Zeder, Fred, Ambassador. Interview with Author. 15 February 1988. For USASDC.

Secondary Sources

Acheson, Dean. *Present at the Creation: My Years in the State Department*. New York: W.W. Norton, 1969.
Adams, H.B., ed. *Diplomatic and Constitutional History*. Vol. XIX. Baltimore, MD: Johns Hopkins Press, 1901.
Adams, Lawrence E. "American Involvement in Perspective." *National Security and International Trusteeship in the Pacific*. William Roger Luis, ed. Annapolis, MD: Naval Institute Press, 1973.
Alexander, Joseph H. *Utmost Savagery: The Three Days of Tarawa*. Annapolis, MD: Naval Institute Press, 2008.
Alkire, William H. *An Introduction to Peoples and Cultures of Micronesia*. 2nd ed. Menlo Park, CA: Cummings, 1977.
Armstrong, Arthur J., and Howard Loomis Hills. "The Negotiations for the Future Political Status of Micronesia (1980–1984)." *The American Journal of International Law* 78.2 (1984): 484–97.
Asian Development Bank. *Report and Recommendation of the President to the Board of Directors on a Proposed Loan to the Republic of the Marshall Islands for the Ebeye Health and Infrastructure Project*. July 1999.
Auten, Brian J. *Carter's Conversion: The Hardening of American Defense Policy*. Columbia: Missouri University Press, 2008.
Bailey, Gilbert. "Freedom on Kwajalein." *Asia* 44 (October 1944): 437–40.
Bailey, Thomas A. *A Diplomatic History of the American People*. 10th ed. Englewood Cliffs, NJ: Prentice-Hall, 1980.
Ballendorf, Dirk A. *A Brief Review of Economic Development in Micronesia from Earliest Times to the Present*. Prepared for Peace Corps Volunteer Trainees in Micronesia. Saipan, Northern Mariana Islands, 1968.
Ballendorf, Dirk A., and Howard Seay. "Catalysts or Barnacles in Micronesia: The First Five Years of the Peace Corps." *In Oceania and Beyond: Essays on the Pacific Since 1945*, ed. Frank P. King. Westport, CT: Greenwood Press, 1976.
"Ballistic Missile Defense: The Emperor's Newest Clothes." Narrator: Kathryn R. Schultz. Washington, D.C.: Center for Defense Information, 9 June 1996.
Barry, Hamlet J., III. "The Marshall Islands." *In Oceania and Beyond: Essays on the Pacific Since 1945*, ed. Frank P. King. Westport, CT: Greenwood Press, 1976.
Bates, George H. "Some Aspects of the Samoan Question." *Century* 37.6 (1889): 947.
Baucom, Donald R. *The Origins of SDI, 1944–1983*. Lawrence: University Press of Kansas, 1992.
Beasley, W.G. *Japanese Imperialism, 1894–1945*. Oxford: Clarendon Press, 1987.
_____. *The Rise of Modern Japan: Political, Economic, and Social Change Since 1850*. New York: St. Martin's Press, 1995.

Bell Labs. *ABM Research and Development at Bell Laboratories: Kwajalein Field Station.* Whippany, NJ: Bell Labs for the U.S. Army Ballistic Missile Defense Systems Command, 1975.
Bemis, Samuel Flagg. "The Yap Island Controversy." *The Pacific Review* 2 (September 1921): 308–28.
Bernstein, Barton, ed. *Politics and Policies of the Truman Administration.* Chicago: Quadrangle, 1970.
Bertell, Rosalie. "Victims of the Nuclear Age." *The Ecologist* (November 1999): 408–11.
Besse, Janet, and Harold D. Lasswell. "Our Columnists on the A-Bomb." *World Politics* 3.1 Johns Hopkins University Press (October 1950): 72–87.
Bischof, Gunter, and Robert L. Dupont, eds. *The Pacific War Revisited.* Baton Rouge: Louisiana State University Press, 1997.
Blakeslee, George H. "The Mandates of the Pacific." *Foreign Affairs* 1 (1922): 98–115.
Bliss, Ella Theodora Crosby. *Micronesia Fifty Years in the Island World: A History of the Mission of the American Board.* Ann Arbor: University of Michigan Press, 2009.
Blum, John M., et al. *The National Experience: A History of the United States.* 4th ed. New York: Harcourt Brace, 1977.
Bogan, Eugene F. "Government of the Trust Territory of the Pacific Islands." *Annals of the American Academy of Political and Social Science* 267 (January 1950): 164–74.
Boorstin, Daniel J. *The Americans: The National Experience.* New York: Vintage, 1965.
Borgwardt, Elizabeth. *A New Deal for the World: America's Vision for Human Rights.* Cambridge, MA: Belknap Press of Harvard University Press, 2005.
Borneman, Walter R. *The Admirals: Nimitz, Halsey, Leahy, and King—The Five-Star Admirals Who Won the War at Sea.* New York: Back Bay, 2013.
Boyer, Paul. "'The Fences Are Gone': American Policymaking in the Dawn of the Nuclear Era." Reviewed work: "The Winning Weapon: The Atomic Bomb in the Cold War, 1945–1950" by Gregg Herken in *Reviews in American History* 10.3, Johns Hopkins University Press (September 1982): 448–53.
Bradley, David. *No Place to Hide.* Boston: Little, Brown, 1948.
Bradley, James. *The Imperial Cruise: A Secret History of Empire and War.* New York: Back Bay, 2010.
Brown, Richard G. "The German Acquisition of the Caroline Islands, 1898–99." In *Germany in the Pacific and Far East, 1870–1914,* eds. John A. Moses and Paul M. Kennedy. Brisbane, Australia: University of Queensland Press, 1977.
Bryan, James A., III, et al. "Poliomyelitis in an Isolated Population: Report of a Type 1 Epidemic in the Marshall Islands, 1963." *American Journal of Epidemiology* 82.3. Johns Hopkins University, 1966.
Buck, Alice. *The Atomic Energy Commission.* United States Department of Energy. Office of Management. Office of the Executive Secretariat. Office of History and Heritage Resources. July 1983. http://www.energy.gov.
Buckley, William F., Jr. "Precision Sailing: The Sun and Stars by Which Sailors Have Navigated from Time Immemorial Have a New Rival in the Skies—Satellites." *The New York Times* 19 May 1985.
Buhl, Lance C. "Mariners and Machines: Resistance to Technological Change in the American Navy, 1865–1869." *The Journal of American History* 61.3 (December 1974): 703–27.
Builder, Carl H. *The Army in the Strategic Planning Process. Who Shall Bell the Cat?* Prepared for the U.S. Army by the Rand Corporation. Santa Monica, CA. 1987.
Bumpers, Dale. "Missile Defense Boondoggle." *Raleigh News and Observer* 26 February 1999: 19A.
Bush, George H.W. "Remarks at the Conclusion of the Pacific Island Nations–U.S. Summit in Honolulu, Hawaii." Center for Cultural Interchange Between East and West. 27 October 1990.
———. "Statement on Signing a Bill Approving Diplomatic Relations Agreements with the Marshall Islands and Micronesia." White House, Washington, D.C. 26 July 1989.

Callahan, James M. *American Relations in the Pacific and the Far East, 1784–1900*. Baltimore, MD: Johns Hopkins Press, 1901.
Carter, Jimmy. *White House Diary*. New York: Farrar, Straus, Giroux, 2010.
Carucci, Laurence Marshall. *In Anxious Anticipation of Kuwajleen's Uneven Fruits: A Cultural History of the Significant Locations and Important Resources of Kuwajleen Atoll*. Huntsville, AL: U.S. Army Strategic Defense Command, 1996.
_____. "The Source of the Force in Marshallese Cosmology." In The *Pacific Theater: Island Representations of World War II*, eds. Geoffrey M. White and Lamont Lindstrom. Pacific Islands Monograph Series, No. 8. Honolulu: University of Hawai'i Press, 1989.
Clark, Roger S. "Self-Determination and Free Association—Should the United Nations Terminate the Pacific Islands Trust?" *Harvard International Law Journal* 21.1 (Winter 1980): 2–86.
Clyde, Paul H. *Japan's Pacific Mandate*. New York: Macmillan, 1935.
Cobbs, Elizabeth A. "Decolonization, the Cold War, and the Foreign Policy of the Peace Corps." *Diplomatic History* 20.1 (1996): 79–105.
Coffman, Tom. *Nation Within: The Story of America's Annexation of the Nation of Hawai'i*. Honolulu: EpiCenter Press, 1998.
Connell, John. *Marshall Islands. Country Report No. 8: Migration, Employment, and Development in the Pacific*. Noumea, New Caledonia: South Pacific Commission, 1983.
_____. "The New Micronesia: Pitfalls and Problems of Dependent Development." *Pacific Studies*. 14.2 (1991): 87–120.
"Constitutional Law: Executive Agreements. International Law: Executive Authority Concerning Future Political Status of the Trust Territory of the Pacific Islands." *Michigan Law Review* 66.6 (April 1968): 1277–1292.
Converse, Elizabeth. "The United States as Trustee." *Far Eastern Survey* 18.22 (1949): 260–63.
Cooper, John M. *Reconsidering Woodrow Wilson: Progressivism, Internationalism, War, and Peace*. Baltimore, MD: Johns Hopkins Press, 2008.
_____. *Woodrow Wilson: A Biography*. New York: Vintage Press, 2009.
Crapol, Edward P. *James G. Blaine: Architect of Empire*. Biographies in American Foreign Policy, 4. Washington, D.C.: Rowman and Littlefield, 1999.
Crocombe, Ron, and Ahmed Ali. *Politics in Micronesia*. Vol. 3 of the series *Politics of the Pacific Islands*. Suva, Fiji: Institute of Pacific Studies of the University of the South Pacific, 1988.
Currie-McDaniel, Ruth. *The U.S. Army Strategic Defense Command: Its History and Role in the Strategic Defense Initiative*. Huntsville, AL: Historical Office, U.S. Army Strategic Defense Command, 1986.
_____, Claus R. Martel, and James A. Walker. *The U.S. Army Space and Strategic Defense Command: Historic Overview*. 4th ed. Huntsville, AL: Historical Office, U.S. Army Strategic Defense Command, 1993.
Curtis, Carol. *Handicrafts*. Alele National Archives, Library, and Museum. Majuro, Marshall Islands.
Davenport, Coral. "Rising Seas Are Claiming a Vulnerable Nation." *The New York Times* 2 December 2015.
Davis, Vincent. *Postwar Defense Policy and US Navy, 1943–1946*. Chapel Hill: University of North Carolina Press, 1966.
Dennis, Alfred L.P. *Adventures in American Diplomacy, 1896–1906*. New York: E.P. Dutton, 1928.
Denoon, Donald, ed. *The Cambridge History of the Pacific Islanders*. Cambridge: Cambridge University Press, 1997.
DeSmith, Stanley A. *Microstates and Micronesia: Problems of America's Pacific Islands and Other Minute Territories*. New York: New York University Press, 1970.
_____. *Options for Micronesia: A Potential Crisis for America's Pacific Trust Territory*. New York: New York University Center for International Studies, 1969.

Dever, Greg. *Ebeye, Marshall Islands: A Public Health Hazard*. Honolulu: Micronesia Support Committee, 1978.
Dibblin, Jane. *Day of Two Suns: U.S. Nuclear Testing and the Pacific Islanders*. London: Virago Press, 1988.
Dorrance, John C. *The United States and the Pacific Islands*. The Washington Papers 158. Westport, CT: Praeger, 1992.
Dower, John W. *War Without Mercy: Race and Power in the Pacific War*. New York: Pantheon, 1986.
Doyle, William A. "The United States' Strategic Trust in the Pacific." Dissertation. Air War College at the Air University, 1965.
Drucker, Philip. "Anthropology in Trust Territory Administration." *The Scientific Monthly* 72.5 (May 1951): 306–12.
Dudden, Arthur Power. *The American Pacific: From the Old China Trade to the Present*. New York: Oxford University Press, 1992.
_____, ed. *The American Empire in the Pacific. The Pacific World: Lands, Peoples and History of the Pacific, 1500–1900*. Vol. 9. Trowbridge, Wiltshire, England: Cromwell Press, 2004.
Dulles, Foster Rhea. *America in the Pacific: A Century of Expansion*. Boston: Houghton Mifflin, 1938.
Dyer, Thomas G. *Theodore Roosevelt and the Idea of Race*. Baton Rouge: Louisiana State University Press, 1992.
Emerson, Rupert. "American Policy Toward Pacific Dependencies." *Pacific Affairs* 20.3 (1947): 259–75.
"Excerpts from Unofficial Account of President Nixon's Meeting with Reporters." Special to *The New York Times* 26 July 1969.
Falgout, Suzanne, Lin Poyer, and Laurence M. Carucci. *Memories of War: Micronesians in the Pacific War*. Honolulu: Hawai'i University Press, 2008.
Fallows, James. "The Philippines: The Bases Dilemma." *Atlantic* 261.2 (1988): 18–30.
Federated States of Micronesia. *Report on Compact Negotiations, 2 November 2001*. Palikir, Pohnpei: Federated States of Micronesia Information Service, 2001.
Finney, John W. "Nike Zeus Intercepts a Missile Fired from U.S. Over Pacific." *The New York Times* 20 July 1962.
Firth, Stewart. "German Firms in the Pacific Islands, 1857–1914." In *Germany in the Pacific and Far East, 1870–1914*, eds. John A. Moses and Paul M. Kennedy. Brisbane, Australia: University of Queensland Press, 1977.
_____. *Nuclear Playground: Fight for an Independent and Nuclear Free Pacific*. Honolulu: University of Hawai'i Press, 1987.
_____. "Sovereignty and Independence in the Contemporary Pacific." *The Contemporary Pacific* 1 and 2 (Spring and Fall 1989): 75–76.
FitzGerald, Frances. *Way Out There in the Blue: Reagan, Star Wars and the End of the Cold War*. New York: Simon & Schuster, 2001.
Foltos, Lester J. "The New Pacific Barrier: America's Search for Security in the Pacific, 1945–47." *Diplomatic History* 13.3 (1989): 317–42.
Forrestal, James, and Walter Mills. *The Forrestal Diaries*. New York: Viking Press, 1951.
Foster, John W. *American Diplomacy in the Orient*. Boston: Houghton, Mifflin, 1904.
French, Howard W. "A Pacific Puzzle: Connecting Dots into a Nation." *Majuro Journal* 30 June 2001: A4.
Friedman, Hal M. *Arguing Over the American Lake: Bureaucracy and Rivalry in the U.S. Pacific, 1945–1947*. Williams-Ford Texas A&M University Military History Series No. 126. College Station: Texas A&M University Press, 2009.
_____. "The Beast in Paradise: The United States Navy in Micronesia, 1943–1947." *The Pacific Historical Review* 62.2 (May 1993): 173–95.
_____. *Creating an American Lake: US Imperialism and Strategic Security in a Pacific Basin, 1945–1947*. Contributions in Military Studies 198. Westport, CT: Praeger, 2001.

_____. *Governing the American Lake: US Defense and Administration of the Pacific Basin, 1945–1947*. East Lansing: Michigan State University Press, 2007.
Galbraith, Kate, Glenda Bendure, and Ned Friary. *Micronesia*. 3rd ed. A Lonely Planet Travel Survival Kit. Oakland, CA: Lonely Planet, 2000.
Gale, Roger W. *The Americanization of Micronesia: A Study of the Consolidation of U.S. Rule in the Pacific*. Washington, D.C.: University Press of America, 1979.
Garrett, John. *Where Nets Were Cast: Christianity in Oceania Since World War II*. Suva, Fiji: Institute of Pacific Studies, 1997.
Gereben, Janos. "Cleveland Bears His Role in Micronesian Policy." *Honolulu Star-Bulletin* 30 July 1971: A1.
Gerig, Benjamin. "Significance of the Trusteeship System." *Annals of the American Academy of Political and Social Science* 255 (January 1948): 39–47.
Gilchrist, Huntington. *Imperialism and the Mandates System*. Published for the League of Nations Non-Partisan Association by the Margaret C. Peabody Fund. New York: Margaret C. Peabody Fund, 1928.
_____. "The Japanese Islands: Annexation or Trusteeship?" *Foreign Affairs* XXII (1944): 635–42.
Glain, Stephen. *State vs. Defense: The Battle to Define America's Empire*. New York: Crown, 2011.
Glanz, James. "Cast of Star Wars Makes Comeback in Bush Plan." *The New York Times* 22 July 2001: 10.
Godbold, E. Stanly, Jr. *Jimmy and Rosalynn Carter: The Georgia Years, 1924–1974*. New York: Oxford University Press, 2010.
Goodrich, Leland M., and Marie J. Carroll, eds. *Documents on American Foreign Relations, Volume VI: July 1943–June 1944*. Boston: World Peace Foundation, 1945.
Graebner, Norman A. "James Polk." In *The American Empire in the Pacific: From Trade to Strategic Balance, 1700–1922. The Pacific World: Lands, Peoples and History of the Pacific, 1500–1900*. Vol. 9, ed. Arthur Power Dudden. Burlington, VT: Ashgate Variorum, 2004.
Graham, Daniel O. *High Frontier: A New National Strategy*. Washington, D.C.: High Frontier, 1982.
Gray, J.A.C. *American Samoa: A History of American Samoa and Its United States Naval Administration*. Annapolis, MD: U.S. Naval Institute, 1960.
Greenberger, Allen J. "Japan as a Colonial Power: The Micronesian Example." *Asian Profile* 2.2 (April 1974): 151–63.
Haglelgam, John R. "A Brief History." Regent Professor, College of Micronesia, Federated States of Micronesia.
Hamilton, Gail. *Biography of James G. Blaine*. Norwich, CT: Henry Bill Publishing, 1895.
Hanley, Charles J. "Islanders' Fears Rising with Tides: Nation Status, Culture at Risk." *Asheville Citizen-Times* 8 December 2010: A10.
Hanlon, David. "Micronesia: Writing and Rewriting the Histories of a Nonentity." *Pacific Studies* 12.2 (March 1989): 1–21.
_____. "Patterns of Colonial Rule in Micronesia to 1942." In *Tides of History: The Pacific Islands in the Twentieth Century*, eds. Kerry R. Howe, Robert C. Kiste, and Brij V. Lal, 93–118. Honolulu: University of Hawai'i Press, 1994.
_____. *Remaking Micronesia: Discourses Over Development in a Pacific Territory, 1944–1982*. Honolulu: University of Hawai'i Press, 1998.
Hastings, Max. *Retribution: The Battle for Japan, 1944–45*. New York: Knopf, 2008.
Hatanaka, Sachiko. *Culture Change in Micronesia Under the Japanese Administration*. Programme of Participation, No. 4. Paris: UNESCO, 1973.
Heffer, Jean. *The United States and the Pacific: History of a Frontier*. Trans. W. Donald Wilson. Notre Dame, IN: University of Notre Dame Press, 2002.
Heiferman, Ronald Ian. *The Cairo Conference of 1943: Roosevelt, Churchill, Chiang Kai-shek and Madame Chiang*. Jefferson, NC: McFarland, 2011.

Heine, Carl. "Current Developments in the Pacific: Micronesia's Future Political Status Commission, Its Rendezvous with Destiny." *Journal of Pacific History* 4 (1969): 127–32.

———. *Micronesia at the Crossroads: A Reappraisal of the Micronesian Political Dilemma*. An East-West Center Book. Honolulu: University of Hawai'i Press, 1974.

Henning, Joseph M. *Outposts of Civilization: Race Religion and Formative Years of American-Japanese Relations*. New York: New York University Press, 2000.

Herwig, Holger H. *Politics of Frustration: The United States in German Naval Planning, 1889–1941*. New York: Little, Brown, 1976.

Hess, Jim. "Republic of the Marshall Islands." Political Reviews, Micronesia. *The Contemporary Pacific* (Spring 1997): 210–17.

Hezel, Francis X. *First Taint of Civilization: A History of the Caroline and Marshall Islands in Pre-Colonial Days, 1521–1885*. Pacific Islands Monograph Series, Book 1. Honolulu: University of Hawai'i Press, 2000.

———. "Looking Ahead to the End of Trusteeship, Trust Territory of the Pacific Islands." *Journal of Pacific History* 4 (1978): 204–10.

———. *Making Sense of Micronesia: The Logic of Pacific Island Culture*. Honolulu: University of Hawai'i Press, 2013.

———. *The New Shape of Old Island Cultures: A Half Century of Social Change in Micronesia*. Honolulu: University of Hawai'i Press, 2001.

———. *Reflections on Micronesia: The Collected Papers of Father Francis X. Hezel*. Working Papers Series. Honolulu: University of Hawai'i at Manoa, 1982.

———. *Strangers in Their Own Land: A Century of Colonial Rule in the Caroline and Marshall Islands*. Pacific Islands Monograph Series 13. Honolulu: University of Hawai'i Press, 2003.

Hills, Howard Loomis. "Compact of Free Association for Micronesia: Constitutional and International Law Issues." *International Lawyer* 18.3 (Summer 1984): 583–608.

Hinckley, Ronald H. *People, Polls, and Policymakers: American Public Opinion and National Security*. New York: Macmillan, 1992.

Hiser, David and Melinda Berge. "New Nations in the Pacific." *National Geographic* (October 1986): 460–500.

Hitch, Thomas K. "The Administration of America's Pacific Islands." *Political Science Quarterly* 61.3 (September 1946): 384–407.

Hobbs, William Herbert. "In the Mandated Pacific Islands." *Michigan Alumnus Quarterly Review* 49.15 20 e 1943. Ann Arbor: The Alumni Association of the University of Michigan, 1943.

Hoffman, Elizabeth Cobbs. *All You Need Is Love: The Peace Corps and the Spirit of the 1960s*. Cambridge, MA: Harvard University Press, 1998.

———. "Bernath Lecture: Diplomatic History and the Meaning of Life: Toward a Global American History." *Diplomatic History* 21.4 (1997): 499–518.

Hollingsworth, J. Rogers, ed. *American Expansion in the Late Nineteenth Century: Colonialist or Anticolonialist?* New York: Holt, Rinehart and Winston, 1968.

Hotta, Eri. *Japan 1941: Countdown to Infamy*. New York: Knopf, 2013.

Howe, K.R., Robert C. Kiste, and Brij V. Lal, eds. *Tides of History: The Pacific Islands in the Twentieth Century*. Honolulu: University of Hawai'i Press, 1994.

Hughes, Daniel T., and Sherwood G. Ligenfelter, eds. *Political Development in Micronesia*. Columbus: Ohio State University Press, 1974.

Hull, Cordell. *The Memoirs of Cordell Hull*. 2 Vols. New York: Macmillan, 1948.

Hunt, Linda. *Secret Agenda: The United States Government, Nazi Scientists, and Project Paperclip, 1945–1990*. New York: St. Martin's Press, 1991.

Hunt, Michael H. *Ideology and U.S. Foreign Policy*. New Haven, CT: Yale University Press, 1987.

Ickes, Harold L. "The Navy at Its Worst." *Collier's Weekly* 118 (31 August 1946): 22–23.

Ide, Henry C. "The Imbroglio in Samoa." *North American Review* 168 (1899): 511.

———. "Our Interest in Samoa." *North American Review* 165 (1897): 489.

Igarashi, Masahiro. *Associated Statehood in International Law*. The Hague: Kluver Law International, 2002.
Ikenberry, G. John, ed. *The Crisis of American Foreign Policy: Wilsonianism in the Twenty-First Century*. Princeton, NJ: Princeton University Press, 2009.
"Introducing the Republic of the Marshall Islands." *Asian Culture Quarterly* 17.2 (1989): 83–89.
Iriye, Akira. *Japan and the Wider World: From the Mid-Nineteenth Century to the Present*. London: Longman, 1997.
_____. *Pacific Estrangement: Japanese and American Expansion, 1897–1911*. Harvard Studies in American-East Asian Relations. Boston: Harvard University Press, 1972.
Islands of Micronesia Under the Administration of U.S. Naval Military Government. Pacific Ocean Areas. Maps. Honolulu: The United States Commercial Company, 1946.
Jacobsen, Annie. *Operation Paperclip: The Secret Intelligence Program That Brought Nazi Scientists to America*. Boston: Little, Brown, 2014.
Jetnil-Kijiner, Kathy. "Carl Heine Remembered: A Marshall Islands Legacy." Special on behalf of the Heine family to *Yokwe Online*. 14 April 2011.
Johnson, Donald D. "The Trust Territory of the Pacific Islands." *Current History* 58.341 (1970): 233–39; 246.
Johnson, Giff. *Collision Course at Kwajalein: Marshall Islanders in the Shadow of the Bomb*. Honolulu: Pacific Concerns Resource Center, 1984.
_____. *Don't Ever Whisper—Darlene Keju: Pacific Health Pioneer, Champion for Nuclear Survivors*. CreateSpace Independent Publishing Platform, 2013.
_____. "Ebeye: Apartheid, U.S. Style." *The Nation* 25 December 1976: 22.
_____. "Ebeye and Kwajalein: A Tale of Two Islands." *The Progressive* 43.2 (1979): 47.
_____. "Marshall Islands." Political Reviews, Micronesia. *The Contemporary Pacific* (Spring 1993): 141–44.
_____. "Marshall Islands: Politics in the Marshall Islands." In *Micronesian Politics*, ed. Ron Crocombe. Suva, Fiji: Institute of Pacific Studies, University of the South Pacific, 1988: 67–85.
_____. "Nuclear Legacy: Islands Laid Waste." *OCEANS* (1980): 57–60.
Johnson, Giff, ed. *The Marshall Islands Journal*. 2010–2016.
Johnstone, Andrew. "Creating a 'Democratic Foreign Policy': The State Department's Division of Public Liaison and Public Opinion, 1944–1953." *Diplomatic History* 35.3 (2011): 483–503.
Johnstone, William C. "The United States as a Pacific Power." *Current History* 58.344 (1970): 193–243.
Jones, Howard. *Crucible of Power: A History of American Foreign Relations from 1897*. Washington, D.C.: Rowman and Littlefield, 2008.
Jones, Marcus. "Strategy as Character: Bismarck and the Prussian-German Question, 1862–1878." In *The Shaping of Grand Strategy, Policy, Diplomacy, and War*, eds. Williamson Murray, Richard Hart Sinnreich and James Lacey. Cambridge: Cambridge University Press, 2011.
Kahn, E.J., Jr. *A Reporter in Micronesia*. New York: W.W. Norton, 1966.
Karig, Walter. *The Fortunate Islands, a Pacific Interlude: An Account of the Pleasant Lands and People in the U.S. Trust Territories of the Pacific*. New York: Rinehart, 1948.
Kastor, Peter J. *America's Struggle with Empire: A Documentary History*. Washington, D.C.: CQ Press, 2010.
Kawamura, Noriko. "Wilsonian Idealism and Japanese Claims at the Paris Peace Conference." *Pacific Historical Review* 66.4 (November 1997): 503–26.
Keim, Jeanette. "Forty Years of German-American Political Relations." Dissertation. University of Pennsylvania, 1919.
Keith, Jeffrey A. "Civilization, Race, and the Japan Expedition's Cultural Diplomacy, 1853–1854." *Diplomatic History* 35.2 (April 2011): 179–202.
Kelin, Daniel A., II, ed. *Marshall Islands: Legends and Stories*. Honolulu: Bess Press, 2003.

Kennedy, Ross A. *The Will to Believe: Woodrow Wilson, World War I, and America's Strategy for Peace and Security.* Kent, OH: Kent State University Press, 2009.
Kent, Glenn A. *A Suggested Policy Framework for Strategic Defenses.* Prepared for the Ford Foundation. Santa Monica, CA: The RAND Corporation, 1987.
Kentarō, Kaneko. "A Japanese Monroe Doctrine and Manchuria." *Contemporary Japan* 1.1 (1932): 176–84.
Kenworthy, E.W. "Pacific Trust: Has U.S. Failed?" *The New York Times* 30 July 1967: 138.
Kimball, Warren F. *Forged in War: Roosevelt, Churchill, and the Second World War.* Chicago: Ivan R. Dee, 1997.
Kissinger, Henry. *The White House Years.* Boston: Little, Brown, 1979.
Kiste, Robert C. *The Bikinians: A Study in Forced Migration.* Menlo Park, CA: Cummings, 1974.
———. "Overview of U.S. Policy." In *History of the Trust Territory of the Pacific Islands: Proceedings of the Ninth Annual Pacific Islands Conference,* ed. Karen Knudsen. Working Papers. Honolulu: University of Hawaii at Manoa, 1985.
Kluge, P.F. *The Edge of Paradise: America in Micronesia.* Honolulu: University of Hawai'i Press, 1991.
Knudsen, Karen, ed. *History of the Trust Territory of the Pacific Islands: Proceedings of the Ninth Annual Pacific Islands Conference.* Working Papers. Honolulu: University of Hawai'i at Manoa, 1985.
Kolko, Gabriel. *The Politics of War: The World and United States Foreign Policy, 1943–1945.* New York: Pantheon, 1990.
Kristof, Nicholas D. "An Atomic Age Eden (But Don't Eat the Coconuts)." *The New York Times* 5 March 1997.
———. "Yankee, Go Home. Send Cash." *The New York Times* 30 March 1997.
Kupferman, David W. "Marshall Islands." Political Reviews, Micronesia. *The Contemporary Pacific* 21.1 (2009): 124–30.
———. "Marshall Islands." Political Reviews, Micronesia. *The Contemporary Pacific* 22.1 (2010): 137–44.
———. "Marshall Islands." Political Reviews, Micronesia. *The Contemporary Pacific* 23.2 (2011): 184–90.
———. "Pacific Currents: The Republic of the Marshall Islands Since 1990." *The Journal of Pacific History* 46.1 (June 2011): 75–88.
Labby, David. *The Demystification of Yap: Dialectics of Culture on a Micronesian Island.* Chicago: University of Chicago Press, 1976.
LaFeber, Walter. *The American Age: United States Foreign Policy at Home and Abroad, Vol. 2: Since 1896.* New York: W.W. Norton, 1994.
———. *The American Search for Opportunity, 1865–1913.* The Cambridge History of American Foreign Relations Volume II. Cambridge: Cambridge University Press, 1998.
———. *The Clash: U.S.-Japanese Relations Throughout History.* New York: W.W. Norton, 1998.
———. *The New Empire: An Interpretation of American Expansion 1860–1898.* Ithaca, NY: Cornell University Press, 1998.
Lawrence, W.H. "Work Is Rushed on Pacific Bases." *The New York Times* 24 February 1946: 71.
Leech, Margaret. *In the Days of McKinley.* New York: Harper Brothers, 1959.
Lehman, John F., Jr. *Command of the Seas.* New York: Macmillan, 1988.
Leibowitz, Arnold H. *Colonial Emancipation in the Pacific and the Caribbean: A Legal and Political Analysis.* New York: Praeger, 1976.
———. *Defining Status: A Comprehensive Analysis of U.S. Territorial Relations.* Dordrecht, Netherlands: Martinus Nijhoff, 1989.
Levin, N. Gordon, Jr., ed. *Woodrow Wilson and the Paris Peace Conference.* 2nd ed. Lexington, MA: D.C. Heath and Company, 1972.
Levy, Neil M. *Micronesia Handbook.* 5th ed. Moon Travel Handbooks. Emeryville, CA: Avalon Travel Publishing, 2000.

Louis, W. Roger, ed. *National Security and International Trusteeship in the Pacific.* Annapolis, MD: Naval Institute Press, 1973.
Love, Eric T. *Race Over Empire: Racism and U.S. Imperialism, 1865–1900.* Chapel Hill: University of North Carolina Press, 2004.
Lutz, Catherine A. "The Compact of Free Association, Micronesian Non-Independence, and U.S. Policy." *Bulletin of Concerned Asian Scholars* 18.2 (April-June 1986): 21–27.
Lynch, David M. "United States Policy Toward Micronesia, 1945–1972." Dissertation. West Virginia University, 1973.
Machiavelli, Niccolo. *The Prince.* Oxford: Oxford University Press, 2005.
MacLennan, Nancy. "U.S. Will Bar U.N. from Atom Tests: But Will Answer Questions on Welfare of Inhabitants of Pacific Islands." Special to *The New York Times* 5 December 1947: 16.
MacMillan, Margaret. *Paris 1919: Six Months That Changed the World.* New York: Random House, 2001.
Maga, Timothy P. *John F. Kennedy and a New Pacific Community, 1961–63.* New York: Saint Martin's Press, 1990.
Magstadt, Thomas K. *An Empire If You Can Keep It: Power and Principle in American Foreign Policy.* Washington, D.C.: CQ Press, 2004.
Mahan, A.T. "A Twentieth-Century Outlook." *Harper's New Monthly Magazine* (September 1897): 521–33.
_____. *The Influence of Sea Power Upon History, 1660–1783.* New York: Harper, 1897.
"Majuro: News About Former President Imata Kabua and Judge Charles Henry. Former Marshalls President Seeks Rental Repayment." Contributed by *Yokwe Online* to *The Marshall Islands Journal News.* 11 November 2002.
Manela, Erez. *The Wilsonian Moment: Self-Determination and the International Origins of Anticolonial Nationalism.* Oxford Studies in International History. Oxford: Oxford University Press, 2009.
_____. "Woodrow Who?" *Diplomatic History* 35.1 (27 December 2010): 75–80. Review of *Reconsidering Woodrow Wilson: Progressivism, Internationalism, War, and Peace,* ed. John Milton Cooper. Baltimore, MD: Johns Hopkins University Press, 2008.
Margold, Jane, and Donna Belardo. "Matrilineal Heritage: A Look at the Power of Contemporary Micronesian Women." In *Women in Asia and the Pacific: Towards an East-West Dialogue,* ed. Madeleine J. Goodman. Honolulu: Distributed for the Women's Studies Program by the University of Hawai'i Press, 1985.
Martel, Gordon, ed. *American Foreign Relations Reconsidered, 1890–1993.* London: Routledge, 1994.
Mason, Leonard, ed. *The Laura Report.* An East-West Center Book. Honolulu: University of Hawai'i Press, 1967.
_____. "A Marshallese Nation Emerges from the Political Fragmentation of American Micronesia." *Pacific Studies* 13.1 (1989): 1–46.
May, Glenn Anthony. "The Unfathomable Other: Historical Studies of U.S. Philippine Relations." *Pacific Passage: The Study of American-East Asian Relations on the Eve of the Twenty-First Century,* ed. Warren I. Cohen. New York: Columbia University Press, 1996.
McDougall, Walter A. *Let the Sea Make a Noise: A History of the North Pacific from Magellan to MacArthur.* New York: HarperCollins, 2004.
McElroy, Robert. *Grover Cleveland: The Man and the Statesman.* 2 vols. New York: Harper, 1923.
McHenry, Donald F. *Micronesia, Trust Betrayed: Altruism vs. Self Interest in American Foreign Policy.* Washington, D.C.: Carnegie Endowment for International Peace, 1975.
McMullen, Ronald. "Lilliput Revisited: The Case for Free Association." *Journal of Public and International Affairs* 4 (Fall 1983): 50–66.
McNeill, J.H. "The Strategic Trust Territory in International Law." Dissertation. London School of Economics and Political Science, 1974.

Meller, Norman. *Constitutionalism in Micronesia*. Institute for Polynesian Studies: Brigham Young University–Hawaii Campus, 1985.

_____. *The Congress of Micronesia: Development of the Legislative Process in the Trust Territory of the Pacific Islands*. Honolulu: University of Hawai'i Press, 1969.

Merrill, Dennis, and Thomas G. Paterson, eds. *Major Problems in American Foreign Relations: Volume 2, Since 1914*. 7th edition. Boston: Wadsworth, 2010.

Michal, Edward J. "Protected States: The Political Status of the Federated States of Micronesia and the Republic of the Marshall Islands." *The Contemporary Pacific* 5.2 (1993): 303–32.

Micronesian Support Committee. *Marshall Islands, A Chronology: 1944–1983*. 3rd ed. Honolulu: Maka'ainana Media, 1983.

Miller, Byron S. "A Law Is Passed: The Atomic Energy Act of 1946." *The University of Chicago Law Review* 15.4 (Summer 1948): 799–821.

Miller, David Hunter. *My Diary at the Conference of Paris*. New York: G.P. Putnam's Sons, 1928.

_____. *The Drafting of the Covenant*. 2 vols. New York: G.P. Putnam's Sons, 1928.

Mink, Patsy T. "Micronesia: Our Bungled Trust" *Texas International Law Forum* 6.2 (January 1971): 181–207.

"Missile Interceptor Passes Critical Test." *The Sunday Gazette* 3 October 1999: A11.

Mitchell, Christopher K. "Food from the Sea in Micronesia: Micronesia Is Capable of Satisfying Its Needs for Marine Products." *Micronesian Reporter: The Journal of Micronesia* XXIII.4 (4th Quarter 1975): 13–30.

Moore, Robert W. "Our New Military Wards, the Marshalls." *National Geographic* 88.3 (1945): 325–52.

Moos, Felix, and Grant Kohn Goodman, eds. *United States and Japan in the Western Pacific: Micronesia and Papua New Guinea*. Boulder, CO: Westview Press, 1981.

Morgan, William Michael. *Pacific Gibraltar: U.S.–Japanese Rivalry Over the Annexation of Hawai'i, 1885–1898*. Annapolis, MD: Naval Institute Press, 2011.

Morison, Samuel Eliot. *The Two-Ocean War: The Definitive Short History of the United States Navy in World War II*. New York: Ballantine, 1972.

Moses, John A., and Paul M. Kennedy, eds. *Germany in the Pacific and Far East, 1870–1914*. Brisbane, Australia: University of Queensland Press, 1977.

Murray, Steve. "The Americanization of Micronesia: Paradise Lost." *Ramparts* (February 1971): 35–37.

Nelson, Anna Kasten, ed. *The Policymakers: Shaping American Foreign Policy from 1947 to the Present*. Washington, D.C.: Rowman and Littlefield, 2009.

Neu, Charles E. *The Troubled Encounter: The United States and Japan*. Malabar, FL: Krieger, 1979.

Nevin, David. *The American Touch in Micronesia*. New York: Norton, 1977.

"Nike-Zeus Hit." *The New York Times* 19 July 1962.

Nufer, Harold F. *Micronesia Under American Rule: An Evaluation of the Strategic Trusteeship (1947–77)*. Hicksville, NY: Exposition Press, 1978.

O'Hanlon, Michael. "Star Wars Strikes Back." *Foreign Affairs* 78.6 (1999): 68–82.

Ogden, Michael R. "Republic of the Marshall Islands." Political Reviews, Micronesia. *The Contemporary Pacific* (Spring 1996): 164–69.

Omicinski, John. "'Star Wars' Lost, but Missile Defense Drive Lives." *Asheville Citizen-Times* 24 May 1998: A13.

Osorio, Jonathan K. *Dismembering Lahui: A History of the Hawaiian Nation to 1887*. Honolulu: University of Hawai'i Press, 2002.

Pacific Concerns Resource Centre. "Kwajalein Missile Tests Endanger Arms Control Treaties." Media Release. 20 January 2000.

Pacific Islands Development Program/Center for Pacific islands Studies. "Marshall's Foreign Minister: Washington Mood Favorable to Compact Renegotiation." *The Marshall Islands Journal* 14 August 1997.

"Pacific Islands Report," Political Reviews, Micronesia. *The Contemporary Pacific* (6 December 2001).
_____. *The Contemporary Pacific* (25 October 2010).
Patterson, Thomas G. *American Foreign Policy: A History*. Lexington, MA: D.C. Heath, 1977.
Paulding, Hiram. *Journal of a Cruise of the United States Schooner Dolphin*. New York: G. & C. & H. Carvill, 1831.
Paullin, Charles Oscar. *Diplomatic Negotiations of American Naval Officers, 1778–1883*. The Albert Shaw Lectures on Diplomatic History, 1911. Baltimore, MD: Johns Hopkins, 1912.
Payson, Jackson Treat. *The Far East: A Political and Diplomatic History*. New York: Harper, 1928.
"Peace Corps Dispatches 25,000th Aide Overseas." *The New York Times* 5 December 1966.
Peacock, Karen M. "Online Access to the Trust Territory Archives Photograph Collection." *The Contemporary Pacific* 7 (1995): 177–87.
Peattie, Mark R. "The Nan'yō: Japan in the South Pacific," in *The Japanese Colonial Empire, 1895–1945*, eds. Mark R. Peattie and Ramon H. Myers. Princeton, NJ: Princeton University Press, 1987.
_____. *Nan'yō: The Rise and Fall of the Japanese in Micronesia, 1885–1945*. Pacific Islands Monograph Series, No. 4. Honolulu: University of Hawai'i Press, 1988.
Perry, William. "The Problems Facing the Judiciary in the Marshall Islands." *Changing Micronesia* (6 May 1975).
Peterson, Glenn. "Breadfruit or Rice?: The Political Economics of a Vote in Micronesia." *Science and Society* (1979–80): 472–85.
_____. "Lessons Learned: The Micronesian Quest for Independence in the Context of American Imperial History." *Micronesian Journal of the Humanities and Social Sciences* 3, no. 1–2 (December 2004): 45–63.
Philbrick, Nathaniel. *Sea of Glory: America's Voyage of Discovery, the U.S. Exploring Expedition, 1838–1842*. New York: Viking, 2003.
Piccard, Paul J. *Science and Public Policy: More Literature for a Field*. Reviewed work. "A Peril and a Hope: The Scientists' Movement in America, 1945–1944," by Alice Kimball Smith. Blackwell Publishing on behalf of the American Society for Public Administration: 225–28.
Picturesque Cuba, Porto Rico, Hawaii and the Philippines: A Photographic Panorama of Our New Possessions. Springfield, OH: Mast, Crowell and Kirkpatrick, 1898.
Pike, Francis. *Hirohito's War: The Pacific War, 1941–1945*. London: Bloomsbury, 2015.
Porter, David. *Journal of a Cruise Made to the Pacific Ocean*. 2 vols. New York: Wiley and Halsted, 1822.
Prados, John. "The Wave Maker: Bill Casey in the Reagan Years." In *The Policymakers: Shaping American Foreign Policy from 1947 to the Present*, ed. Anna Kasten Nelson. Washington, D.C.: Rowman and Littlefield, 2009.
Price, Willard. *America's Paradise Lost*. New York: John Day Company, 1966.
"Problems of Peace" Lectures Delivered at the Geneva Institute of International Relations, 1927. Second Series. London: Oxford University Press, 1928.
Purcell, Daniel C., Jr. "The Economics of Exploitation." *Journal of Pacific History* XI (1976): 3–4.
Quigg, Philip W. "Coming of Age in Micronesia." *Foreign Affairs* (April 1969): 493–508.
Ranney, Austin, and Howard R. Penniman. *Democracy in the Islands: The Micronesian Plebiscites of 1983*. Washington, D.C.: American Enterprise Institute for Public Policy Research, 1985.
Raum, Tom. "Star Wars Sequel: Conservatives Won't Let Missile Defense Idea Die." *Asheville Citizen-Times* 14 August 1998.
Rearden, Steven L. "Paul H. Nitze and NSC 68: 'Militarizing' the Cold War." In *The Policy Makers: Shaping American Foreign Policy from 1947 to the Present*, ed. Anna Kasten Nelson. Lanham, MD: Rowman and Littlefield, 2009: 5–28.

Reichhardt, Tony. "Catch a Falling Missile: The U.S. Air Force Practices Firing Its ICBMs at a Target in the South Pacific. This Is What It's Like to Live in the Bull's Eye." *Air & Space* (December 1997/January 1998): 27–37.
Rejcek, Peter. "Army to Celebrate 226th Birthday: Range to Honor Former President with New Name." *The Kwajalein Hourglass* 41.45 (8 June 2001): 1, 4.
Republic of the Marshall Islands. *Marshall Islands Guidebook*. Updated and revised. Majuro, Marshall Islands: Micronitor News, 1989.
Reynolds, William. *The Private Journal of William Reynolds: United States Exploring Expedition, 1838–1842*, ed. Nathaniel Philbrick and Thomas Philbrick. New York: Penguin, 2004.
Rhodes, Benjamin D. *United States Foreign Policy in the Interwar Period, 1918–1941: The Golden Age of American Diplomatic and Military Complacency*. Praeger Studies in Political Communication. Santa Barbara, CA: Praeger, 2001.
Richard, Dorothy E. *United States Naval Administration of the Trust Territory of the Pacific Islands. Vol. 1, The Wartime Military Government Period*. Office of the Chief of Naval Operations. Washington, D.C.: U.S. Government Printing Office, 1957.
_____. "Trusteeship and the United Nations," typed manuscript, c. 1950.
Roehrs, Mark D., and William A. Renzi. *World War II in the Pacific*. 2nd ed. New York: Routledge, 2003.
Rogers, Robert F. *Destiny's Landfall: A History of Guam*. Honolulu: University of Hawai'i Press, 1995.
Rottman, Gordon L. *The Marshall Islands 1944: Operation Flintlock, the Capture of Kwajalein and Eniwetok*. Campaign 146. Oxford: Osprey, 2004.
Sady, Emil J. "The Department of the Interior and Pacific Island Administration." *Public Administration Review* (Winter 1950): 13–19.
Saxon, Wolfgang. "Amata Kabua, 68, President of Marshall Islands, Is Dead." *The New York Times* 16 December 1996.
Sayre, Francis B. "American Trusteeship Policy in the Pacific." *Foreign Policy* XXII.4 (January 1947): 406–16.
Schellhorn, Kai M. "Politics in the South Pacific Region." *Contemporary Southeast Asia*. 13.2 (1991): 188–199.
Schlesinger, Stephen C. *Act of Creation: The Founding of the United Nations*. New York: Basic Books, 2004.
Schmidt, Dana Adams. "Pentagon Disputes Study of Spraying Devastation." Special to the *New York Times* 9 January 1971: 3.
Schulte, Bret. "For Pacific Islanders, Hopes and Troubles in Arkansas." *The New York Times* 5 July 2012.
Schwalbenberg, Henry M. "Compact of Free Association: More Association than Free." *Pacific Magazine* 7.3 (32) (March-April 1982): 28–31.
_____. "Compact of Free Association: More Association than Free." *Pacific Magazine* 7.3 (33) (May-June 1982): 28–31.
_____. "Current Developments in the Pacific: Marshallese Political Developments: No to Commonwealth." *The Journal of Pacific History* 20.2 (1985): 105–15.
Schwartz, John. "Back to Court, Decades After Atomic Tests." *The New York Times* 6 August 2008: A23.
Scott, David Clark. "Pacific Islands Battle High Suicide Rates Among Youth." *The Christian Science Monitor* 18 May 1989.
Senese, Donald J. "The United States in Micronesia: From Trust Territory to Freely Associated States." *The Journal of Social, Political and Economic Studies* 18.4 (1993): 413–26.
Slaughter, Anne-Marie. "Wilsonianism in the Twenty-First Century." In *The Crisis of American Foreign Policy: Wilsonianism in the Twenty-First Century*, ed. G. John Ikenberry. Princeton, NJ: Princeton University Press, 2009.
Smith, Gary. *Micronesia: Decolonisation and U.S. Military Interests in the Trust Territories [Sic]*

of the Pacific Islands. Canberra, Australia: Pacific Research Centre, Australian National University, 1991.
Smith, Roy H., and Michael C. Pugh. "Micronesian Trust Territories—Imperialism Continues?" *Pacific Review* 4, I (1991): 36–44.
Snowbarger, Willis Edward. "The Development of Pearl Harbor." Dissertation. University of California, Berkeley, Graduate Division, Northern Section, 1950.
"Soviet Urges Arbitration of Kwajalein Claim Issue." *The New York Times* 8 June 1962.
Sparrow, Bartholomew H. *The Insular Cases and the Emergence of American Empire.* Landmark Law Cases and American Society. Lawrence: University Press of Kansas, 2006.
Spector, Ronald. *Eagle Against the Sun: The American War with Japan.* New York: Vintage, 1985.
Spoehr, Alexander. *Strategic Trust: The Making of a Nuclear Free Pacific.* New York: Cinema Guild, 1984.
Stanley, David. *Micronesia Handbook: Guide to an American Lake.* Chico, CA: Moon Publications, 1985.
Statham, E. Robert, Jr. *Colonial Constitutionalism: The Tyranny of United States' Offshore Territorial Policy and Relations.* Lanham, MD: Lexington Books, 2002.
Stege, Kristina E. "Marshall Islands." Political Reviews, Micronesia. *The Contemporary Pacific* (Spring 2002): 198–202.
_____. "Marshall Islands." Political Reviews, Micronesia. *The Contemporary Pacific* (Spring 2004): 126–31.
Steigerwald, David. "The Reclamation of Woodrow Wilson." *Diplomatic History* 23.1 (1999): 79–99.
_____. *Wilsonian Idealism in America.* Ithaca, NY: Cornell University Press, 1994.
Stenninius, Edward R., Jr., et al. "Joint Statement by the Representatives of the United States, the United Kingdom, and the Union of Soviet Socialist Republics." *World Affairs* (December 1944): 231–40.
Strauss, David M. "Marshall Islands Terminates Service of Another Chief Justice," *Pacific Islands Report* (2 July 2000): 1.
Summers, Harry G., Jr. "War: Deter, Fight, Terminate. The Purpose of War Is a Better Peace." *Naval College Review* (January/February 1986): 18–29.
Takahiro, Fukada. "Marshall Islands, Nuke Test Victim Call for Nonproliferation." *Japan Times* 17 April 2008.
Taylor, A.J.P. *Bismarck: The Man and the Statesman.* New York: Vintage, 1967.
Taylor, Stuart, Jr. "Reagan Supports Cleanup of Atoll Contaminated by U.S. Atom Tests." Special to *The New York Times* 14 March 1985: A12.
Thomas, Evan. *The War Lovers: Roosevelt, Lodge, Hearst, and the Rush to Empire, 1898.* New York: Back Bay Books, 2011.
Thornburgh, Dick, Glenn Reichardt, and Jon Stanley. *The Nuclear Claims Tribunal of the Republic of the Marshall Islands: An Independent Examination and Assessment of Its Decision-Making Processes.* Washington, D.C.: Kirkpatrick and Lockhart LLP, 2003.
Throntveit, Trygve. "The Fable of the Fourteen Points: Woodrow Wilson and National Self-Determination." *Diplomatic History* 35.3 (June 2011): 445–81.
Tobin, Jack A. "The Resettlement of the Enewetak People: A Study of a Displaced Community in the Marshall Islands." Dissertation. University of California, 1967.
_____. *Stories from the Marshall Islands.* PALI Language Texts: Micronesia. Honolulu: Hawai'i University Press, 2002.
Toll, Ian W. *The Conquering Tide: War in the Pacific Islands, 1942–1944.* Pacific War Trilogy. New York: W.W. Norton, 2015.
Townsend, Mary Evelyn. *The Rise and Fall of Germany's Colonial Empire, 1884–1918.* New York: Macmillan, 1930.
Truman, Harry S. *Memoirs by Harry S. Truman, Vol. 1: Year of Decisions.* New York: Doubleday, 1955.
Trumbull, Robert. *Paradise in Trust: A Report on Americans in Micronesia, 1946–1958.* New York: William Sloane Associates, 1959.

Tyler, Alice Felt. *The Foreign Policy of James G. Blaine.* Minneapolis: University of Minnesota Press, 1927.
"U.S. Military Gets Green Light on Kwajalein Lease." Pacific Islands Report, Political Reviews, Micronesia. *The Contemporary Pacific* (25 October 2010).
Uyehara, Mitsuo. *The Prophetic Vision of Keopuolani, the Sacred Queen of Hawaii.* Honolulu: Hawaiian Almanac Publishing, 1982.
Van Cleve, Ruth G. *The Office of Territorial Affairs.* Praeger Library of U.S. Government Departments and Agencies. New York: Praeger, 1974.
Vila, Bryan, and Cynthia Morris. *Micronesian Blues: The Adventures of an American Cop in Paradise.* Boulder, CO: Paladin Press, 2009.
Wakeman, Edgar A. *Report of Captain E. Wakeman to W.H. Webb on the Islands of the Samoan Group.* New York: Slote and Janes, 1872.
Walsh, Julianne M. "Marshall Islands." Political Reviews, Micronesia. *The Contemporary Pacific* (Spring 2000): 204–11.
———. "Marshall Islands." Political Reviews, Micronesia. *The Contemporary Pacific* (Spring 2001): 211–16.
———. "Micronesia in Review: Issues and Events, 1 July 1998–30 June 1999." *The Contemporary Pacific* 12.1 (2000): 204–211.
Ward, R Gerard, ed. *American Activities in the Central Pacific, 1790–1870: A History, Geography, and Ethnography Pertaining to American Involvement and Americans in the Pacific. Taken from Contemporary Newspapers, etc.* Vol. 7. Upper Saddle River, NJ: Gregg Press, 1967.
Webb, James H., Jr. *Micronesia and U.S. Pacific Strategy: A Blueprint for the 1980s.* Praeger Special Studies in International Politics and Government. New York: Praeger, 1974.
Weisgall, Jonathan M. *Operation Crossroads: The Atomic Tests at Bikini Atoll.* Annapolis, MD: Naval Institute Press, 1994.
Welch, Richard E. *Response to Imperialism: The United States and the Philippine-American War, 1899–1902.* Chapel Hill: University of North Carolina Press, 1987.
———, ed. "Hawaii and the Debate Begun: Alfred T. Mahan versus Carl Schurz." *Imperialists vs. Anti-Imperialists: The Debate Over Expansionism in the 1890's.* Itasca, IL: F.E. Peacock, 1972.
Westwick, Peter J. "'Space-Strike Weapons' and the Soviet Response to SDI." *Diplomatic History* 32.5 (November 2008): 955–79.
Whaley, Floyd. "U.S.-Philippine War Games Start Amid China Standoff." *The New York Times* 17 April 2012: A8.
White, Donald W. *The American Century: The Rise and Decline of the United States as a World Power.* New Haven, CT: Yale University Press, 1996.
White, Geoffrey M., and Lamont Lindstrom, eds. the *Pacific Theater: Island Representations of World War II.* Pacific Islands Monograph Series, No. 8. Honolulu: University of Hawai'i Press, 1989.
Wilkes, Charles. *Narrative of the United States' Exploring Expedition During ... 1838–1842.* Condensed and Abridged. History of Travel. London: British Library Historical Print Collections, 2011.
Wilkes, Daniel. "Bikini Breath of Death." *The Science News-Letter* 50.6 (10 August 1946): 84–85.
Wilkes, Owen, Megan van Frank, and Peter Hayes. *Chasing Gravity's Rainbow: Kwajalein and US Ballistic Missile Testing.* Canberra Papers on Strategy and Defense No. 81. Canberra, Australia: Nautilus Pacific Research, 1991.
Williams, Ian. "Freedom at Last: The United Nations Security Council Has Cut United States Colonial Ties with Three Pacific Trust Territories, but Reactions Have Been Mixed." *Pacific Islands Monthly* (February 1991): 10–12.
Willens, Howard P., and Deanne C. Siemer. *National Security and Self-Determination: United States Policy in Micronesia (1961–1972).* Westport, CT: Praeger, 2000.
Winchester, Simon. *Pacific: Silicon Chips and Surfboards, Coral Reefs and Atom Bombs, Brutal*

Dictators, Fading Empires, and the Coming Collision of the World's Superpowers. New York: Harper, 2015.
Wood, Junius B. "Japan's Mandate in the Pacific." *Asia* XXI.9 (September 1921): 747–53.
Woodruff, J. Lyon. "The Story of the Samoan Disaster." *Cosmopolitan* 20 (1895): 5–16.
Wright, Burton. *Eastern Mandates: The U.S. Army Campaigns of World War II*. Publication 72-23. Washington, D.C.: Center of Military History, 1993.
Yamasaki, Naomasa. *Micronesia and Micronesians*. Preliminary Paper Prepared for Second General Session of the Institute of Pacific Relations. Honolulu, Hawai'i, 15–29 July 1927. University of Hawai'i Archives.
Yanaihara, Tadao. *Pacific Islands Under Japanese Mandate*. International Research Series, Institute of Pacific Relations. Westport, CT: Greenwood Press, 1940.

Index

Numbers in **_bold italics_** refer to pages with photographs.

Acheson, Dean 147–48
Adams, John 12
Adams, John Quincy 12, 14, 28
Adams-Onis Treaty 12
Admiralty Area **_48_**, 59
Advance Research Projects Agency *see* U.S. Army
Advanced Ballistic Missile Defense Agency (ABMDA) *see* U.S. Army
Aelon Kein 15, 180n23
Ahlert (German commander) 24, 124
Ailinglapalap 16–17
Ainiken Dri-Majol 133, 140–41
Albright, Madeleine 161
Allen, George 193n56
al Qaeda 161, 164
American Board of Commissioners for Foreign Missions 16
American Lake 36
American Peace Commission *see* McKinley, William
Anglo-American Washington Conference (Trident Conference 1943), 57
Anglo-Japan Naval Alliance (1902) 37–38, 44
Annexationist Club 28
Anti-Ballistic Missile Systems (ABM Treaty) 137–38, 163; MAD (Mutual Assured Destruction) 137, 147
Armbruster, Thomas 173
Asian Development Bank 157, 163
Aspinall, Wayne 105, 109, 114, 116
Atlantic Charter 55, 72–75
The Atlas *see* U.S. Air Force
ATLAS D *see* U.S. Air Force
Atomic Energy Act (1946) 85

Balfour, Arthur 42
Ballistic Missile Agency *see* U.S. Army
Ballistic Missile Defense Organization (BMDO) *see* U.S. Army

Balos, Ataji 131, 169
Bartlett, Roscoe 170
Bataan Death March 56
Bayard, Thomas F. 28
Bergquist, L.C. 64–65
Berlin General Act 33
Bhagavad Gita 148–49
Bikini Atoll 85, 148
Bingham, Hiram 17
Bishop, Clyde 170
Bismarck, Otto von 21–22, 26–28, 31–33
Blaine, James G. 25–31
Blue Area 75–76
Bolkeim, Jalle 95, 99
Boston Congregationalist mission 17, 45
Boxers *see* Fists of Righteous Harmony
Braun, Wernher von 92; *see also* Operation Paperclip
Bravo series 85, 148, 157–58, 194n23, 194n36
Brown, Elizabeth 110, 114
Brzezinski, Zbigniew 132–34, 136, 139, 193n62
Bulow, Bernhard von 32, 40
Bundy, McGeorge 104, 106–07
Burton, Phil 136
Bush, George Herbert Walker 141, 157
Bush, George W. 161, 163, 165, 171

Cairo Conference (1943) 73
Cairo Declaration 75
Califano, Joseph 116
Camp David Accords (1978) 135, 138
Campbell, Kurt 173
Campbell, Martha 171
Capelle, Adolph 21
Capelle, Donald 178
Carter, Jimmy 132–42, 147
Carter Doctrine 139
Carver, John 104, 109–10, 114–16, 128
Casablanca Conference (1943) 56

Casey, William (Bill) 150
Cecil, Robert 41
Centers for Disease Control (CDC) 109
Central Pacific strategy 62, 74
Chamorros 48
Cheney, Dick 161
China Incident 52
China market 34
Chinese Eastern Railway 36–37; *see also* South Manchuria Railway
Churchill, Winston 55, 56, 72–75, 77
CinCPac/CinCPOA Supply Section *see* U.S. Navy
Clark, William 11–12
Cleveland, Grover 27–29, 182n38
Cleveland, Harland 104, 110
Climate Conference, Copenhagen (2009), 177
Clinton, Hillary 171, 177
Clinton, William Jefferson 157, 161
Code Orange *see* U.S. Navy
Cold War 4, 84–86, 92, 102, 106, 137–38, 147, 152, 155–57, 163, 165
Collier's magazine 81
Columbia University 65–66, 74
Compact Negotiations, Office of *see under* U.S. Department of State
Compact of Free Association 4–5, 124–25, 134–35, 145, 151–52, 154–55, 158- 62, 165–66, 168, 170, 173- 74, 178, 195n14; Trust Fund 162, 166, 172, 174
Congress of Micronesia 110–19, 121–26, 128–31, 133, 152–53, 155; Commission on Future Political Status" 116–18, 131, 125, 153; Council of Micronesia 113; Inter-District Advisory Committee to the High Commissioner 113; Joint Committee on Future Status 123, 125; Subcommittee, Eastern District Hearings 126, 129–30
Congregational mission 15–17, 19–20
Cook, James 12, 15, 24
Corlett, Charles H. 62, 185n30
Corner, Frank 103, 110
Council of Iroij *see* Traditional Rights Court
Council of Micronesia *see* Congress of Micronesia
Crane, Glenn 96
Crowe, William J. 123
Cuban Missile Crisis 106

Davenport, Coral 177
deBrum, Jose 21
deBrum, Oscar 144
deBrum, Tony 139–40, 142, 144–45, 157–60, 169, 171–72, 176–78, 197n2
"Declaration by United Nations" (1942) 73
DEFENDER research project *see* U.S. Army
DeLauer, Richard D. 147, 149–50
Denfeld, I. Louis 83

Deutsche Handels- und Plantagen Gesellschaft (DHPG) 21
Dewey George 31
Doane, Edward 16–18
Doane, Sarah 16
Dole, Sanford B. 28
Dribo, Handel 140–42
Dumbarton Oaks Talks 73
d'Urville, Dumont 8

Ebeye: improvement program 97–98; landownership rights 70, 87–91, 135–36, 140; village council 87–88
"Ebeye problem" 70, 87
Eden, Anthony 77
Einstein, Albert 84, 158
Eisenhower, Dwight D. 112, 148, 188n52
Ellice Islands 27
Eniwetok Atoll 62, 85
Erlichman, John 115
Executive Coordinating Committee (1944–45) 74–77, 80; *see also* Roosevelt, Franklin D.; Truman, Harry S.

Fairlamb, John 161–63, 165–66
Federated States of Micronesia 130–31, 135, 139, 163–64, 188n53, 196n38
Fists of Righteous Harmony (Boxers) 34
Floyd D. Spence National Defense Authority Act (2001) 170
USS *Flying Fish* 14
Ford, Gerald 130–31, 138
Forrestal, James Vincent 76
Forrestal, Michael Vincent 106
Fortas, Abraham (Abe) 79
Four Principles 122–23
Fox, Eugene 151
Franklin, Benjamin 2, 179n1
Freely Associated States 103, 127–28, 135, 139, 155, 162, 163–64, 171; *see also* Compact of Free Association

GAO *see* U.S. General Accounting Office
Garfield, James 27
Gaspar Rico *see* Taongi Atoll
German-Spanish Treaty (1899) 32–33
Germany first strategy 56
Gilbert Islands 7, 17, 27, 43, 57–59
Gilliland, Thomas 90–91
Goding, M. Wilfred 105, 113
Goldberg, Arthur 110, 115
Gorbachev, Mikhail 155
Graham, Daniel 147–48, 150
Grant, Ulysses S. 26
Guam Doctrine *see* Nixon Doctrine
Gulick, Luther H. 45

Handy, Ichabod 16
haole 25, 28–29, 51, 183n22
Harrison, Benjamin 27, 29
Hawaiian League 28

Hay, John 33–34, 52
Hearst, William Randolph 30
Heine, Carl 122, 129–30, 197n7
Heine, Dwight 112–14, 121
Heine, Hilda 178, 197n7
Hickel, Walter Joseph 118, 121–23
High Frontier 148, 150
Hilo Principles 132, 134, 139, 143–45, 167–68
Hitler, Adolf 51, 55, 56
Hodel, Donald Paul 168
Homing Overlay Experiment (HOE) *see* U.S. Army
Hoover, Herbert 52
House, Edward M. 42
Hughes, Charles Evans 43–44
Hughes, William 41
Hull, Cordell 73, 75
Hummel, Arthur W. 123
Hunt, Bryan 65–66
Hussein, Saddam 165

Ickes, Harold L. 81–82
Independent Advisory Committee on Human Radiation Experiments (ACHRE) 157–58
Inter-District Advisory Committee to the High Commissioner 112–13
Interim Use Agreement (1982) 145
Intermediate-Range Nuclear Forces (INF) Treaty 155–56
International Court of Justice 157–58
International Monetary Fund (IMF) 157, 163
Iran-Contra Affair 150
Island State Security Conference, Honolulu (July 2003), 165–66

Jackson, Andrew 12
Jackson, John B. 32
Jaluit: Company 21–23, 26, 35; Roman Catholic mission 16, 18
Japanese Congregational Church 45
Japan's "twenty-one demands" 37, 40–41
Jefferson, Thomas 11–12
Jesuit 23, 45
Jewell, Sally 173
Johnson, Lyndon B. 109, 113–16, 133, 137

Kaahumanu, Queen 16
Kabua, *Paramount Iroij of the Ralik Chain* 22–24, 35, 124, 144
Kabua, Amata, *Iroij* 95, 98, 112–14, 116, 119, 121–22, 124, 126–29, 130, 133, 135, 140–42, 144–45, 152, 155–57, 159, 165, 167, 191n16
Kabua, Imata, *Iroij* 140–41, 159–60, 167, 169–70, 172
Kabua, K., *Iroij* 99; *see also* "Memorandum of Concurrence" (April 1968)
Kabua, Kabua, *Paramount Iroij* 167
Kabua, L., *Iroij* 99; *see also* "Memorandum of Concurrence" (April 1968)

Kaibuke, *Chief Iroij of the Ralik chain* 16–18
Kai-shek, Chiang 73
Kanoa 17
Kaysen, Carl 104, 106
Kennedy, John F. 95, 102–109, 114–16, 123–24, 133, 137, 188n52; National Security Action Memorandum (NSAM) No. 145 (4/18/1962) 104–105, 108, 116; NSAM No. 191 (10/1/1962) 191n16; NSAM No. 229 (3/21/1963) 106–107; NSAM No. 243 (5/9/1963) 107; NSAM No. 268 (10/25/1963) 108
Kerry, John 173, 177
Khrushchev, Nikita 102, 106
Kia'aina, Esther Puakela 173
King, Ernest J. 56–57
Kissinger, Henry 120–24, 128, 131, 142, 192n11
Korea 37, 41
Kristof, Nicholas 159–60
Kwajalein Atoll Corporation (KAC) 140–41, 144, 167–68, 196n50
Kwajalein Atoll Development Authority (KADA) 168–69, 172, 196n50
Kwajalein, Battle of 3, 57–64, 74, 83; Operation Flintlock 57, 62
Kwajalein Land Use Agreement (LUA) 5, 10, 47, 71, 94, 112, 119, 140–41, 144, 153, 166–72, 189n34
Kwajalein Missile Range (KMR) 100, 106, 120, 131, 133, 135, 137–38, 143, 151–52, 156, 170
Kwajalein Naval Station 90
Kwajalein Negotiation Commission (KNC) 165–66
Kwajalein Test Site 96, 100

Laminini, *Iroij* 69–70
Lansing, Robert 37, 40–41
Lansing-Ishii Agreement 37, 40–41
Lawrence Livermore Laboratory 149
League of Nations 40–44, 46, 48–51, 73, 75, 79, 187n36; Class C (mandate) 43–44; Covenant of the League 40–42, 44; "equality of nations" 41–43; Japanese mandate 3, 56, 74–77, 182n29; mandate system 42–45, 51, 73, 77, 79; "racial equality" clause, 41–43
Leo XIII, Pope 26–27
Lewis, Meriwether 11–12
Lilienthal, David 85
Liliuokalani, Queen 28–29
Lodge, Henry Cabot 30, 43–44, 75
Loeak, Anjua 99, 193n59; *see also* "Memorandum of Concurrence" (April 1968)
Loeak, Christopher 166, 169, 173–78
Long, John D. 30, 39–40
Louisiana Purchase 11–12

MacArthur, Douglas 56–57
Madrid Protocol (1877) 22

Mahan, Alfred 29–30, 41
Majuro, Battle of 59
Majuro Declaration for Climate Leadership 174
Malayo-Polynesian 7
Manchukuo 50–52
Mandate system *see* League of Nations
Manhattan Project 84, 148–49
Manifest Destiny 12
Mansfield, Mike 79, 81
Marehalau, Jesse B. 164
Marshall, George C. 56
Marshall, John 15
Marshall Islands Interim Use Agreement (1982) 145
McCarthy, Eugene 116
McCoy, Janet 141, 143, 145
McElroy, Neil 92
McFarland, Robert 147
McHenry, Donald 110, 132, 135
McKay, Douglas 112
McKinley, William 3, 29–34, 37, 39, 41, 148; McKinley Executive Order (1898) 32, 65; McKinley Tariff 29
McNamara, Robert 96, 100, 110, 137
Meiji Restoration 35–36
Meller, Norman 112
Memorandum of Concurrence (April 1968), 99–100
Micronesian Constitutional Convention (1975) 130
Micronesian Future Political Status Talks: First Round (1969) 121–22, 125; Second Round (1970) 122–123; Third Round (1971) 124; Fourth Round (1972) 124; Fifth Round (1972) 125, 128; Sixth Round (1972) 126; Seventh Round (1973) 128–29; Eighth Round (1976) 131
Micronesian Nuclear Claims Commission 139
Micronesian Status Negotiations, Office of (1971) 123, 125, 133, 136, 141
Micronesian Support Committee (MSC) 141–42
Mid-Atoll Corridor 93, 96–98, **97**, 140, 156
Midway, Battle of 56, 58–59, 65, 74
Military Use and Operating Rights Agreement (MUORA) 5, 161–62, 165–66, 169–70
Miller, David Hunter 39, 41, 43, 183n24
Missile X Program *see* U.S. Air Force
Monroe Doctrine 20, 27, 30, 40, 73
Morris, Greta 169
Morton, Rogers 123
Moscow Conference (1943) 73
Muller, Philip 160, 173, 178
Mutual Assured Destruction *see* ABM Treaty

Namur *see* Roi-Namur
Nanyo, *South Seas see* League of Nations: Mandate system

National Geographic Genographic Legacy Fund 9
National Security Act (1947) 86
Neas, Maynard 90
Nemaira 17
Nemra, Casten 178
Ngiraked, John 116
NIKE-X *see* U.S. Army;
NIKE-X Project Office *see* U.S. Army
NIKE-ZEUS *see* U.S. Army
Nimitz, Chester W. 57–59, 62, 67
Nitze, Paul H. 147–48
Nixon, Richard 100, 115, 118–21, 128–29, 130, 137–38, 163
Nixon Doctrine 120
Northern Marianas 119, 130, 135, 188n52
Northwest Ordinance 11
Note, Keasai 160–61, 166, 168–69
Nuclear Age Peace Foundation 176
Nuclear Claims Tribunal 145, 157–58
Nuclear Compensation Fund 145;

Obama, Barrack 2, 5, 171, 173–175, ***174***, 177–78
Obama, Michelle 173, ***174***
Open Door notes (1899) 34, 52
Operation Crossroads 85, 148; *see also* Bikini Atoll
Operation Flintlock *see* Battle of Kwajalein
Operation Homecoming 143–44
Operation Paperclip 92
Oppenheimer, J. Robert 148–49, 158, 194n37
Orange Plan *see* U.S. Navy: Code Orange
Oregon Territory 14

Pacific and adjacent theaters (1943) **55**
Pacific Islands Forum 171; Post Forum Dialogue, 171
Pacific Military Conference 57
Pacific Missile Range Facility, Kwajalein 93, 96–97
Pacific Range Electromagnetic Signature Studies Program (PRESS) *see* U.S. Army
Pacific triangulation 27
Pago Pago 26–27, 33
Palau 32, 35, 48–49, 78, 84, 116, 121, 124–26, 135, 139
Panama Canal Treaties (1977) 135, 138, 145
USS *Panay* 52
Paris Climate Agreement *see* UN Climate Change Conference, Paris (2015)
Paul C. Aiken & Smith 91
Peace Corps 103, 115, 129
PEACEKEEPER missile *see* U.S. Air Force, MX Missile System
USS *Peacock* 14
Pearl Harbor 26, 29, 34, 50, 53, 55–59, 63, 65–66, 161, 182n1, 185n1
Pearl River 24, 29, 36
Pedro, Fred 176–77
USS *Pennsylvania* 64

phosphate mining 28, 47
Pierson, George 16–18
Pierson, Nancy 16–18
Polk, James K. 14
Port Arthur 36, 53
Portsmouth Peace Conference 36–37, 40
Protestant World Council of Churches 143
Puerto Rico 32, 42

"racial equality" clause *see* League of Nations
Rainbow series plan *see* U.S. Navy
Ralik Chain 8, 16, 22, 44, 96
Ratak Chain 8, 59, 96
Reagan, Ronald 136–39, 141, 145–52, 154–56, 161, 164, 170, 172, 176–77; Executive Order No. 12569 155; National Security Directive 119, 150
Reciprocity Treaty of 1875–1876 *see* United States–Hawaii Reciprocity Treaty (1875–76)
Republic of the Marshall Islands (RMI) 4–5, 7, 145, 152–78; Constitutional Convention 135, 167; Treason and Sedition Act (1988) 156; United Democratic Party 160 169
Reynolds, William 14
Richardson, Robert C., Jr. 62
Robertson and Hernsheim 21
Rodman, Peter W. 164
Ronald Reagan Ballistic Missile Defense Test Site (RTS) 170, 172–73, 197n54
Roosevelt, Franklin D. 3, 52, 55–56, 72–76, 84; Executive Coordinating Committee (1944–45) 74–76; Naval Act (1938) 52–53
Roosevelt, Theodore (Teddy) 30, 37–38, 40–41
Root-Takahira Agreement (1908) 37
Rosenblatt, Peter R. 133–34, 136, 139–40, 142
Rostow, Walt 116
Rotger (German commander of the SMS *Nautilus*) 22
Rusk, Dean 110
Russo-Japanese War 36–37

Sabin Oral Polio Vaccine 109
SAFEGUARD Command (SAFSCOM) *see* U.S. Army
Salii, Lazarus 116, 121–25
Samoa 24, 26–28, 33, 57, 65, 81, 83, 182n29, 182n57
San Francisco Conference 75–77; *see also* United Nations: Charter
Sandwich Islands 15, 25
Schultz, George 149
Scowcroft, Brent 147
Scowcroft Report 147, 151
SDI *see* Strategic Defense Initiative
Seiberling, John 145–46
self-determination 2, 7, 73–75, 78, 83, 101–04, 122–23, 151, 165

SENTINEL System Command (SENSCOM) *see* U.S. Army
Seward, William 26
Shoecraft, R.K. 95, 98–99
Short, Albert V. 162–63
Shufeldt, Robert W. 26
Sino-Japanese War (1894–95) 36
Smith, Holland M. 62, 185n30
Smith, Robert C. (Bob) 170
Smuts, Jan C. 42
Snow, Benjamin G. 45
Solomon, Anthony N. 107–110; Solomon Report 107–110, 118, 124; Solomon Task Force 107, 114
South Manchuria Railway 36–37; *see also* Chinese Eastern Railway
South Seas Bureau 44–49
"South Sea Islands Company" 35
Space and Missile Defense Command (USASMDC) *see* U.S. Army
Spanish-American War 3, 34, 40
SPARTAN missile *see* U.S. Army
SPRINT missile *see* U.S. Army
Spruance, Raymond A. 59–62, 185n30
Stalin, Joseph 73–75, 86
Star Wars 150
Starbird, Alfred 100
Status of Forces Agreement (SOFA) *see* U.S. Army
Stayman, Allen P. 161–63
Stettinius, Edward J. 75–76
Stimson, Henry 52, 76
Strategic Arms Limitation Talks (SALT) 137; SALT II 138–39
Strategic Defense Command (USASDC) *see* U.S. Army
Strategic Defense Initiative (SDI) 150–52, 155, 161, 164–65
Strategic Defense Initiative Organization (SDIO) 150–51
strategic denial 5, 134, 142–43, 152, 154, 156, 162–64
strategic trust 3–4, 75, 79–80, 83–85, 87, 101, 134, 152, 154
strategic trusteeship 104
Strong, Josiah 30
Sturgeon, G.H. 64–64
Suzuki-Goto Expedition (1883) 35

Taft-Katsura Memo (1905) 37
Taongi Atoll 32, 39
Tarawa, Battle of 57–59
Teheran Conference (1943) 73
Teller, Edward 85, 147–49, 151
Tet Offensive 116
Tetsutaro Sato 36
Thomas, Elvert D. 84
Thurston, Lorrin A. 28–29
Tituila Island 26
Tobin, Jack 89
Tobolar, Coconut Boy 180n9

Tobolar Copra Company 9, 47, 179n9
Tobolar, the Mother of Mothers 9
Tomeing, Litokwa 133, 169–71
Tracy, Benjamin 29
Traditional Rights Court 167
Trident Conference *see* Anglo-American Washington Conference
Trident II (D-5) missile *see* U.S. Navy
Tripartite Pact 53, 55, 72
Truman, Harry 3–4, 72, 75–77, 80–87, 109, 111, 147–148, 188n52; Executive Coordinating Committee 75–77, 80; Executive Order 9875 80–81, 83; Executive Order 10265 84; National Security Council Paper Number NSC-68 *"United States Objectives and Programs for National Security"* 147–48; Truman Doctrine 86
Trust Territory Conference on Self-Government (1953) 112
Trust Territory of the Pacific Islands (TTPI) 3–4, 79–81–84, 87–91, 93–95, 97–101, 103–107, 109–136, 139, 141–43, 151–54, 157, 162, 164, 167–68, 170
Turner, Richmond Kelly 185n30
Tyler, John 24–25, 31
Tyler Doctrine 25

Udall, Stewart 97, 105, 108, 115
Ukicho, Taguchi 35
United Nations: Charter 77–78, 80–81; Climate Change Conference, Paris (2015) 177–78; "Declaration by United Nations" (1942) 73; General Assembly 75, 78–79, 102–103, 187n36; Nuclear Non-Proliferation Treaty (1968) 176; Resolution 742, "attainment of self-government" 102; Resolution 1514, "Declaration on Colonialism" 102; Resolution 1541, "Principles of Self-Government" 102–103; Security Council 77–80, 132, 154, 157; Trusteeship Agreement 77–79, 83, 107, 125, 132, 154–55; Trusteeship Committee 131–32; Trusteeship Council 77–81, 83–84, 103, 109, 112–114, 154–57; *see also* San Francisco Conference
U.S. Air Force: Air Force System Test Target Program 138; the Atlas 92; ATLAS D 94; Missile X Program 138; MX missile system 139, 142, 146
U.S. Ambassador's Fund for Cultural Preservation 9
U.S. Army: Advance Research Projects Agency 93; Advanced Ballistic Missile Defense Agency (ABMDA) 100, 106; Army Forces Strategic Command 172–73; Ballistic Missile Agency 92; Ballistic Missile Defense Organization (BMDO) 138, 163; DEFENDER research project 100, 106; Garrison—Kwajalein Atoll 172–73; Homing Overlay Experiment (HOE) 151; Kwajalein Atoll (USAKA) 156, 170;

Nuclear Claims Tribunal 145, 157–58; Memo-of-Understanding (MOU) (9/15/1961) 93; Memo-of-Understanding (MOU) (April 1982) 142; NIKE-X missile 95–96, 100, 119–120; NIKE-X Project Office 98–99; NIKE-ZEUS missile 92–96, 105–107, 190n15, 191n16; Pacific Range Electromagnetic Signature Studies Program (PRESS) 93; SAFEGUARD Command (SAFSCOM) 119–20, 137–38; SENTINEL System Command (SENSCOM) 100; Space and Missile Defense Command (USASMDC) 161–62, 170; SPARTAN missile 119–120; SPRINT missile 96, 119–120; Status of Forces Agreement (SOFA) 161–62, 169–70; Strategic Defense Command (USASDC) 151, 156, 161–62, 170
U.S. Department of State: Compact negotiations, Office of 161, 168; Compact, reauthorization 134, 155, 158, 165–66, 170
U.S. Exploring Expedition (1838–1842) 12, *13*, 14
U.S. General Accounting Office 163–65, 196n37
United States–Hawaii Reciprocity Treaty (1875–76) 25–26, 36
U.S. National Institutes of Health: "Emergency Health Crisis" proclamation (2013) 89
U.S. Navy: CinCPac/CinCPOA Supply Section 66; Civil Affairs (Military Government) Section at Pearl Harbor 65; Code Orange 30, 53; Legislative Advisory Committee, Inter-District Advisory Committee 111, 113; Proclamation Number One 67–68, 71, 83; Proclamation Number Two 68; Proclamation Number Four 68; Proclamation Number Five 71; Rainbow series plan 53, 57; Trident II (D-5) missile, 147; Ultra, military intelligence 59
U.S. Senate Foreign Relations Committee (1919) 40, 43
USSR 73–75, 78, 80, 84–86, 106, 131, 137–39, 146–47, 150, 152, 155–57, 165

van Buren, Martin 12
Vandenberg, Arthur, Jr. 75
Vandenberg Air Force Base 92, 94, 106, 156
Vaughn, Jack H. 115
Versailles Peace Conference 3, 39, 41–44, 51, 77
Vietnam War 114, 116, 119–20, 123, 133–34, 138
Voice of the Marshalls *see Ainiken Dri-Majol*

Wake Island 32–33, 50, 56, 78, 81, 172
Wall, John F. 151
Washington Conference (1887) 27–28
Washington Naval Conference (1921–1922),

43–44, 184n42; Five-Power Treaty 44; Four-Power Treaty 44
Watergate 129–30, 138
Webster, Daniel 24–25
Weinberger, Caspar 141, 147, 149
Wiles, E.E. 91
Wilhelm, II, Kaiser 28, 32–33
Wilkes, Charles 12–14, 24, 26, 180n13, 180n19
Williams, Franklin Haydn 123–25, 128, 131
Wilson, Woodrow 3, 39–44, 73, 75–76, 183n24; State of the Union Speech (1913) 73; "Wilsonian Moment" 42
Women United Together in the Marshall Islands 10, 178, 179–80n9
World Bank 157

World Council of Churches *see* Protestant World Council of Churches
Wright, Carlton H. 82

Yalta Conference 74–75
Yamamoto Isoroku 53, 55–56, 185n1
Yap 26, 38–39, 43–44, 48–49, 84, 129, 135, 186n29, 196n38
Yarnell, Harry 74
yellow peril 41
Youth to Youth In Health 9

Zackios, Gerald M. 164–66, 169, 197n53
Zeder, Fred M. 82, 141–43, 145–46, 193n56
Zeus Corridor 93, 96

www.ingramcontent.com/pod-product-compliance
Ingram Content Group UK Ltd.
Pitfield, Milton Keynes, MK11 3LW, UK
UKHW041948140426
5217IPUK00014B/705